ABT

ALLEN COUNTY PUBLIC LIBRARY

3 1833 03590 2581

MW00999635

746.92 G91H
Gross, Elaine.
Halston

WITHDRAWN

18/99

ALLEN COUNTY PUBLIC LIBRARY
FORT WAYNE, INDIANA 46802

You may return this book to any location of
the Allen County Public Library.

DEMCO

✓

HALSTON
An American Original

HALSTON

An American Original

ELAINE GROSS & FRED ROTTMAN

HarperCollins*Publishers*

EDITOR: JOSEPH MONTEBELLO

ASSOCIATE EDITOR: ANJA SCHMIDT

DESIGNER: JOEL AVIROM

DESIGN ASSISTANTS: MEGHAN DAY HEALEY AND JASON SNYDER

PAGE III: *Halston in his Olympic Tower office, 1979.*

PAGES VI–VII: *The Skimp, photographed in Halston's town house, as seen on the front page of* WWD, *November 4, 1974.*

Photograph and illustration credits appear on page 237.

HALSTON. Copyright © 1999 by Elaine Gross and Fred Rottman. All rights reserved. Printed in Italy. No part of this book may be used or reproduced in any manner whatsoever without written permission except in the case of brief quotations embodied in critical articles and reviews. For information address HarperCollins Publishers, Inc., 10 East 53rd Street, New York, NY 10022.

HarperCollins books may be purchased for educational, business, or sales promotional use. For information please write: Special Markets Department, HarperCollins Publishers, Inc., 10 East 53rd Street, New York, NY 10022.

FIRST EDITION

Library of Congress Cataloging-in-Publication Data

Gross, Elaine.
    Halston : an American original / Elaine Gross and Fred Rottman—
1st ed.
        p. cm.
    Includes bibliographical references and index.
    ISBN 0-06-019318-2
    1. Halston, 1932–1990. 2. Costume designers—United States—
Biography. 3. Costume design—United States—History—20th
century.   I. Rottman, Fred. II. Title.
TT505.H25676   1999
746.9'2'092—dc21
    [B]
                                                99-19332

99 00 01 02 03 ❖/MNT 10 9 8 7 6 5 4 3 2 1

To my parents, for their unwavering and continual support, and to Ashley, my fashion guru. —E.G.

—————

To my wife, Vivienne, and son, Harrison, for their great patience and support during this project. And to my parents for their unconditional love and support. —F.R.

CONTENTS

ACKNOWLEDGMENTS

The authors would like to thank certain individuals for their generosity of time and effort, without which this book would not have been possible.

Dorothy Globus and Valerie Steele of the Museum at the Fashion Institute of Technology, for giving us open-door access to the Halston Archives and all of its treasures. Ena Szkoda, also of the Museum at FIT, for sharing with us her time and the years of knowledge she acquired studying Halston's art and craft. Irving Solero, photographer at the Museum at the Fashion Institute of Technology, for patiently and expertly reproducing materials from the Halston Archives.

Lauren Rosenblum and Lori Friedman of Fairchild Publications, for allowing us into their archives of both words and pictures, which enabled us to reconstruct Halston's complete fashion history.

Gregory Monfries of *People* magazine, for his invaluable help. Akira Maki, for re-creating some of Halston's most unique patterns. Bill Dugan and Nancy North Dugan, for freely giving their time and information. B. Jeffrey Madoff of Madoff Productions, for allowing us into his video archives. Elizabeth Connelly, for her invaluable assistance as a researcher.

A special thank-you to our editor, Joseph Montebello, for acknowledging the need to chronicle Halston's contributions, and to his associate, Anja Schmidt, for guiding us through the day-to-day production of the project.

Elaine gives special thanks to Hope Hood, for being the best coach anybody could ever have, and to Linda Konner, for encouragement and assistance throughout the process of developing this book.

Fred would like to thank Piero and Francesco Picchi for their understanding and support during the past year.

We give special thanks to all of Halston's colleagues, clients and friends who allowed us a peek into their memories.

FOREWORD
by Dorothy Twining Globus

Roy Halston Frowick did more than just contribute to establishing America as a recognized force in the international fashion arena; with his minimal designs and use of luxurious materials, he elevated American sportswear to a new level. Over the course of his career, Halston developed a series of interchangeable and seasonless separates. His most successful clothes were imaginative variations on time-proven classics. The man-tailored shirt became a shirtdress. The twin set was elongated to a floor-length coat and dress. Pajamas became outerwear, and caftans were not for camouflage anymore, but to attract attention. Simple and streamlined, his designs were perfectly suited to the 1970s, when minimalism began to influence both art and life.

The Museum at the Fashion Institute of Technology had a close relationship with Halston and has consistently collected his designs. Our costume collection houses more than 300 examples of his garments, hats and accessories. We presented the first major retrospective of his work in October 1991, titled "Halston: Absolute Modernism." The Halston Archive was established at the Museum in 1993, founded upon a generous donation of materials from Halston Borghese Inc. Its extensive holdings include sketches, patterns, swatches, runway photographs and related ephemera dating from the early days of Halston's career until its end. With these rich resources, the Museum has become a major center for the study of Halston. Fashion designers, scholars, journalists and television crews have all drawn upon its contents.

It is with great pleasure that the Museum at the Fashion Institute of Technology has made its resources available to the authors of *Halston: An American Original*. Now the important insights and information they discovered in their research can be shared. These pages reveal Halston's practical and democratic approach to fashion design. As you will see, his vision, more than any specific style or design element, is undoubtedly Halston's chief contribution to the history of fashion.

—Dorothy Twining Globus,
director, the Museum at the Fashion Institute of Technology

3 1833 03590 2581

INTRODUCTION:
The Halston Mystique

If fashion's Seventh Avenue had a Hollywood-style walk of fame, the biggest and shiniest star would belong to Halston, America's first true fashion celebrity. Nine years after his death, his name still conjures up images of luxury and fashion excellence commonly associated only with the toniest of European couturiers.

Before him, Claire McCardell's casual sportswear and Norman Norell's European-inspired glamour wardrobes made major contributions to the American fashion scene. But it wasn't until Halston, with his special blend of luxurious, comfortable and gimmick-free fashions, that America truly found an original, and a role model for its fashion future.

Behind the grandiose image lived a man with an innate talent for foretelling the fashion needs of a changing generation of women. He mixed couture-level garment construction with the reality of modern lifestyles. Both in spirit and in detail, he led fashion's redefinition from the pie-in-the-sky dictates of a handful of designers to apparel driven by women's needs. With a unique interpretation of sensuality, movement, proportion and simplicity that caused *Women's Wear Daily* (*WWD*) to nickname him "Mr. Clean," he invented a way of dressing that revolutionized his, and our, fashion times.

Although some may remember him most as the designer of Jackie Kennedy's inaugural pillbox hat, in fact all of 1970s contemporary fashion was defined by Halston. Every woman, from royalty and celebrities to middle-American housewives, wore his designs or was scented with his fragrance. A simple black, block-lettered name and logo became an adjective for fashion elegance, much as Rolls-Royce was for luxury cars.

It is impossible to clearly separate Halston, the man, from the designer or the business. There was a synergy to his life and work that zigzagged in and out of all his activities. Any more than you can isolate a single ingredient from a master chef's recipe, these facets cannot be extracted and examined individually. The whole was more than the sum of its parts.

Timing is everything, and Halston's life and career can be summed up as the timely convergence of a number of unique personal and social elements. Had they

Halston in his New York town house, 1978. © Harry Benson

occurred either separately or during another era, he would probably not have had the far-reaching impact he did.

The 1950s, when Halston began his fashion career as a milliner, was a time when a woman would sooner dare utter profanities in public than walk out of the house without wearing a chapeau. The places where he learned and perfected his design and personal skills as a milliner during the early to mid-1960s—the Ambassador Hotel in Chicago, Lilly Daché and Bergdorf Goodman in New York—were repositories for the wealthy and celebrated hoi polloi. There he learned the genteel art of catering to the carriage trade who demanded European-style, custom-made attire and a level of service to match. At the same time, he intuited the slow disappearance of this kind of conspicuous consumption and the beginnings of a pro-American fashion attitude that would lead to the growth of more democratic fashion in the form of ready-to-wear.

When Halston opened his apparel business in 1968, he astutely tapped into the antiestablishment, freethinking, open-minded, more casual approach to life that was emerging. Vietnam War protests and the Watergate political scandal, the rise of discos, Beatlemania and the London fashion scene, widespread recreational drug use and the burgeoning women's and sexual liberation movements all helped change the scope of most women's expectations, lifestyles and, therefore, fashion needs.

Halston's movie-star good looks and charismatic star qualities ushered in a newfound celebrity status for fashion designers. Almost daily, his name appeared in the fashion and society columns alongside those of his equally famous clients. They were naturally attracted to each other and their celebrity transferred both ways.

Halston was interviewed on every subject from his daily grooming habits ("wash hair every day, shave twice a day, and wash face with own signature soap") and his favorite recipes (cottage cheese dressing for crudités, caviar on a baked

© *The* New Yorker *Collection, 1978.*
Dana Fradon from cartoonbank.com.
All Rights Reserved.

"I dreamt I was sitting in on a National Security Council meeting,
and guess what. Liza Minnelli and Halston were there, too!"

potato, cold salmon mousse) to how he stays fit (eats an early breakfast, follows rigid exercise program) and his working habits (likes to work late into the evening so he can concentrate without being disturbed, books appointments for himself "rather like a doctor").

Halston was featured in two *New Yorker* cartoons and appeared on every talk show from Merv Griffin, and Phil Donahue, to Dinah Shore, and *Good Morning America*, and capped it all off with a featured role in a special fashion episode of *The Love Boat*. Halston was spoofed on the April 11, 1987, edition of *Saturday Night Live*, with the late Phil Hartman impersonating the designer in a mock interview on the fictitious *Pat Stevens Show*. Halston's name was mentioned in two popular songs—Billy Joel's "Big Shot" (1978) and Sister Sledge's disco favorite "He's the Greatest Dancer" (1978). Upon Halston's insistence, whenever Sister Sledge's song played over the speakers in his office, fittings would come to a halt until after the line "Halston, Gucci, Fiorucci" was heard.

On the set of The Love Boat *with designer Gloria Vanderbilt, 1981.*

Through a conscious effort, he attained one-name celebrity status and palled around with such luminaries as artist Andy Warhol. "Andy was the ultimate voyeur and Halston was the ultimate host. So whenever you were around them, you knew there was going to be some fun, mischief and hijinx," says film director Joel Schumacher, a longtime friend and short-time coworker of Halston's. "I think they both loved celebrities and the spotlight."

Like an actor who rehearses for weeks on end to make it seem as though he is not acting at all, Halston liked to make his fashions seem effortless and easy, and exhibited a contradictory mix of grandeur and bare-knuckled hard work. His reputation as a social butterfly was blown so out of proportion that it somewhat tarnished and overshadowed his legacy as a brilliant fashion designer.

More than any other designer before him, Halston's celebrity and style put American fashion on the map and helped make New York City the internationally recognized fashion capital it is today—on equal footing with the long-standing meccas of Paris, London and Milan.

When corporate America began to take over the fashion industry, Halston was caught in its early machinations. He was on the cutting edge of the business world's conglomerate fever of the 1970s and 1980s, and became a small cog in the big wheel of huge corporations. But without any precedent to guide him, he unwittingly shared his name and valuable trademark with a corporation that both allowed him to build a dynamic business and later forced him out of active design duty. It was a world that he could never fully adapt to, a world where the concept of supporting the integrity and creativity of the fashion arts was secondary to dollars-and-cents accountability. But through his triumphs and errors, he laid the foundation for today's fashion superstars to market themselves into global empires and worldwide recognition without losing control of the products that carry their names.

BELOW:
Halston and Liza Minnelli,
slow dancing.
OPPOSITE:
Left to right: Halston, Loulou de
La Falaise, Yves St. Laurent,
Nan Kempner and Steve Rubell
at Studio 54 party celebrating the
launch of St. Laurent's Opium
perfume.
OVERLEAF:
Pearlized sequins on silk halter dress,
January 1974. © Neal Barr

Halston's fashion genius was at its best when he had total control of the creative process. When his business grew to colossal proportions, some think that it was his inability to delegate responsibility that precipitated his decline. But before that happened, Halston took the fragrance and cosmetics industry by storm, creating a perfume that for more than ten years was listed as one of the top ten sellers. The Halston fragrance was sold in a unique bean-shaped, Elsa Peretti–designed bottle that is still one of the most famous perfume bottles in history.

Halston rang all the bells on the meter that measures success. And in recognition, his peers awarded him five Coty Fashion Critics Awards, the Oscars of the fashion industry, for his groundbreaking millinery and fashion designs.

Halston was a man with many faces who selectively revealed different aspects of himself depending upon whom he was with. "It was a little bit like watching the Wizard of Oz in operation behind the curtains," says his former assistant Bill Dugan.

The uptown and regal Halston easily conversed and played with true royalty such as the Duchess of Windsor and the Baroness Marie Hélène de Rothschild, and Hollywood royalty like Gloria Swanson and Elizabeth Taylor. The downtown and down-to-earth Halston treated Viola, his longtime, in-office cook as though she were a queen, and could "get real" with eccentric and bohemian friends such as rock singer Monty Rock III and artist Andy Warhol.

The glamorous Halston could stage the most dramatic entrance at Studio 54 or design a breathtaking environment for his Olympic Tower offices. Yet the practical Halston never forgot he was designing clothes for real people of all types and shapes.

First and foremost, however, he was the focused and serious fashion designer who put his work and ambition before all else, demanding perfection in all things, from himself and from those who worked for him. But through it all he interjected a playful, cutting wit, dry sense of humor and a steady stream of practical jokes.

But he was something of an enigma, even to his closest friends.

"I think I got as close to him as anybody," said Liza Minnelli at the dedication of the Halston Archive at the Fashion Institute of Technology. "But he was still such a gentleman that there was a certain line that one never crossed with him. And yet he knew everything about me. He was always there if I needed him—as a friend, as a designer, as a brother. He was wonderful. But you know, he had this wonderful kind of style where you really didn't intrude on his life."

Because of his simple and focused fashion view, during the 1970s many fashion critics called Halston the antidesigner. In contrast, he always thought of himself as just a dressmaker who thoroughly enjoyed but was somewhat bemused by the level of his success. Today we know that he was actually the predesigner whose mystique and design concepts changed the scenery and the rules of fashion's future.

Neal Barr

HALSTON
An American Original

HIS STORY

Roy Halston Frowick was born on April 23, 1932, in Des Moines, Iowa, the second of four siblings—brother Robert, two years older; sister Sue, five years younger; and brother Donald, fourteen years younger. Roy was named after his father's brother, and received his middle name from his maternal grandfather, Halston Holmes.

"The name's been with me since childhood," Halston said of what would become one of the most famous names in fashion, "to prevent confusing me with my Uncle Roy."

During Roy's early years, the Frowicks lived in a two-room bungalow in a lower-middle-class neighborhood of Des Moines with woods across the way that Robert remembers Roy imaginatively named "the enchanted forest." Roy's father, James Edward Frowick, of Norwegian descent, was an accountant with a passion for inventing that he hoped would one day bring financial rewards, but never did. His mother, Hallie May, a devoted housewife, doted on her children and imparted to them her Midwestern family values and down-to-earth character. She was always busying herself with a sewing, knitting or crocheting project; young Roy assuredly picked up some of her creativity.

Front-page notoriety came early to Roy, an omen of things to come. At age two, he was named the Healthiest City Boy at the 1934 Iowa State Fair. And when he was five, a photo of Roy giving a May Day basket to the prettiest girl in the neighborhood appeared on the front page of a Des Moines newspaper.

The family began to notice Roy's fashion talents when he was about six, when sister Sue was drafted into becoming his first house model. She recalls an outfit that he embellished by weaving chicken feathers through a straw hat and then inserting feathers into the buttonholes of her jacket. Roy encouraged her to model this first original for the family camera.

Following a series of moves to Lake of the Ozarks, Kentucky and Missouri during the World War II years, in 1943 the family put down roots in Evansville, Indiana, where Roy worked as a soda jerk at the Merry-Go-Round Drive-In. In high school, stylishly dressed Roy was already acutely aware of the importance of appearance and volunteered advice to family and friends. While brother Bob spent weekends on the sports field, Roy, already drawn to the finer things in life, attended the

Halston with models and masked assistants at the Sixty-eighth Street showroom.

races with the owner of the restaurant where he worked. Many of his friends were naturally culled from among the so-called better families in the community.

For Sue's thirteenth birthday, Roy, now eighteen, gave her a complete fashion makeover. He bought her a black and white quilted, sleeveless dress and insisted on accessorizing it with her first pair of high heels, three inches high and bright red. Roy pressed Sue to stroll down Main Street while he walked three feet behind to monitor the reactions to his efforts.

After graduating from Benjamin Bosse High School in 1950, Roy studied one semester at Indiana University while working as a clerk at International Harvester. But he was always thinking about fashion.

"It's very strange, but very true. I always wanted to be in the fashion business, from the time I was about four or five years old," Halston said. "I was always fascinated with it, and always wanted to make things, and actually did make things when I was really young. And it was very difficult for me as a young man because I wasn't much encouraged in that world of fashion. Everybody discouraged you right down the pike, and you were not supposed to do what I was doing, which was making hats. I guess you had to be smaller and a little bit more fey."

In the early 1980s, when publicity writer Barbara Bonn asked what his parents thought of his career, he replied, "Well, a six-foot, two-inch milliner was not exactly what my mother had in mind for me."

That was when a combination of fate and determination took over. Midwesterners say they can never totally divest themselves of their roots, but at least on the surface, Roy began to put that life behind him forever when he moved to Chicago in 1952. Karma played an important role in moving him along and up his personal career path.

"I think people are born for their destinies," said Halston. "Certain people are gifted to use their hands, or voices or minds. I'm fortunate enough to be such a person."

Chance stepped in when European-raised André Basil, a well-placed friend and lover twenty-five years his senior, gave Fro, as he was now called, a luxurious place to live in Chicago. He also gave him the opportunity to hobnob with Chicago society and the means to turn his hatmaking hobby into a lucrative career.

Fashion journalist Peg Zwecker gave Fro his first press coverage in her column in the *Chicago Daily News* and introduced him to Chicago's native design genius, Charles James, someone who was to play an important role in Halston's future. Another fortuitous introduction by Zwecker, to famed New York milliner Lilly Daché, led to a job and a move to New York City in 1957.

New York's pace was a perfect fit for Halston's curious and fast-moving mind. And while working for Daché another chance introduction, to the *directrice* of

Bergdorf Goodman's custom millinery salon, led to a nine-year affiliation with the store. Fate was on Halston's side when he discovered a young and beautiful Texan, Berkley Johnson, working behind the hat and accessories counter at Bergdorf Goodman. He wasted no time making her his fit model. (She later introduced him to family friend Estelle Marsh Watlington, who in 1968 gave Halston the financial backing he needed to leave Bergdorf Goodman and start his own business.)

"Mr. Halston" the milliner, was Bergdorf Goodman's star customer magnet, but it took great effort and considerable persuasive skills to convince Andrew Goodman, the store's chief executive, to allow him to design an apparel collection exclusively for the store and to open a special boutique in which to sell it. With that under his belt, a year later he felt ready to test his skills under his own umbrella.

Luck may have opened the doors to opportunity, but it was hard work, cunning and a love for fashion that propelled Halston to the heights he eventually climbed. Once he found his calling, he never lost sight of the goal that he was to have the good fortune to fulfill—to become one of the most important fashion designers in the world. Drive, talent and intelligence made it happen.

What the fashion press in the 1970s labeled as Halston's "overnight success" was actually founded on many years spent developing his trade. From the moment that Halston started his own business, it set off a domino series of events that projected the fashion world off in a direction it is still following today.

Working out of his apartment at 360 East Fifty-fifth Street, in 1968 Halston formulated a plan and mobilized a team of friends to join him in the business that, by the end of that year, would have a home of its own and a name, Halston Ltd.

This was the beginning of a career-long practice of hiring and surrounding himself with friends, almost seamlessly blending his personal and professional life. Bill Dugan, who became a Halston design assistant in 1972 and worked by his side for twelve years, knew Halston socially and was hired very casually at a party celebrating Halston's second Coty Award. D. D. Ryan had been a client before becoming part of his team and was hired after a similar conversation at Studio 54.

"I have a fabulous group of friends whom I love more than anything," Halston told *WWD* in 1971. "I see them every night, usually for dinner in people's houses. Or we may go dancing, to an amusing party, try a new restaurant. But no matter how terrific the party is, I always leave by 12:30 or 1, because I do need a little sleep."

Halston loved people "who do things, who work and have a constructive life," which characterized those with whom he formed the closest attachments—interior designer Angelo Donghia, model-turned-jewelry-designer Elsa Peretti, illustrator Joe Eula, performers Liza Minnelli and Elizabeth Taylor, designer Charles James and sometime artist Victor Hugo. By their very nature, some of these strong personalities were destined to clash, and many did, sometimes ending the relationships abruptly and permanently.

Peretti and Halston eventually quarreled over the fees she was paid for the design of his perfume bottle. She had agreed on a onetime $25,000 design fee (the equivalent of $100,000 to $150,000 today), which included unlimited use of her name, says Paul Wilmot, then vice president of sales promotion for Halston Fragrances. As payment she chose a sable peacoat made by licensee Ben Kahn instead of money. When a miniature version of the bottle on a chain was used for a gift with purchase, the promotional gift was so successful, Peretti later felt she had not been properly compensated and in a fury destroyed the coat by throwing it into the fireplace at Halston's town house.

Halston Ltd.'s original foursome was a powerhouse of young creative talent. Joanne Creveling, now running her own public relations firm, helped Halston write the business prospectus for the company. She and Halston met in the mid-1960s at the Fire Island home of mutual friend, interior designer Angelo Donghia, and quickly became friends. She had been trained in retailing, business and public relations at Macy's.

Joel Schumacher, now a Hollywood film director, also met Halston at Donghia's Fire Island home where he says Halston was a constant houseguest. Schumacher had been a partner in the trendsetting and phenomenally successful New York City store Paraphernalia, a haven for 1960s "youthquake" and London fashion. At Halston, he was in charge of knitwear and also brought his retailing and merchandising expertise to the mix.

"I had crashed and burned on drugs already by the time Halston came to see me," Schumacher frankly reveals. "I didn't want to work in fashion anymore. I don't know if he gave me a job out of the kindness of his heart, to save my life, because I was lost. But he wanted someone who he felt had made a dent in this world. I was there for comic relief. I was more exotic, daring and iconoclastic than the others. Halston always liked that in me."

Halston knew Frances Stein when she had been an accessories and fashion editor and featured his hats on the pages of *Glamour* and *Harper's Bazaar*. She brought her excellent taste and a reputation as a style setter of her day. Stein currently works for Chanel in Paris.

A great risk taker throughout his career, Halston consistently pushed the envelope beyond the accepted business and fashion practices of the time. He was simply following his own concepts and visions without concern for what others were doing. The first risk he took was leaving his prominent position at Bergdorf Goodman to venture out on his own. The second was locating his showroom far from the garment center.

In 1968, with an estimated $125,000 investment from Estelle Marsh Watlington, Halston began looking for a space to rent.

"After he left Bergdorf Goodman, he only had enough money to last him for a year," remembers Michael Marsh, Estelle's son. His mother met Halston during a visit to New York and they got along so well that they immediately struck a deal. "My mother and Halston wrote an agreement on a piece of paper or an envelope. It later made my mother's financial advisors crazy."

Halston first looked for a suitable showroom nearby the Fifty-seventh Street and Fifth Avenue art gallery and fashion hub frequented by the elite. He was about to lease the former Alexander Iolas art gallery on West Fifty-seventh Street when the previous owner suddenly reappeared with new financing and reclaimed his space. Out of desperation, he rented the third floor of a six-story town house at East Sixty-eighth Street and Madison Avenue that was owned by Phoebe of Phoebe's Whamburger restaurant. (It also happened to be the building where Franklin Delano Roosevelt spent some of his childhood years.) Madison Avenue was not yet the fashionable street it is now, but Halston was virtually sitting in the backyards of the wealthy women who would become his clients.

OPPOSITE TOP:
Elsa Peretti and Halston at a party at Studio 54.
OPPOSITE BOTTOM:
The new Halston Ltd. team, August 1968. Left to right: Halston, Frances Stein, Joel Schumacher, Joanne Creveling.

Michael Marsh started working for Halston in August 1968 and remembers four months of intense activity getting the showroom ready. Taking another risk, Halston allowed Donghia to decorate the showroom in a cozy but elegant East Indian mood that was different from anything anyone had ever seen at the time. "I never understood gold chairs and white walls," said Halston, referring to the standard decor of Parisian couturiers' salons.

For about six months, Marsh worked for Halston as carpenter, errand boy and menswear model, and at the same time monitored the family's investment. "Halston started the business like one of those old Judy Garland, Mickey Rooney films," Marsh remembers. "It was, 'OK kids. Let's put on a show.'"

Walls were torn out and the space was rebuilt. With the help of a small budget and a lot of talented friends, Halston created a souk-like oasis on the Upper East Side, draping the walls, the furniture and ottomans in hundreds of yards of ethnic batik prints from Donghia's fabric line. Oriental bric-a-brac accented the sisal carpeting and animal horn furniture, and the ever-present smell of Rigaud candles wafted through the air. It was quite a contrast from the gray-walled, carpetless atmosphere that most Seventh Avenue designers were working in at the time.

"There were twenty or thirty different kinds of batiks," Creveling recalls. "The curtains alone would have one border and then a different kind of tieback and a different kind of heading. It was something you might have seen in the East Village."

"It was all draped, and had a very unpretentious feeling to it," says Schumacher. "It didn't feel like a couture salon, but like someone's living room. It was very comfortable."

Shortly after the salon opened, in December 1968, *Life* and *Look* magazines photographed fashion spreads in the salon.

Also unlike the garment center, the showroom's doors were locked at noon and lunch was served to whatever clients or friends had been invited or dropped by. And not a sandwich from the corner deli, but a freshly made salad, cheese and quiche fare accompanied by a good bottle of wine.

"It wasn't my intention to go into a made-to-order business," Halston said, "but the first day I opened up I had Mrs. William Paley come to me at nine-thirty that morning to buy some clothes. I wasn't prepared to make clothes for private people because I didn't have that kind of staff, you know, but, of course, she is probably the number-one client you could possibly want as a designer. My second client was Jane Engelhard, who is one of the loveliest, nicest ladies I have ever met in my life, who came to me with a whole Christmas list . . . took me in the corner and asked me if I needed some money. Thank God, I didn't, but I'll never forget it. All of a sudden, I was in the made-to-order business. I made every mistake known, but I did the dream of every American designer, which is to remove yourself from the marketplace, have a made-to-order business, have your own building, have the fame, fortune and notoriety, a good clientele and so forth."

The business grew very quickly and as space in the building became available, Halston added floors, eventually taking over the entire building. The third floor had the made-to-order salon where Halston's "special" clients were assisted, with a small design workroom in back. He initially shared the fourth floor with hairdresser Sebou, but later took over the whole floor, with his office in front and design offices in the back. After he acquired the fifth floor, the fourth-floor dressmaking workroom was moved there, along with the tailoring and millinery workrooms. At times, the fifth floor was also a living space for visitors such as Elsa Peretti.

Halston's first showroom/salon on East Sixty-eighth Street designed by Angelo Donghia.

Designer boutiques and the importance of designer labels were a new phenomenon in 1969 when Halston opened his first in-store boutique in Bloomingdale's, New York City, and another a few days later in Halle Bros., Cleveland.

"It was just the beginning of designers becoming front row and center, rather than in the background," says Ellin Saltzman, who was fashion director for Saks Fifth Avenue. "It's hard to imagine that throughout the early 1970s, everything in the store had a Saks label on it, not a designer label. I remember writing a paper on it for Saks management using the example that customers now come to stores to buy Halston, not Saks Fifth Avenue. Designers were not considered important people. Then, suddenly, they were. Halston's personality made it happen."

Soon after leaving Bergdorf Goodman, Halston had a meeting with Bloomingdale's chairman Harold Krensky, president Marvin Traub and executive vice president in charge of ready-to-wear Mel Jacobs. "He [Krensky] told me that one of the main problems a store faces today is to get merchandise of the moment," said Halston to *WWD*. "This involves getting it into the store quickly, selling it quickly, and going on to the next thing. And I thought, by golly, that's the way we do it in the hat business . . . in and out fast. Why not clothes? Now we live in the most immediate 'you are there' times. You can be any place in the world instantly due to TV. Fashion should be that way too."

The first Halston boutique opened in Bloomingdale's on the third floor in August 1969, with a core collection of about thirty pieces of clothing and accessories that Halston described as "amusing, not kooky clothes for fast delivery and selling." A small group of new merchandise would be added each month. Halston designed the collection but it was manufactured by outside contractors.

The boutique's decor mimicked Halston's Donghia-designed showroom, and Traub remembers, "Halston wanted to be involved in every detail, down to the shelving. The night before the boutique opened, he stayed up all night to personally sew the drapery and fabrics."

During the next two years, Halston opened similar boutiques in Sakowitz in Houston and Nordstrom-Best in Denver, making his collection exclusive to one store per city. He won a second Coty Award for his collection, cited for its total look.

It wasn't until 1972 that Halston also became a retailer. He created the first retail boutique owned by an American designer to sell his own products off the rack. Only European designers Yves St. Laurent and Valentino were known to previously have done the same. And it was conveniently located on the ground floor of the same building as his showroom in a space vacated by a menswear retailer.

"It was an impetuous move," said Halston to longtime friend, fashion journalist Eugenia Sheppard. Halston started organizing and decorating the boutique only a month prior to the opening.

"I remember Halston in the sixties when he was a young hat maker in Rome at one of my shows. Then I met him again in the seventies and he was the talk of New York—a great designer and the greatest star in New York."

—VALENTINO

The boutique opened on February 7, 1972, without any advertising, but its oversized windows were filled with mannequins modeled after Amanda Burden, one of his most faithful customers. Halston hired two helpers, Roz Rubinstein, formerly of Bendel's, and Stephen Sprouse, a former assistant to Bill Blass, as well as a crew of about seven salesgirls.

In an ironic testimony to its success, *WWD* reported that the boutique was robbed twice in the first month it was open and the trade newspaper called it "the latest gathering ground for the Cat Pack. Every time I turn around I find 50 more Ladies," said Halston. "It's been terrific. I opened in February, which is a slow month, and my biggest problem is getting the stock into the store."

As the product offerings grew, the boutique grew accordingly. Before the concept of "diffusion" or secondary, lower-priced lines was formulated, Halston was selling three different collections at three different price levels all under one roof.

The ground floor, once the Roosevelts' dining and cooking area, held Halston's lower-priced fashions, up to $100 retail, including pullovers and cardigans made of cashmere and stretch terry. A chrome and white staircase led to what Halston called his "orchid palace" on the second floor, where cashmeres and ready-to-wear priced from $100 to $400 were presented to private clients. By this time, Halston had redecorated his salon in the starkly modern, mirror-and-Ultrasuede mood that would remain his signature. It included low-slung couches covered with white Ultrasuede, huge mirrors on rollers, pillows thrown on the bleached pine floor and a few carefully placed orchid plants. The third floor was a club-like meeting place for Halston's special made-to-order customers where they could order items costing one thousand dollars and up.

Halston would eventually open two more boutiques based on this prototype, in Chicago's Water Tower in 1976, and then in the South Coast Plaza in Orange County, California, in 1978.

Decades before Benneton's socially and politically controversial advertising campaigns and Barneys' humorous store windows created a media buzz, the windows of Halston's boutique featured powerful, pungent displays that made social statements about people, politics and the events of the day. Halston's artist friend and lover, Victor Hugo, was responsible for most of the outrageous displays, often with the aide of one of Halston's jack-of-all-trades design assistants, Perucho Valls.

Halston's boutique windows "received sharp criticism from area residents and passersby," said *WWD* on August 11, 1978. "They featured five mannequins dressed in black lingerie shown acting out various forms of violent behavior. Heidi Gates, then the store manager, said one woman complained that the window was 'downgrading [sic] to women.' A neighborhood resident, Sidney Gross, was so incensed by the 'knives, guns and whips' that he sent letters of complaint to six publications."

One of Hugo's finer surrealistic moments was the window he designed to commemorate the Patty Hearst kidnapping. It showed Hearst and terrorist mannequins

*Window display at Halston's
boutique of a mock fashion show,
September 1975.*

armed with machine guns. Another memorable window featured a very pregnant mannequin in a maternity hospital room, surrounded by anxious but very well dressed visitors all wearing red and black. The mannequins in an airport waiting room wore raincoats with Hartmann's color-matched Ultrasuede carry-on bags by their side, while waiting for their Ultrasuede luggage to pass inspection by a makeshift X-ray machine. A surrealistic breakfast scene showed ladies in various styles of chiffon dresses and jumpsuits, frying eggs on the floor and on a hot plate. A space-age male fantasy was re-created with shapely silver "robots" wearing sexy Savage bathing suits, attached with long wires to an invisible power source.

Upon publication of friend Andy Warhol's book *The Philosophy of Andy Warhol*, Hugo tiled the floor of the window with his books. In his *Diaries* entry for November 28, 1976, Andy Warhol mentioned that the turkey bones in Halston's Thanksgiving Day windows had been stolen.

"I thought the windows were spectacular, because up until that point every mannequin that you ever saw either looked like Lisa Taylor or Suzi Parker or Dorian Gray, with wigs and nail polish," remembers Joanne Creveling, who was in charge of window display at Henri Bendel's at the time.

The more traditional Halston windows featured chisel-faced, pure white mannequins without hair, makeup, or accessories, a stark background and garments all of one color. Among the scenes were a mock fashion show, a croquet game on a grassy carpet, and for New Year's Eve, strands of gold and white lights linking mannequins dressed in black velvet and gold metallic ensembles.

Thanks to growing attention by the media—a *Newsweek* cover photo and article that appeared on August 18, 1972, and several appearances on the *Dinah Shore Show*—Halston's boutique was a flurry of activity, and the designer became known outside of the fashion industry and his cult of clients. But it wasn't until two Seventh Avenue angels, Ben Shaw and Guido De Natale, entered the picture that Halston's business became commercially profitable. Both men had a history of financially backing and nurturing highly talented designers such as Dominic Rompolo, Donald Brooks, Chuck Howard and Giorgio di Sant'Angelo. Halston came to their attention in a number of ways.

Beth Levine, who made the shoes for all of Halston's early runway shows, recalls running into Shaw on the street many months prior to his initial meeting with Halston. At the time, he opined that Halston would "never make it." Shortly after Shaw partnered with Halston, Beth's husband, Herbert Levine, sent Shaw a telegram saying, "I'm not worried about you anymore."

Designer Chuck Howard, who knew Halston, Shaw and De Natale, was responsible for making the initial introductions and for arranging their first meeting.

Around the same time, Lynn Manulis of Martha's, the luxury specialty boutique, also brought Halston to the attention of Shaw. Manulis, daughter of the store's owner and namesake, Martha Phillips, knew Halston at Bergdorf Goodman and wanted to sell his designs in her stores. He continually put her off, saying that his workroom was too small to accommodate her needs. But persistence finally prevailed and she convinced Halston to sell her a few jersey skirts and blouses. The minute they were put in the store, they sold out. Next Manulis persuaded him to sell her a half-dozen hand-painted caftans, promising to sell them only in the Palm Beach, Florida, shop. Mrs. Vincent Astor bought the first one and wore it to a party. The next week her friends bought all the remaining pieces.

Halston now took her "little" boutiques more seriously, and he was convinced to do a trunk show in her shop in Bal Harbour, Florida. It was so successful, he stayed on to do a show in Palm Beach. The result was more than two hundred orders, which he was not equipped to produce. Halston suggested canceling the orders, but Martha called her friend Ben Shaw to find a solution.

The negotiations that began in early 1972 with Shaw and De Natale led to a partnership, Halston Originals, that would produce a ready-to-wear collection based on Halston's made-to-order designs, and would oversee the licensing of Halston's name. All equal partners, Shaw and De Natale each invested $150,000, and Halston invested his name and talent. The $300,000 was leveraged into a loan that bankrolled the business. Shaw, who was widely known in the business, directed the public relations. De Natale handled the production and business duties. The partnership began even before they signed on the dotted line.

Halston's first Newsweek *cover with Karen Bjornson wearing an Ultrasuede hat, August 21, 1972.*

Halston Originals operated independently from the Halston Ltd. made-to-order business and boutique, with separate offices on the fourteenth floor of 550 Seventh Avenue. It was an instant and resounding success, says De Natale, because they made line-for-line copies of Halston's custom collection, using the exact same patterns and fit. By limiting distribution to only one major department store and one specialty store per city, the collection was earmarked as something special. The first stores to carry the Halston Originals line were Bergdorf Goodman and Martha's in New York, Neiman Marcus and Lou Lattimore in Dallas, I. Magnin and Giorgio's in Beverly Hills and I. Magnin in San Francisco.

Halston was triumphant when Bergdorf Goodman opened a special boutique for his ready-to-wear and accessories in August 1972, especially since it was in his "old spot" on the second floor where the apparel collections he designed for the retailer had been located, now between boutiques for Givenchy and furs.

"I grew up in this room, looking out those windows at the Plaza," Halston reminisced to *WWD*. Leonard Hankin, executive vice president of the store, pulled out of storage the glass table that Joseph Braswell had designed for Halston's millinery boutique and put it in the new one. "I was sure Halston would remember it, and he did," said Hankin.

"Bergdorf Goodman had sold $40,000 worth of Halston clothes even before its boutique for the designer was opened," Bernadine Morris reported in the *New York Times* on September 20, 1972. In February 1973, less than a year after the Seventh Avenue operation began, Morris reported that the company had booked close to $4 million.

Licensing designer names to products other than the ones they produced was just in its infancy in the early 1970s, so the team slowly and tentatively looked for appropriate vehicles. One of the first, in December 1972, was for a collection of furs with the Dan Grossman Inc. division of Richton International. In 1973, Halston began designing bodywear for Kayser-Roth, Ultrasuede luggage for Hartmann, tennis dresses under the Halston for Palm Beach Masters label, and negotiations were under way for swimwear, menswear and sweaters. With offices next door to the ready-to-wear showroom, Halston III rainwear was opened, a partnership between Shaw, De Natale, Jack Sobel and Abe Isaac, selling outerwear priced at $55 to $125 wholesale.

De Natale's wife, Catherine, then working for the McCall's Pattern Company, a division of Norton Simon Inc. (NSI), was the matchmaker in a deal making line-for-line copies of Halston's top looks—caftan, shirtdress style #704, halter-neck jumpsuit, cardigan suit, soft obi-like sash belt, soft pouch bag—available to the home sewer. She says the patterns were too sophisticated for the average home sewer and were never a great success, but continued for many years because of the marriage between Halston and NSI.

European designers had already learned the value, both for image and income, of having a perfume wear their name. In 1973, Revlon's Norman Norell scent was the only American designer name fragrance.

Revlon was among the first companies that De Natale and Shaw spoke with about licensing a Halston fragrance, but they also approached Max Factor, then the fourth largest cosmetics firm in the United States. Max Factor was a mass-market, drugstore-oriented company that Norton Simon Inc. had purchased the year before for a reported $480 million in stock and that was not profitable, according to market sources. The company needed a designer name to move them into the black and into the department store fragrance market. For the fiscal year ending June 1972, Norton Simon had earnings of $1.5 billion from its many divisions, which included Canada Dry soft drinks, Hunt-Wesson Foods, Johnnie Walker Scotch and *Redbook* and *McCall's* magazines, in addition to Max Factor.

Halston and his partners had verbally reached an agreement for a fragrance license with Max Factor when one of Max Factor's attorneys demanded approval of any future licensing arrangements entered into by Halston Originals.

"I said, 'No way,'" remembers De Natale. "In fact, I told them I didn't want them to take on any other designer fragrances. So we got up and started walking away from the table. The negotiations had really come to a halt. And with that, my attorney said to Max Factor's attorneys, 'If you want to control them, then buy the whole company.' And we left."

A week later NSI's attorneys called, offering to buy both of Halston's companies, Halston Ltd. and Halston Originals. Then negotiations began for the selling price.

"Ben, Halston and I met at a restaurant on Second Avenue and we got drunk. The higher the price went, the drunker we got," reminisces De Natale.

Conflicting figures appeared in the press, but NSI actually purchased Halston Ltd. and Halston Enterprises for $7 million in stock, combining all the Halston operations into Halston Enterprises Inc., a wholly owned subsidiary of the conglomerate. Halston received shares worth approximately $4 million, and reportedly gave $1 million to his initial investor, Mrs. Watlington. Shaw and De Natale split the remaining shares, worth approximately $3 million, giving sales manager Jerry Uchin a previously agreed 10 percent. Their $150,000 investment, just a year and a half before, had been a very profitable one.

Despite claims to the contrary, De Natale says Halston Originals was profitable at the time of the sale to NSI, doing about $3 million in sales, although Halston Ltd. owed Halston Originals about $300,000 for merchandise sold in the Sixty-eighth Street boutique, and he believes that Halston Ltd. was operating at a deficit of about $700,000.

"They weren't buying a very profitable business, because we hadn't been in business that long," says De Natale, who remained with the company, in charge of operations and production for the Seventh Avenue portion of the business. "But they saw the expectations and they bought it on futures."

As an NSI employee, Halston received a salary and an incentive bonus if he met budget, which was to be paid partly in stock options and partly in cash. David

Halston with cook Viola at his Olympic Tower offices, 1982.

Mahoney, then chief executive of NSI, today remembers there also being an "evergreen clause" in the contract, which provided financially for Halston should the company be taken over. Corporate perks were also included, such as access to the company workrooms to make his personal wardrobe, a round-the-clock limousine, a personal secretary to oversee both his home and office activities, a continually refreshed supply of orchids and, of course, Viola, his cook.

In return, there was a limited but open-ended noncompete clause that, according to Malcolm Lewin, who later became Halston's attorney, stipulated that if Halston was no longer employed by NSI, he agreed not to use his name or likeness to create any business that would be "confusingly similar" to those businesses operating under his name at the corporation. Although it was popularly believed that Halston sold his name and trademark to NSI lock, stock and barrel, Lewin insists that the agreement between Halston and NSI set up a dual ownership, which meant that there were two accepted users.

Nobody could have anticipated the ramifications that clause would have about ten years later. Although Halston was not the first fashion designer to become affiliated with a corporation, he was the first to sell a company in its entirety to a corporation, and along with it, his namesake trademark.

"No one would have bought the company without the trademark or without Halston's continuing efforts as a designer," says Michael Lichtenstein, who was managing director of Halston Enterprises for nine years. "He was given what, twenty-five years ago, was considered a very good salary. There was no reason for him to feel that the deal was wrong. In fact, he got a second scoop of money from his stock options when NSI was sold."

"It was a good deal for Halston," agrees Mahoney. "He was getting his money up front. Nobody was offering that kind of money to these other guys [designers]. I can't tell you how many of those other guys came to me to make a comparable deal."

Although many pointed out to Halston the dangers of overexposure, he saw it as "a designer's dream to broaden his public. I will do nothing to jeopardize the Halston name. It took twenty years building it," he told the press. He was pleased to be relieved of business duties and able to concentrate on what he knew and loved best—designing.

Halston's personal relationship with Mahoney was the linchpin in the deal. Although a successful and respected corporate executive, Mahoney accepted and appreciated that working with an artist like Halston was not going to be like working with canned-goods and soft-drink factories.

"I think we understood each other," says Mahoney. "Halston just didn't fit into a pegged hole. When you're talking about a Picasso or a Rembrandt, you can't expect them to fit into a certain structure." Mahoney also understood that in the fashion business, "you're selling hopes and dreams. You can't cost everything out. It really was show business and Halston was the master of it."

With the financial backing of NSI, the show was able to take on the dimensions of a full-blown Broadway revue. Everything else had just been a warm-up for what Halston was now able to do with the budget and business savvy of a huge corporation behind him. He now had the opportunity to build the fashion empire of which he had always dreamed.

With his share of the proceeds of the sale of his companies, Halston decided he could finally afford a new home. He had been considering buying Grace Mirabella's old apartment when Donghia, who had just bought a house, convinced Halston to do the same.

He bought the only town house built in Manhattan since World War II, located at 101 East Sixty-third Street. Although it had been designed for someone else, the building and integrated furniture designed by Paul Rudolph were a perfect fit for Halston, so much so that some say the house inspired some of his future fashions.

The main room, all white and gray, had a gray carpeted fifty-foot sunken living room with twenty-seven-foot ceilings, white walls, a skylight ceiling and huge gray square upholstered chairs. The delustered nylon carpet from licensee Karastan Rug Mills had a suede-like look. At the end of the living room, a twenty-seven-foot glass-walled, mirror-backed greenhouse was landscaped by Robert Lester with giant tropical and bamboo plants costing four thousand dollars.

"Except to sleep or look at TV, I rarely use any room but this, its proportions are so interesting to me," said Halston of the living room. "And it's here that I've discovered that modern is the only way to live. I like the simplification of living with only a few things."

Around the living room was a raised dining area and three levels of suspended balconies reached by a suspended wooden staircase without railings. One level had the

Living room of Halston's East Sixty-third Street town house, 1980. © Harry Benson

master bedroom and a joining giant bath, as well as planned massage and exercise rooms. On another level was a guest wing. The top floor was a studio apartment. In all, it had four bedrooms and four and a half baths plus a garage. Although Halston had collected more than four hundred pieces of art, very few were hung at any one time, keeping the look starkly clean.

The house was often used for business-related parties. When the launch of the Fieldcrest sheet and bath line and the Karastan rug designs was held there, *WWD* reported that he had his mirrored bedroom roped off, museum style, so his visitors would not muss or lie on his bed.

If Mahoney had any doubts about the potential of his new property, they were soon dispelled by an event that Halston was greatly responsible for organizing. Just months after the NSI purchase, Halston was one of five American fashion designers invited to participate in an unprecedented and unrepeated event, a joint French-American fashion show and dinner held in the Queen's Theater at the Palace of Versailles outside Paris. It was a singular event in fashion history, one that was pivotal in helping legitimize American fashion to the world.

The Versailles event began with Eleanor Lambert, the publicist who invented the Coty American Fashion Critics Awards, the Best Dressed List and the American Fashion Week at the Plaza Hotel. She was Halston's publicist from the minute he opened the doors of Halston Ltd. until Norton Simon purchased the company.

While vacationing on the Riviera as a house guest of Gerald Van Der Kemp, the curator of the Palace of Versailles, the two came up with the idea of a fashion show to try to raise at least $250,000 in much-needed funds for the Versailles Restoration Fund. Van Der Kemp offered the Queen's Theater, which hadn't been used for centuries.

"I said the only way I would do it is if the leading French designers would invite American designers, fifty-fifty," says Lambert.

It was a publicist's dream. There were a series of dinners and lunches organized around the event. Mahoney hosted one for two hundred people at Maxim's, at a cost of about $25,000. "The entire cost (show and lunch) is probably less than a half-minute commercial in the United States," Mahoney said at the time. "We've been told the Versailles show will be one of the great things of the world—a happening. And as we are new in this business, this is our way of saying we'd like to offer our support. I think this is a wise use of money."

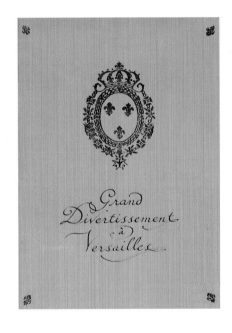

The Americans gave up their Thanksgiving holiday to be in Paris for the November 28, 1973, event. For many of the French in the audience it was the first occasion for them to see what American designers were doing.

"The couture houses were still showing the old-fashioned way, in their showrooms with twelve mannequins every afternoon," says Marc Bohan, then the designer for Christian Dior who was one of the French designers participating in the show.

The fashion elite, royalty and socialites from both sides of the Atlantic gathered for this first, and only, French-American fashion show. It was an elegant and posh spectacle beyond anything the fashion world had seen before or since. The Baronness Marie Hélène de Rothschild organized the French contingent—Hubert de Givenchy, Yves St. Laurent, Pierre Cardin, Emanuel Ungaro and Marc Bohan for Christian Dior. Eleanor Lambert invited five American designers who she felt represented the wide range of American fashion—Stephen Burrows, Anne Klein, Bill Blass, Oscar de la Renta, and Halston.

Halston initially turned down the invitation and later changed his mind, saying, "I always wanted to go, but November was such a busy time for me. However, it's turned into such a big deal that of course I'll go." A decision he would not regret.

The French hired Jean-Louis Barrault to choreograph their part of the spectacle, which was to include performances by Josephine Baker, Rudolf Nureyev, actress Capucine and the strippers/dancers from the Crazy Horse Saloon. Elaborate props, scenery and floats were planned for each of the French designer's segments.

Whether or not it was premeditated, by all accounts the French were less than accommodating toward the Americans when it came to equity in rehearsal time and facilities. The night before the show, the French

OPPOSITE TOP:
Program cover from French-American fashion show at Palace of Versailles, November 28, 1973.
OPPOSITE BOTTOM LEFT:
Queen's Theater at the Palace of Versailles.
OPPOSITE BOTTOM RIGHT:
André Oliver's farewell lunch at Maxim's, November 1973. Left to right: Marc Bohan, André Oliver, Oscar de la Renta, Halston, Joe Eula, Bill Blass.
BELOW LEFT:
A sketch of Liza Minnelli's outfit that Halston designed for the Versailles show.
BELOW RIGHT:
Scene from the opening of the American segment of the Versailles show, 1973.

contingent rehearsed first, but did so until ten o'clock at night, without providing the waiting Americans with basic amenities such as water, food, ashtrays, toilet paper and wastebaskets in the dressing rooms. Requests for certain lighting equipment that were sent to the electricians weeks in advance had not been filled. When it finally came time for the Americans to rehearse, the electricians, past their union's allotted working hours, started to walk out, and the heat in the drafty palace was turned off.

Tensions ran very high on all sides. Halston had a tantrum, but he wasn't the only one. Liza Minnelli, there to star in the show, was a unifying force, knowing that the show must go on. "Part of the reason it seemed so chaotic," says Minnelli, "was because it was a show, not a fashion show. You were dealing with models, not actresses, and you were dealing with stars, not models."

Probably for the first and last time, the American designers stopped bickering among themselves and banded together against a common enemy. They pulled off the greatest American triumph since the French and Indian War.

Each American designer spent between fifteen and twenty thousand dollars for transportation, housing and other production costs. Thanks to Halston, Kay Thompson produced and choreographed the American portion of the show and her goddaughter, Liza Minnelli, both opened and closed it with a song. Halston eventually won over the other designers to his idea of having clothes from all the designers in the opening and closing of the show, which was to prove to be one of the more powerful aspects of the American presentation. A pool of thirty-six models and ten dancers were selected to be used by all. Halston also invited such friends as Andy Warhol and Jane Holzer. In addition to the professional models, Carola Polakov, Betsey Theodoracopulus Kayser and Marisa Berenson also modeled in the show.

The 720 seats in the blue and gold theater built for Marie Antoinette in 1769 were sold out, at $235 per head. The curtain did not go up until 10 P.M., instead of 9, as they were waiting for Princess Grace of Monaco to arrive. Already seated were the Duchess of Windsor, making one of her first public appearances since she was widowed in 1972, and such European dignitaries as the Duchess of La Rochefoucauld, Vicomtesse Jacqueline de Ribes, the Begum Aga Khan and Princess Maria Gabriella of Savoy.

The French portion of the show was first. It was elaborate, lavish and, says Lambert, "was planned to be a twentieth-century version of what would have been a show in the palace at the time of Louis XVI, which they never explained. So it looked very pompous."

"The French really didn't have a theme," says Liza Minnelli. "But I think they got scared when they heard that I was coming, thinking that the Americans were going to have a big show."

A live orchestra provided the ambiance music for the hour-and-a-half long French segment. Each designer's segment had a float in keeping with their designs. Zizi

Jeanmaire was featured in Yves St. Laurent's 1930s-inspired segment, whose float was an elongated, old-fashioned car. Models in Cardin's space-age leotards and tunics entered through a space ship. Actor Louis Jourdan donned rhinoceros ears to dance in and out of a circus wagon in Ungaro's segment, not quite fitting the romantic fur-and-feathers fashion mood. Dior's giant pumpkin carried a chiffon-draped Cinderella, Danielle Darrieux, and her ladies-in-waiting wearing elegant tones of black and beige. Givenchy completed the French segment with nearly transparent evening dresses and an appearance by French actress Capucine. Rudolf Nureyev and Merle Park danced a pas de deux, and the finale featured Josephine Baker, age sixty-seven, with a chorus of strippers from the Crazy Horse Saloon in sequined G-strings.

During the half-time champagne break at 1 A.M., Mahoney remembers thinking to himself, "'They will bury us.' We had no props. Because they couldn't rehearse, Liza's singing was put on tape."

"When the Americans came on there were no sets, just lights, the models, staging and fantastic, hot music, the hit music of the day," remembers Bill Dugan. The entire American segment ran a quick thirty-five minutes. It was all scenery, movement and striking fashion. The models practically danced down the runway.

There could be no finer compliment than the one paid by an unidentified Parisian socialite in *Newsweek* magazine who said of the American designers, "They are like someone who gets invited into your home for dinner and then runs off with your wife and the silverware, as well."

Liza Minnelli opened the American segment wearing a white Halston outfit and sang "Bonjour Paris," written by Thompson especially for the event. Twenty-five years later, Liza remembers the lyrics: "What a lovely night. I'm feeling so fresh and alive. And I'm so glad to arrive. It's all so grand. You see who's here to see. I'm at home in a palace. I feel like I live in Wonderland. *Allo, allo, mes amis. Allo, allo, je suis ici. C'est merveilleux* to be back in Paree. In Paris it's always spring. Makes you want to sing and sing and sing and sing."

When the music cued up for a song from *Funny Face*, the models paraded out onto the runway, dressed by all five designers in beige and off-white rainwear and umbrellas. Then came the individual designer segments, each three minutes long. Stephen Burrows dressed his black models in bold primary-colored jerseys and stuck long quills in their Afro hairdos so they looked like praying mantises. Anne Klein followed with a safari-inspired theme showing djellaba pants and models wearing big turbans with hot African jazz playing in the background. Bill Blass showed Gatsby-esque chiffons, with model Billie Blair dressed as a genie, entrancing the other models to follow her on stage to the tunes of Cole Porter. The last individual segment was presented by Oscar de la Renta with ball gowns in a range of pale satins. Liza closed the show wearing Halston's black and silver sequins and beads, singing "Cabaret" and "Au Revoir Paris" with the entire cast dressed in varying shades of black, the men in tuxedos seated at small white tables.

In the next to last segment of the American portion, Halston's models slithered down the runway peering into hand mirrors and moving to very dramatic music by the Band. The unusual, dramatically bright colors of the outfits—ruby red and bright gold yellow set off by black—stood out from the others. Model China Machado somehow fastened her skirt so you could not even see her head, says Dugan. And model Alva Chinn wore a big hat and boa that was flung open to reveal an exposed right breast and a one-shoulder dress.

At the conclusion of the American performance, the usually sedate and controlled French audience looked like an Annapolis graduation, shouting and throwing their programs in the air. Catherine De Natale, who calls it "the favorite night of my life," remembers sitting in a box next to St. Laurent and Pierre Bergé and seeing them screaming. Mahoney says he had goose pimples.

"The French had never seen a concept like this—get it on, get it off, do it fast and precise. They had never seen people do a fashion show like this and it was just awesome," says Catherine.

"I'll never forget Yves St. Laurent, so long and gangly, coming backstage, picking up Kay and swinging her around," Minnelli remembers. "He said to her, 'The Americans have triumphed again.'"

Ungaro grumbled to *Time* magazine, "We should have realized that the Americans would know how to put on a show."

"I was totally unpleased about the French production," remembers Marc Bohan. "We never saw Jean-Louis Barrault. The French were a bit of this and that. The whole thing was *nul*. Ungaro was not pleased, Bergé was screaming. The American show was the way it always was in America, terribly professional, well put together, like a big show on Broadway. Kay Thompson knew what she was doing."

Bohan also remembers that Halston's fashions stood out from the others because "they were more personal, one style and nothing else. Halston was totally something else, very clean, neat, chic, well cut and plain. No satin, not big drama, just by itself."

Before and after the Versailles gala, business at home turned to establishing the new NSI/Halston relationship. Mahoney instituted one of his few demands, to have an NSI executive in place at Halston's offices. He appointed Ed Gallagher as the first divisional vice president and managing director of Halston Enterprises, but that only lasted about two months. His background with chemical and food vending machine companies was a world apart from fashion.

He was replaced by Michael Lichtenstein, an easygoing but astute former lawyer whose experience at Playtex and Kleinert's allowed him to quickly learn how to negotiate with and around Halston. He knew which battles were worth fighting and which ones to let roll by.

Lichtenstein masterminded a massive licensing program, a five-year plan that, at its peak, had some thirty licenses operating at one time. Only Pierre Cardin and, perhaps, Christian Dior, had as large a stable of companies manufacturing merchandise bearing their names. The Halston logo—simple, black, perfectly straight, unadorned, fine letters on a beige ground, was on its way to becoming the fashion equivalent of Coca-Cola or McDonald's.

Except for the McCall's Pattern Company and Hartmann Luggage, all previous licenses were allowed to lapse and new ones were established. Using the MOR (Merchandising and Operating Results) categories of merchandise, Lichtenstein narrowed down a list of about thirty merchandise categories "prioritized according to their potential dollar value, those that would be a good marketing tool for a designer and those that Halston would not consider an anathema."

In 1974, new licensees included: Halston IV loungewear and robes by Dorian Loungewear Inc., a subsidiary of Loungees Inc., which replaced a previously negotiated arrangement with B. Cohen & Co.; Ben Kahn Furs, replacing previous licenses with Richton and then, A.C. Bang; and the opening of a menswear subsidiary in conjunction with Rapid American Corporation. NSI also bought back Jack Sobel's and Abe Isaac's interests in Halston III rainwear.

In 1975, the new licensees included: Max Factor fragrances; Fieldcrest bed and bath products; Karastan carpets; Halston V sportswear and Halston VI blouses, both manufactured by Manhattan Industries; Sportcraft, a dress line for distribution only in Canada; and the J. Schoeneman Inc. division of Cluett Peabody & Co. for men's tailored clothing and sportswear, replacing Rapid American.

In 1976, the new licensees included: a popular-priced hat collection for Commodore hats, sister company to Designer Collections, for whom Halston already designed wigs; Daniel La Foret for scarves; Kayser-Roth for women's gloves and accessories; Paris Accessories division of Kayser-Roth for men's belts; Cluett Peabody & Co. for men's shirts; Rose Marie Reid for swimwear; Jonathan Logan for beachwear; Bausch & Lomb for eyeglasses and sunglasses; Garolini Inc. for shoes; men's robes, pajamas and swimwear with Weldon; and Misty Harbor for rainwear. The Halston V license of Manhattan Industries changed its product line from sportswear to dresses.

In 1977, licensees were added for: foundations and coordinating daywear with the Vassarette division of Munsingwear; a line for Japan with Micalady, Inc.; Tucker Ties for men's neckwear, handkerchiefs and scarves; and a cosmetics line with Max Factor. H.B. Accessories, a joint venture company, was formed with Richard Bienen as president to manufacture women's handbags, belts and small leathers. (In August 1980, Halston Enterprises sold its share of H.B. Accessories to its owners, but continued the licensee relationship.)

BELOW:
Print ad for Halston-designed sheets and bedding for Fieldcrest.
BOTTOM:
Print ad for Halston-designed Ultrasuede luggage for Hartmann Luggage.

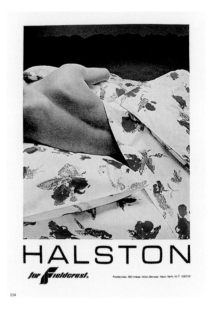

Halston and models show the range of licensed products at the Olympic Tower offices of Halston Enterprises.

RIGHT:
One of a series of four ads that Andy Warhol created for Halston-licensed accessories.

BELOW:
Artist Larry Rivers's painting used as an ad for Halston, 1975. Art © Larry Rivers/Licensed by VAGA, New York

HALSTON

33 EAST 68TH STREET, NEW YORK, N.Y. 10021 U.S.A.

In 1981, Van Heusen Co. was licensed to manufacture and market a line of men's dress and sport shirts.

To celebrate and promote the impressive and wide range of licensed products, Halston hired his friend Andy Warhol to create a series of four illustrated ads—one each for womenswear, menswear, cosmetics and fragrances, and accessories—that artistically, rather than realistically, represented all of the Halston-name products. Another artist, Larry Rivers, lent his own style to a singular Halston ad that showed the artist's concept for a new type of mannequin that had a TV monitor for a face, a cassette player for a voice and was dressed and accessorized by Halston. Friend and fashion illustrator Joe Eula produced many ads in his soft-stroke style, a sophisticated contrast to the very straightforward photography that most other designer companies were using.

The proliferation of licensing agreements was already bringing in $75 million in retail sales annually in 1976, and would grow to over $100 million. As *Signature* magazine detailed in January 1979, "You can wake up on a Halston sheet, toss off a Halston blanket and put your feet down on a Halston rug. You could put on a Halston shirt and a Halston tie and pack a Halston suitcase for a trip on which you'll be served by a Braniff stewardess in a Halston uniform. Your wife might serve you breakfast wearing a Halston bra under her Halston robe before going shopping in her Halston raincoat. And you could bring her Halston perfume in the famous tear-shaped bottle."

It was beginning to seem like Halston would put his name on almost anything. Halston refuted that, telling a *WWD* reporter in 1977, "I'm not interested in doing children's wear or aprons and I've said no to things like a container for a coffee company."

Another product he was happy to pass by was designer jeans. "I only wanted to do it with Levi's. We came close to doing it. I wanted to do a new cut. I didn't want to do the personal endorsement. I'll save that for my old age. Being a stylist is just as respectable. I'm not putting it down, but from my point of view unless I can change something, I don't want to do it. I'm not just in it for the money."

Halston also explained why he declined to put his name on a Lincoln Mercury Mark IV automobile in 1975, although the company wanted to pay him fifty thousand dollars, plus give him a car. "The cars had already been designed and they just wanted me to put my name on it," said Halston. "Why, it looked like a pimp-mobile, with a little bottle on it. . . . I only do what I want to do and I don't want to dress up cars. Putting Ultrasuede on the interior of an automobile is like putting a ruffle on a dress."

Creating a designer fragrance for Max Factor was the primary reason NSI formed Halston Enterprises, and it turned out to be one of the most lucrative fragrance deals of all times. The fragrance's creation, also known as "the battle of the bottle," is a legendary story of Halston's tenacity and unswayable determination to get what he wanted, fighting against all odds, and then being vindicated by success. As with everything Halston designed, he was intimately involved throughout the entire process, including choosing the ribbon used to tie the packages.

Max Factor's very straitlaced executives were disturbed that Halston rejected their suggested bottle design and were taken aback by Halston's emissaries, Joe Eula and Elsa Peretti. Halston developed a bottle design with Elsa Peretti based upon the shapes she had been using for her jewelry. It had a curved neck that was difficult to manufacture and impossible to fill on the normal assembly lines. Creating a leak-proof stopper was another challenge.

"I wanted a bottle that will be a collector's item," said Halston. "It was horrendous. But I'm a fighter. And after nights of work, we finally worked it out."

Max Factor wanted to call the perfume Halston Nights or Halston Romance, says Lichtenstein, but the designer refused to give it any name other than his own. He also refused to let them permanently paint his name on the bottle, demanding that his name only be on a little paper sticker around the neck that had to be removed when it was opened. Halston wanted it to be a beautiful object by itself when sitting on a woman's dressing table. He also wanted a plain box, printed only with his name, but, "we found, to his dismay, that the law required a certain amount of legal writing and sourcing, and so that was stuck on the bottom in the smallest type possible," remembers Lichtenstein.

Developing gift-with-purchase items to entice sales was, and still is, important for any fragrance, but Halston would not approve something as mundane as an umbrella. His idea was to give away Halston with Halston—a solid fragrance in a miniature Peretti bean-shaped compact, and the fragrance in miniature versions of the bottle on a sterling silver chain.

Paul Wilmot, who was vice president of public relations for Halston Fragrances, says these were so successful that "we had to limit the number of stores who would get the miniature bottles. We were doing a few thousand per year on just that item."

It took two years for the team—Halston, Peretti, Eula, Lichtenstein and Max Factor—to develop the fragrance under the tutelage of the fragrance developers at International Flavors and Fragrances. They all had to first learn the language and nuances of the perfumer's craft. After the fact, Halston told *WWD*, "Sweetheart, it was absolutely horrendous. For months and months and months I worked. It was an incredible experience. After two months of courtship, I began to discriminate the smells. And it was really very liberating. I must have smelled hundreds and hundreds of perfumes. And they were either too green, or too hot, or too dull or too boring. Nothing seemed right. It was endless."

Halston was finally satisfied with an unusual blend that contained a new, never before used essential oil. When it was finally right, he tested it on a few of his friends. They knew they had it right when at a restaurant, Charles Revson, the CEO of Revlon, approached one of his wealthy friends at another table to ask what fragrance she was wearing. It was the Halston fragrance that had not yet been released.

The fragrance was ready earlier than planned, so Halston insisted on a spring launch when everyone else wanted to wait for the more customary pre-Christmas, fall debut. Max Factor also did not want to spend the money for a grand Halston-style launch party, so Halston volunteered his new town house.

Samples of the fragrance would be given to everyone attending the launch party, and Max Factor's public relations director wanted to display them on a table

Halston regarding an array of
Elsa Peretti–designed Halston
fragrance bottles. © Arnold Newman

Halston cosmetics.

set up inside the entrance to Halston's house. Halston balked: "This is going to be a party in my home. You can give out the fragrance in advance, send it to their homes and they'll wear it to the party."

By this time, Max Factor's PR man was so intimidated by Halston that he wasn't going to take anything for granted, so before making a move he asked Halston how he thought the fragrance gifts should be delivered to the press. Lichtenstein distinctly remembers Halston reply, in his cool, deadpan style, "With midgets!"

"The Max Factor people were ready to die," says Lichtenstein. "They saw a failure looming and, in fact, they were sort of delighted. They said, 'We're going to do everything he wants. We'll show him.'"

Instead, Halston showed them. Although the fragrance was launched in the middle of a minirecession, after the first week it was on sale, a Bloomingdale's merchandise manager called the sixty-dollar-an-ounce perfume "the best introduction I've ever seen for a fashion fragrance," counting forty thousand dollars in sales. In the first three months, $1.5 million worth of perfume was sold. For more than a decade, the Halston fragrance ranked in the top ten luxury fragrances and, at its height, sold about $100 million worth of products a year, with Halston Enterprises receiving about $10 million in royalties. To this day, it is probably one of the most distinctive and recognizable bottles in the history of fragrances and the scent is still distributed by French Fragrances International.

Two men's fragrances were launched right on the heels of the success of the women's. Z-14, a heavier, more American cologne, and 1-12, a lighter, European-type counterpart, were both given their laboratory names. The women's and men's lines were soon expanded to include grooming and body care products. In 1977, a cosmetics line was launched, but was never a big success. They were packaged in versions of Elsa Peretti's designs, an asymmetrical heart compact and a lipstick tube extruded in the shape of the heart. Wilmot thought they were just too big and clunky, but there were other reasons for its less-than-stellar results.

"Calvin Klein and Ralph Lauren all had cosmetics lines out and they all failed," Wilmot recounts. "Women just have never wanted to take direction from fashion designers for their cosmetics colors. It is overreaching their sphere of authority."

Against Halston's advice and without his creative input, the $100-an-ounce Halston Night fragrance was launched in 1981, and it never achieved great success. Halston's only contribution was the pointed bottle, which was adapted from an object in his collection, a bird's beak.

"It was a bomb," says Wilmot. "There is a danger when the designer is out of ideas and the perfume company is more involved in marketing, not creating. It's not a knock on Halston. Everyone was getting launch fever. Halston had already made his statement."

Even later, when Halston was no longer actively involved, the parent company that owned his name and trademark created fragrances such as Halston Couture and Catalyst.

The mid- to late 1970s were busy years for Halston. He insisted upon personally designing collections for all the licensees and there were a bevy of special uniform design and endorsement projects. Several of these exercised his ever-active, promotionally minded imagination.

In 1974, Montgomery Ward teamed up with Halston, in a limited licensing arrangement through February 1977, to provide uniforms for the U.S. athletes who would be competing in the summer 1976 Pan American Games in Sao Paolo, Brazil; the summer 1976 Olympic Games in Montreal; and the winter 1976 Olympics in Innsbruck, Austria. In addition to Ward donating the uniforms to the team, the garments would also be sold exclusively through the Montgomery Ward catalog and stores.

The Fall–Winter 1975 and Spring–Summer 1976 Montgomery Ward catalogs that were distributed to more than six million households bore the official seal of the

BELOW:

*Olympic Team uniforms designed
by Halston for Montgomery Ward,
shown in Fall–Winter 1975 catalog.*

BOTTOM:

*Halston-designed uniforms for Braniff
Airlines' flight personnel.*

OPPOSITE:

*Halston and Halstonettes in Acapulco
during Braniff junket.*

U.S. Olympic Team and piggybacked on the retailer's "Spirit of '76" Bicentennial promotion. All of this appealed to Halston's patriotic nature.

Halston's Olympic designs included a wool-nylon blend melton zip front jacket with hood; peacoats and nylon parkas for men and women; a man's polyester double-knit blazer suit and polyester/cotton raincoat; a printed polyester knit shirtdress with self-sash and a woman's polyester gabardine pantsuit.

In 1976, after wearing Pucci-designed uniforms for ten years, Braniff Airlines asked Halston to update the look of all of the airline's personnel. He designed eight women's and six men's flight attendant uniforms in beige, brown and ivory and topped them with Ultrasuede coats. Under the coats were gabardine suits with either pants or skirts. Crepe blouses and dresses of ivory matte jersey printed with subtle Hs were also part of the women's outfits. The men wore two-button suits with matching vests, an ivory shirt and printed tie. The outfits were accessorized with big Ultrasuede shoulder bags and, for the women, leather boots.

When told of Braniff's request, Halston's quick mind immediately expanded it into a media marvel. He suggested that Braniff throw a big party in Acapulco to introduce the new uniforms, and it so happened that they were working with the Mexican government to help build tourist traffic to the resort. Braniff took advantage of it to also introduce their new luxury plane with leather seats in the first class section. Halston's licensees bought an eight-page advertising supplement in *WWD* to publicize it.

The Braniff promotion was just one example of how once Halston latched onto an idea it mushroomed with lightning speed. He could instantly see all the ramifications.

"You could go into Halston with an idea and he had a brilliant, intuitive way of grasping its real value," says Lichtenstein. With Braniff, "his imagination went on and it became three days and three nights to remember in Acapulco. We flew 250 people down for the weekend. One hundred and fifty of them were Beautiful People whose names were important. One hundred of them were press, who were more important." Among the guests were Lady Bird Johnson, Henry and Nancy Kissinger, Gloria and Loel Guinness, Mrs. Alexander Calder (whose artist husband had once designed the outside of a fleet of Braniff planes), Emilio Pucci, Warren Avis and young movie stars Deborah Raffin and Susan Blakely.

Mary Wells, a big customer of Halston's made-to-order collection, and her husband, Harding

Lawrence, president and chairman of the board of Braniff, hosted many of the junket's parties at their villa. On the second night, Halston presented a dinner and fashion show at the Taj Mahal restaurant with a runway constructed across a reflecting pool. One day, there was a cruise with eleven yachts that started at the Club de Yates and ended in Puerto Marquez Bay for a beach barbecue. On Sunday, a series of brunches were served under the palm trees of five private villas. Peter Duchin and his band led the final evening's dinner entertainment and Salute to Mexico.

Taking advantage of the ninety-degree, balmy Acapulco weather, another fashion show was held at the outdoor theater of the Acapulco Cultural and Convention Center. A muslin tent was erected as a dressing room, but no one thought to leave openings for ventilation.

"We started doing the show without thinking," remembers design assistant Bill Dugan, who at the last minute was called upon to model a steward's uniform in the show. "The girls were modeling chiffons and dripping wet. Halston asked for some fans but started to slash the canvas. He was shirtless during the entire show."

The trip was a nonstop fashion show. At each event, Halston and his Greek chorus of models, by then known as the Halstonettes, made *en masse* grand entrances wearing preplanned, coordinated outfits. One night they wore printed matte jersey; on another they all wore various tones of pale charmeuse. The most memorable entrance was at the beachside picnic, when all the models and Halston

entered the cove in boats, each one wearing a different style of black bathing suit, huge mirrored lens sunglasses from recently signed licensee Bausch & Lomb, huge black straw hats and Peretti's diamonds by the yard.

With fond remembrances of his own scouting days, in 1978 Halston gladly accepted the request to design new uniforms for the adult staff and leaders of the Girl Scouts of the U.S.A., and did so without charging a design or royalty fee. Mainbocher had done the same in 1948. Joe Eula contributed color sketches of the collection and Halston's workroom provided the prototypes for production.

The first thing Halston did was tone down the Girl Scouts' standard emerald green to a sophisticated, more wearer-friendly shade of sage. He designed a five-part group of durable-press, soil-release finished, machine-washable, textured polyester gabardine separates—jackets, vests, skirts and pants—all finished off with ivory, silk-like polyester blouses and a self-fabric oblong scarf that doubled as either an ascot or a sash belt. For a casual mood, straight-legged pants could be worn with long-sleeved, open notched-collar blouses and a vest or jacket. For more formal occasions, there was a gently gathered, modified A-line four-panel skirt worn with a softly shaped and elongated three-button jacket. It was topped off with a new preshaped beret or a visor.

The uniforms were officially installed at a reception at Olympic Tower in May 1978, where adult Girl Scouts volunteered to be models. Halston also displayed them in the windows of his Madison Avenue boutique with boxes of Girl Scout cookies placed around the mannequins' feet, cookies spilling out onto the floor. As a thank-you, the Girls Scouts presented Halston with a Steuben ashtray and a pair of beaded white moccasins made by members of the Southern Cheyenne Indian tribe.

"Just what I wanted," said Halston to the crowd. "When I was living in Iowa, we went fishing up north near Indian territory and I always admired the feather headdresses and moccasins." But he told *WWD* that he wasn't sure if he would wear them to disco or just display them in his home.

That same year, the New York City Police Department, in cooperation with the *New York Post*, asked Halston to submit ideas for reoutfitting the winter uniforms for the force's twenty-four thousand women and men in blue. Again, he waived his usual design fee, telling the *Post*, "I live in New York. I work in New York. I have a good time in New York and I like doing things to help New York."

After declaring their current winter garb uncomfortable, outdated and unsuitable for New York's extreme weather, Halston designed a shiny black quilted down jacket with a hood and hat in weatherproof nylon, and stretch gabardine pants tucked into pile-lined boots.

"The Police Department never followed through, they never even had the model made," says Lichtenstein. "But we got all the publicity we could get from it."

In 1979, Avis, the car rental company that had been recently acquired by Norton Simon, asked Halston to create their first designer uniforms. Until then, their seven thousand employees wore red uniforms with accents of blue, brown and gray. Halston retained the signature Avis orangey-red but combined it with gray and white. There were a total of about twenty-five different polyester-cotton blend pieces that were manufactured by Fashionaire, including outerwear, a seven-piece women's wardrobe, a special shirt for managers, an initial-A belt buckle and a men's wardrobe consisting of sweater, vest, jacket, gray slacks, white shirt and tie.

"They had road shows for employees at Avis offices in dozens of cities where they gave away fragrance samples," remembers Mike Karan, then an Avis rental sales agent in Boston, and now a vice president of the company. "When I look back, it is where we are going today with the uniforms. We're trying to get back to that look. It definitely worked."

ABOVE:
Halston-designed uniforms for Avis Rent-A-Car personnel.
OPPOSITE:
Halston-designed adult Girl Scout uniforms.

ABOVE:
Halston admires the view from the
raw space of his new office in Olympic
Tower, January 1978.
OPPOSITE TOP:
Halston's Olympic Tower office.
OPPOSITE BOTTOM:
Halston in assistants' room at
Olympic Tower. Perucho Valls (left),
Johanna Ricchardi (right), and
D. D. Ryan (in distance).

In 1977, after Norton Simon put its growth plans for Halston Enterprises into effect, it became clear that, with a staff of about seventy people, the company was rapidly out growing its space on Sixty-eighth Street. A safety inspection showed that the building was a fire hazard, and Lichtenstein did not want to take the chance that they might have "the most fashionable re-enactment of the Triangle Shirt Waist Company Factory fire." So he began scouring the real estate market at a time when most commercial space was renting for eight to ten dollars a square foot. Lichtenstein found several suitable spots, including the very expensive twelve dollars a foot space in the new Olympic Tower building at Fifty-first Street off of Fifth Avenue.

When Halston saw the twenty-first floor of the Olympic Tower building he fell in love with the spectacular views. In many ways it was an unusual space. It was the last floor separating the building's lower floor offices from the upper apartments, and because it was positioned just under the air-conditioning and electrical wiring, it was one and a half stories high with eighteen-foot ceilings. The view from one side stretched down to Wall Street, and from the other, up to Harlem. It felt like you were floating over Fifth Avenue, with the tops of the spires of St. Patrick's Cathedral visible at eye level and almost at touching distance, right outside the window.

Halston saw the potential of the raw space, and as soon as David Mahoney approved it, he immersed himself in its design. He wanted it to be a flexible space that could serve as both a showroom and a theater for fashion shows. With the architects Gruzen & Partners, Halston produced a modern crystal palace in the middle of midtown Manhattan.

The northern half of the twelve-thousand-square-foot floor became a spectacular workroom that could still be considered state-of-the-art. The workroom staff, who had been working in small, cramped spaces in the Sixty-eighth Street brownstone, were thrilled.

"You had sixty-five sewing machines in some of the most expensive real estate in New York," says Sassy Johnson Connor, who ran Halston's made-to-order department for eight years of her ten-year employment with Halston.

All the walls were mirrored, including the ninety-foot-long main room, which reflected the New York skyline. The room was separated into four sections—Halston's office, a conference room and two rooms for private customers—all divided by eighteen-foot-high mirrored doors. Each door weighed one and a half tons and were masterfully engineered to Halston's specifications so they could be opened and closed with a light pull. When the doors were all folded back, it left an open space large enough to create a theater that seated three hundred.

Andy Warhol ultimately chose the color for the rug, saying a strong color like red was needed to anchor the space and counteract the floating feeling. Even so, Connor remembers one client, Lady Dudley, who was afraid of heights and when

she came for fittings, screens were put up in the hallway because she could not enter the windowed fitting rooms.

Licensee Karastan made the red carpet with a pattern of connecting Hs. And Charles Fister designed the huge blood-red, lacquered Parsons tables that were everywhere, including one that served as Halston's desk. The design included a closed-circuit TV for shows, theatrical lighting and its own air-conditioning and heating system.

"He knew every single detail of what he wanted there, including which side of the door the handle should be on and how high they should be," says Faye Robeson, Halston's personal secretary. "The architects originally wanted the doors to be electrically opened with the touch of a button, but Halston rejected that, didn't trust that they might not work when they were needed."

While the offices were still under construction Halston held a staff Christmas party there, complete with a decorated Christmas tree and a feast catered by Glorious Foods. A bus was rented to transport the staff, and Halston, from Sixty-eighth Street to Fifty-first Street. "His greatest joy was showing the people in the workroom what their new environment would be. Their environment was better than his, their lighting was the best. He didn't stint with them at all," remembers Robeson.

For his office, Halston chose the area that looked out over St. Patrick's Cathedral. Many a visitor became flustered and intimidated by the sight of Halston, in his uniform of head-to-toe black and mirrored glasses, sitting directly in front of the church spires, which seemed to be protruding from his head.

Halston demanded a stark, pristine environment. Sassy Johnson Connor remembers she was not allowed to have any papers on her desk or a filing cabinet in her office. "It was just as though nobody lived there. I had to come up with a little desk and filing cabinets in a little alcove where the seamstresses were. And Halston's office, for everything that was going on, was always kind of sparse."

The Spring–Summer 1978 made-to-order collection was the first shown at Olympic Tower. Halston planned it to begin at dusk; the city lights outside a dramatic backdrop that almost upstaged the clothes. Liza Minnelli helped her friend christen the runway by modeling a black dress in the show's finale. She presented a long-stemmed rose to Elizabeth Taylor, who was seated in the front row.

"Imagine if you were in stately procession and looking out the window you saw as a backdrop Notre Dame Cathedral. That was the feeling we had at the Halston opening. But it was more exciting," said journalist Sally Kirkland in the *RAM Report*. "Over the years I have sat in Dior's Grand Salon in Paris, in the Italian couturiers' palazzos and, in the glamour days of Hollywood, in Adrian's white-columned mansion reminiscent of *Gone With The Wind*. But this was the most exciting way to see some of the most exciting clothes produced anywhere, not just in New York."

Mahoney may have jokingly referred to the Olympic Tower offices as "the most expensive loft in New York," but he knew it was a bargain considering the amount

Liza Minnelli models in finale of first fashion show at Olympic Tower, the made-to-order collection for Summer 1978.

A celebrity-filled front row was typical at Halston fashion shows at Olympic Tower. Left to right: Carol Channing, Liza Minnelli, an unidentified man, Martha Graham, Doris Duke, D. D. Ryan.

of publicity it generated and how well it was used. Important openings and public relations events were held there, such as a star-studded party to celebrate Halston being given the annual Martha Graham Award. A candlelit buffet party was given for eighty NATO officers, including Halston's brother Robert, in 1983. Overlooking the cathedral was a perfect place for the Mahoneys' St. Patrick's Day party, the green lights of the Empire State Building visible in the distance.

Halston's Olympic Tower fashion shows became the hottest ticket in town, always attended by celebrities and society clients. And he directed and styled them himself. The power of the media was just coming into prominence and Halston, as much showman as fashion designer, innately understood how to use it to his advantage. Where one was seated at his show became as political as the floor plan at the United Nations. The fourteen front-row seats on the St. Patrick's side were for the stars—Liza, Elizabeth, Martha Graham, Berry or Marisa Berenson, Bianca Jagger and others, like Pamela Harriman, who were rarely in town. Next best would be the front seats along the sides of the runway.

"We would ruminate over who got the best seats. If Halston didn't like what we did, he would move it around," says Connor. "Women would get mad at the door and mad at me. I would have to apologize and not let them know that Halston had moved them from the front row." By Halston's instruction, Connor would handwrite the place cards and envelopes that sat on each chair.

The gifts given to the press were a detail Halston never overlooked. For one press show, sixteen thousand dollars was spent on gifts to be left on the seats, every bag containing an expensive sterling silver compact and a sterling silver–encased lipstick from his cosmetics line.

LEFT:
Halston poses with models after fashion show, Elsa Peretti at his right, June 1970.

BELOW:
Hot fashions for Spring 1973 photographed in a firehouse with models Karen Bjornson, Anjelica Huston and Naomi Sims.

The seeds of today's supermodel era were planted at Halston's fashion shows. Halston and Giorgio di Sant'Angelo were among the first designers to challenge the unspoken rule that runway and photographic models were two different species that were never to be mixed. The Halstonettes, as *WWD* called them, were the top eight models of the day, whom Halston used regularly for shows, print photography and as "dates" for benefits and social events. Because Halston's clothes had few if any accessories, enabling quick backstage changes, he was able to use eight models when other designers used as many as twenty. Halston was amused by the tongue-in-cheek reference to Radio City Music Hall's Rockettes. Before he got serious, former model Pat Cleveland remembers him standing in front of the line of models waiting for the fashion show to begin, announcing "left foot forward, right foot forward," like the famous dancers.

The earliest Halstonettes included Naomi Sims, Elsa Peretti, Pat Cleveland, Marina Schiano, China Machado, Anjelica Huston and his house models, first Diane Morgan, then Heidi Lieberfarb. Later house models Karen Bjornson and Shirley Ferro were added, as well as Connie Cook, Carla Araque, Alva Chinn, Nancy Gregor, Margaret Donohue and Chris Royer. Nancy North Dugan modeled in Halston's shows but was also a house model for the Halston Originals ready-to-wear line. Tony Spinelli, Martin Snaric and Pat Anderson were the main male models.

Many thought Halston needed to be surrounded by people, perhaps to camouflage a deep-seated but rarely seen shyness and insecurity. "I think he used them at parties as a buffer, also," says Connor of the Halstonettes. "He was surrounded by people all the time and he needed that on some level. He was like the patriarchal father with the children. He had a lot of control over them."

Naomi Sims modeled in Halston's very first show along with her friend Elsa

Halston pitches the new looks for Fall 1976 at Yankee Stadium.

Peretti. As part of his entourage, Sims was escorted around town in Halston's super-stretch limousine. When she stopped modeling to start her own wig and cosmetics business, she changed roles and became one of his regular clients. For that first show on Sixty-eighth Street, Sims remembers that Halston "had all the dresses ready for us when we arrived and we fit them to a T."

Before moving to Los Angeles to concentrate on acting, Anjelica Huston modeled for many top designers. "I was very frightened and he was very strict with me," says Huston of her first meeting with Halston. "Halston was the big cheese at the time and I was very excited because he had called the agency and asked if I would go up to see him. He made me walk up and down in front of him. He appraised me, and asked me to walk a bit slower. As I walked, I started to think it was sort of amusing and could see that he was sort of breaking down a bit too. The first time I modeled in a show for him, I put my arms over my head. After the show he took me aside and said, 'We don't do that at Halston.'"

Elsa Peretti left her wealthy Italian family to come to the United States to model in 1968, just when Halston was opening his business. He encouraged her to pursue jewelry design and personally arranged for her jewelry to be sold first at Blooming-dale's, and then at Tiffany and Company. Dugan says that Peretti told him that Halston taught her a great lesson, to always make her jewelry in three sizes—small for the Japanese, large for the Americans, and medium for everyone else.

Beautiful as the models were, sometimes Halston remade them into his own image. "He wanted them to look better and feel comfortable with themselves," says Bill Dugan. Connie Cook's blond hair was cut boyishly short. Elsa Peretti was also encouraged to wear a short hairstyle. Shirley Ferro arrived in Halston's office with bleached-blond hair down to her waist, but it did not stay that way very long. It was immediately cut and dyed back to its natural brown color.

The photographer Stanley (Stash) Papich says Halston turned Karen Bjornson into a butterfly. Stash knew her before Halston, when he had taken her photos as Miss Cincinnati. "Halston redid her look and turned her from All-American into chic," he says. She became the face most people instantly identified with Halston, captured on the cover of *Newsweek* magazine, and had the distinction of wearing the first Ultrasuede dress and of opening his fashion shows.

Eighteen-year-old Bjornson came to New York from the Midwest to become a model and was having little success until the day that her agency, Wilhelmina, sent her to see Halston.

"That first encounter was magical," says Bjornson. "Halston was having coffee with someone and he had me try on clothes from the collection. I started working as his house model that day. In the beginning, he was my employer, but I grew up through the relationship and at the end, he was a great friend." So much so that when she got married in 1977, Halston not only made her wedding dress but also hosted the wedding reception in his town house.

As a house model, Halston actually designed and fitted his collections on Bjornson. She sometimes became so attached to certain garments that it was difficult to see other models wearing them during the fashion shows.

"I would stand like a piece of sculpture and he would be the artist creating the design," she remembers. "Halston would pin the tape to create the décolletage, or would cut the fabric to create a ruffle. He was always concerned with how the garment worked, not just how it looked. He would ask me how I felt wearing the outfit, would ask me to walk to see how it moved, asked me to sit down to see if the wraparound wrapped enough.

"He had a certain vision of you [the model] and he would design a whole season's wardrobe for you, from sportswear to evening wear. It was very exciting to be a part of that. When you're the house model, and working on the designs with him, it becomes a very close relationship, and that continued after I left the industry," says Bjornson, who keeps a picture of Halston in her kitchen.

Not only models were subjected to his inscrutable attentions. His personal secretary, Faye Robeson, was convinced to stop dyeing her hair black and let it go gray. Pat Ast, a friend and Andy Warhol character actress, was originally hired as a salesperson for the custom salon. Before she became his first plus-size model, Halston changed her looks from dowdy to chic. He encouraged her to change and henna her hair, get a good cut, and let it be natural and frizzy.

Tony Spinelli, one of the male Halstonettes, first met the designer in 1970 when doing a test shoot with photographer Charles Tracy. He wore Halston clothes and had Halston girls, Elsa Peretti and Marina Schiano, on each arm. Spinelli later became the advertising face for Halston's men's fragrances.

"He was very generous, gave me time and talked to me," says Spinelli. "We had this real estate relationship. We were both investing in properties at the time and I would ask him advice and he always advised me correctly. Whenever I went on talk shows, I would ask him advice about how to handle being on TV, what to say and what not to say. He was so good about it."

He was also generous with model Anjelica Huston. "When I went to California he gave me all these beautiful dresses to take with me. He was sort of secretly sentimental. He was initially very frightening, but once he was on your side, it was nice. And you felt you had accomplished something by winning him over."

"A divine swan" is how Pat Cleveland describes the designer, and traveling with him in his "limo life" was like traveling with a king where "the bottom of your feet never touched the pavement." The "Duchess of Cleveland," as she was nicknamed, was very young when she first started working for Halston, and whenever they would attend an evening event he would personally pick her up at her mother's house in his limo, like a big brother. When the doors were closed "he was so plain and teasing," Cleveland says. "But when clients came, he was much more dignified and reserved. He would stick out that amazing chin a bit when it was time for us to behave properly. Everyone thought he had a ten-ton jaw, but underneath he was like the ugly duckling. He was very vulnerable."

Each of the Halstonettes had a different look and were chosen to complement each other. And at a time when the typical model was five feet, eight inches tall, the Halstonettes were five feet, ten inches and taller. "He wanted all sorts of women to think, well, that's me in that dress," says Nancy North Dugan.

Heidi Lieberfarb was small, an American Twiggy type with curly strawberry-blond hair, big blue eyes and a freckled nose. Rail-thin Karen Bjornson with narrow shoulders, long legs and arms and blue eyes was a delicate country doll, his Cinderella, and always wore white, black, gold, beige or pale pink. Chris Royer was his athletic tomboy. Nancy North Dugan had the perfect measurements for fitting and was never allowed to wear red but always light blue. Elsa Peretti and Naomi Sims were slinky. Pat Cleveland says she was his "grand-size poodle" and always wore the things that moved, like capes and anything red. Anjelica Huston remembers wearing mostly simple and sporty clothes, like trench coats and cashmere tubes.

At fashion shows, Halston would be backstage, giving his final approval to the outfits before the models walked out on the runway. "He sent you out the door and made you feel like the woman who might be buying the clothes, like you were going out for the evening with his approval," says Bjornson.

Halston and his troupe once again made fashion history when he was the first American designer invited to show his clothes in China. In early 1979, China had just opened its borders. A fourteen-member trade delegation from the country's silk industry visited the United States and Halston's showroom and production facilities. As a friendly hands-across-the-ocean exchange, the designer was invited to visit China's silk-producing cities to offer advice on the demands of the American market. This was at the same time that Halston's Japanese licensee, Kosugi Sangyo Inc., was about to launch the Halston apparel line, and the Halston fragrance was being launched in Paris, both requesting a personal appearance.

Halston parlayed this into a six-hundred-thousand-dollar around-the-world tour, hitting three continents and six cities in twenty-four days. A third of the cost was paid by the Japanese licensee; funds were also provided by the Chinese government, about $165,000 was paid by the perfume division, and the rest was funded by Norton Simon.

Seeing is believing and understanding, said Halston, so he decided to bring the Halston and American spirit to China with a traveling fashion show. "I don't think

"Halston was really the first American designer to make an original American statement, particularly in a time when fashion was so derivative of European designs. It sounds corny, but he was the quintessential American designer."

—BILL BLASS

BELOW LEFT:
Halston visits his boutique in Tokyo's Isetan department store, September 1980.

BELOW RIGHT:
Japanese dinner with Halstonettes and Bianca Jagger (at Halston's right), September 1980.

BOTTOM LEFT:
A mao tai toast in China during World Tour, September 1980.

BOTTOM RIGHT:
Model Alva Chinn shows Halston garments to Chinese apparel industry executives, September 1980.

they realize the facets of society we have here. I want them to see the different walks of life of the affluent Americans we dress, and that our needs are quite large," Halston said.

This was to be Halston's finest directorial hour. "I want to have it like a little movie. It makes it more amusing and removes the whole curse of it being just a business thing. If we directed our whole planet the way we would a play or a movie, it would make life more interesting for everyone," Halston explained.

Weeks were spent preparing the shoes and the color-coordinated clothes for the entire "corps de ballet" of twenty-eight people, including models, assistants, executives and friends. Friend and photographer Hiro, who had lived in both Japan and China, was a calming force and documented the expedition.

For every occasion in every city there was a special outfit for everyone on the trip. "The only thing I didn't furnish was their underwear and something to sleep

in," said Halston. "That's the fascination of it—to be able to edit a wardrobe down to the pieces necessary for a world tour."

"We were like migrating birds, well-choreographed, all color-coordinated," remembers Pat Cleveland.

Red jogging outfits were for sleeping on the plane. Pajamas made of silk from the Chinatex mills were worn for banquets given by the Chinese. Red, white and blue separates were the uniform for an American-style banquet thrown by Halston in Beijing. Iridescent taffeta pants outfits were provided for a geisha party in Kyoto, "because everyone will be sitting on the floor." Waterproof silk taffeta jackets were worn when visiting the Great Wall of China. Ruffled dresses were worn at the dinner party in Paris. Black kimonos were worn backstage and Elsa Peretti silver heart-on-a-cord compacts were worn around their necks at all times, like a logo. It was one continuous photo op.

Halston and entourage visit the Great Wall of China outside Beijing. Left to right, back row: Pat Cleveland, Martin Snaric, Chris Royer, Margaret Donohue, D. D. Ryan, Connie Cook, Halston, Karen Bjornson, Tony Spinelli, Nancy North Dugan, Bill Dugan. Front row: Pat Anderson, Alva Chinn, Peter Eng, Carla Araque, Perucho Valls, Victor Hugo.

The entourage piled into nine identical limousines to go to Kennedy Airport, "dressed in sportswear in complementary shades of red, black, beige and ivory, so anyone could stand next to anyone else and not clash—sunglasses as glossy black and secludingly impenetrable as the limos, watched as piece after piece of matching brown Ultrasuede luggage covered the sidewalks," a *WWD* editor reported. "Halston always looked crisp, was efficient, looking as if he had been dry cleaned along with his black pants and turtleneck."

The first stop was Los Angeles for two days and a fashion show at Bullock's department store in conjunction with the Costume Council of the Los Angeles Art Museum.

Then came five days in Japan that included a fashion show at the Imperial Hotel in Tokyo with a giant mirrored runway followed by a reception featuring a twelve-foot ice carving of the Statue of Liberty, all arranged by the licensee. The show brought the Manhattan skyline and sounds of the city to Tokyo, with the clothes shown in scenes with projected backdrops depicting Central Park, a beach, a cocktail party and other all-American activities.

Paris, last stop on the World Tour: Halston with disco queen Regine, who is wearing a Halston.

Other business involved a visit to the Isetan department store where the Halston boutique was opened, and a press reception for the launch of the men's fragrances. For fun, Japanese designers Hanae Mori and Issey Miyake gave a dinner party to welcome Halston to their country. And everyone, including Halston, learned to dance like a geisha at dinner at the Jisaku restaurant. They spent a few days in Kyoto just to see the sights.

As soon as the group arrived in Beijing and settled into the state guest houses where they were residing, everyone went to the Friendship Stores to buy Mao outfits, which they all wore at the same time. Halston was introduced to *mao tai*, the powerful Chinese liquor, and he returned the favor with an American-style banquet with baked fish, roast pork filet, leg of lamb, apple pie, California wine and I Love NY buttons, arranged with the help of the American embassy.

The fashion show took place in an auditorium in Shanghai attended by fashion and textile manufacturers from all over China. The Chinese had never before seen clothes like this and had no concept of where someone might wear the sexy, sheer, flesh-baring numbers. They were so shocked that when Halston introduced the question-and-answer period that was planned to follow the show, everyone was too timid to say anything. In a moment of inspiration, Halston asked if they would like to look at the clothes and had the racks pulled in to let them touch, look, try on and examine the workmanship.

"It was one of the most dramatic half hours that I've spent in fashion," says Michael Lichtenstein. "People really communing over the work, not over the personality. They were so excited to see fabrics like this, to have the cuts explained. Halston really made it happen with his quick mind."

The last stop before going home was five days in Paris, mainly for R and R, but also for a Black theme party Halston gave at Regine's club to promote the perfume launch.

In 1980, Halston's relationship with NSI was working well for everybody. Although Mahoney said that NSI "sold more Canada Dry in Pittsburgh than the total of Halston sales," the company was making money on the fragrance. Halston was pleased because he had his creative freedom and nothing short of an empire.

"He was like a rocket," says Mahoney. "He just kept going up and up and up. It seemed like everything was going right."

The tide started to turn when the corporation decided it needed to increase revenues and opened a new division, Halston Sportswear, with separate offices headed by C. Crawford Mills Jr., previously head of the Halston V and VI divisions of Manhattan Industries. There are several reasons why Halston Sportswear, a "bridge" line before the term was invented, lasted only two seasons—Halston was not comfortable designing sportswear separates, and he would not delegate the design responsibility to anyone else.

BELOW LEFT:
Buffalo-check wool-nylon shirtjacket and scarf created for Halston Sportswear and Halston III for JCPenney.
© *Rico Puhlmann*
BELOW:
Halston Sportswear ad.

Halston's perfectionism and need to control and approve absolutely every item that carried his name was both one of his greatest assets and greatest faults. A self-professed workaholic, he loved his profession, but when the added pressures of designing for such a large number of licensees conflicted with his artistic temperament, it was a recipe for disaster.

Halston Sportswear was disbanded shortly before, and probably because of, an impending deal with JCPenney. The midpriced retailer had been searching for a designer name to associate with as part of a program to improve its fashion image. But it was not the first time the retailer had done so, says Lois Ziegler, who was fashion director for JCPenney. In 1965, to capitalize on the trend to teen-oriented British fashion, the retailer had done special collections and promotions with Mary Quant, and home furnishings collections were also developed with designer Cathy Hardwick. JCPenney targeted Halston when his name came out on top for both recognition and credibility in a customer survey on American designers.

Around this time, in 1981 and 1982, the pressures and demands of Halston's growing design empire, in combination with his highly publicized, self-destructive lifestyle, began to take its toll on his personality and his designs. His temper flared more frequently and erratically, and the buzz around the office was that he started to believe his own press releases, which puffed up his talents and his importance. His fashion shows had lost their edge and the press began referring to them as *déjà vu*.

In a meeting that was infamous among Halston's staff, Robert "Kam" Kammerschen, then executive vice president of five NSI holdings, showed Halston how little his company meant within the big corporate picture. With flowcharts, he showed how the corporation would have made more profit if they had taken the money they used to purchase Halston and put it in the bank.

That was the mood when Mahoney presented Halston with the details of a licensing deal that had already been negotiated with JCPenney but needed his approval to move forward. It was also the signpost most often designated as the beginning of the end of Halston's active designing career.

In September 1982, Norton Simon announced a licensing deal between Halston Enterprises and JCPenney that was called "a new era in the history of American fashion and retailing," and "the most significant design-licensing agreement in the history of the fashion industry." The multimillion dollar, six-year agreement represented $1 billion in retail sales. With a conservative estimate of $100 million in wholesale sales per year, the 5 percent royalty would easily bring NSI an annual income of $5 million.

Starting with the Fall 1983 season, JCPenney exclusively sold womenswear designed by Halston under the Halston III label. (The rainwear line that had been called Halston III had been discontinued years before.) Children's and men's apparel and home furnishings were to be added later. The collections, priced at the upper end of Penney's range, were sold in their catalogs and in 550 selected Penney's stores in specially designed and fixtured Halston boutiques.

The great disparity between his made-to-order customers and the JCPenney audience was questioned, but Halston seemed to be genuinely pleased to have the opportunity to dress all of America.

"I'm a very prolific designer," Halston declared. "I didn't sell myself out like some of the others did. As long as you keep your style and your standards, it can only enhance your name by reaching a broader audience.

"You know me, I'm as American as apple pie. I'm the original Mr. Sweater Set. I like casual clothes and have never been able to make them. When I was a kid, I always shopped in JCPenney. Remember, I come from Des Moines, Iowa."

On June 7, 1983, a big fashion show with one thousand spectators was held in the Hall of Ocean Life at the American Museum of Natural History. In the show were casual separates, some of the same styles in his better ready-to-wear line but toned down with fabrics and construction that met Penney's price range—from twenty-two dollars for a sweater up to two hundred dollars for a wool melton wrap coat. The line was divided into three groups—the Collections group of coordinated separates, the Collectibles group of volume-priced items that changed from season to season, and the Lifestyle group of functional apparel for career, sports, activewear and special occasions, including denim. The look was pure Halston and recognizable even without a visible logo. It included argyle twin sets, black and red buffalo-check skirts cut on the bias, fly-front shirts, ascot blouses with petal collars, cape-like stoles in Shetland wool, a shirtwaist dress in an H-print fabric, beaded tops and knit dresses.

The show was repeated in twenty-one cities across the country, with Halston appearing via videotape. Ten million dollars was spent on an advertising campaign, including magazine advertising, radio and TV spots. Within one month of the merchandise being in the stores it had received 33 percent sell through.

"When I first heard about the JCPenney clothes, I thought, gee, how great that in this economy, with a small amount of money, women could have Halston designs," says Polly Mellen, former fashion editor and creative director of *Vogue* magazine, and currently with *Allure* magazine. "But when I saw the clothes, it was clear they didn't know how to make them. The spiral pant became just baggy pants. The prints were too bourgeois. I don't think he needed to do that, it wasn't his strength."

Before agreeing to the JCPenney venture, Norton Simon had conducted studies to determine if sales of either the Halston fragrance or apparel might be affected. They found nothing significant to indicate that it would. But the backlash from Halston's upscale retail outlets was swift and furious.

Bergdorf Goodman was the first of his prestige retail clients to jump ship, discontinuing sales of his ready-to-wear and cosmetics. Ira Neimark, president and

CEO of the store, was quoted in *WWD* as saying, "We decided that designers as well as retailers must decide who their customers are. They made their decision and we made ours."

"It was so silly because obviously Bergdorf Goodman in New York City and the Penney stores around the country were running totally different lines," says Lois Ziegler, formerly of Penney's. "It might have been an excuse on their part. I thought it was a compliment to Penney's."

"If the store hadn't made such a stink about it, I don't think their carriage trade clientele would even have known about it," agrees Ellin Saltzman, former fashion director of Saks Fifth Avenue. "As far as I was concerned, there wasn't a reason why he couldn't do both. The customers had nothing to do with each other. The clothes certainly didn't look like the ones he was showing at Olympic Tower."

"A two-thousand-dollar beaded dress is quite different from a ninety-dollar wash-and-wear dress," said Halston. "It's so noncompetitive. Penney's doesn't even have a store in New York City."

Today, with designer labels available at all price levels and in all types of stores, it might still be considered an audacious move for a top-level designer to sell to a mass marketer, but it would not be as surprising or as shocking. But in 1982, the idea of the same designer selling merchandise to Bergdorf Goodman and JCPenney at the same time was too great a stretch of the imagination.

At the time, Ben Kahn Furs said it was dropping the Halston license due to a change in company policy to promote its own name. Today, owner Ernie Graf admits the real reason was the JCPenney deal. But even then, most retailers took a wait-and-see attitude and the majority concluded that there would be no adverse effect to Halston fragrance or apparel sales. Unfortunately, Halston's status image had already been tarnished in the press.

What nobody mentioned at the time, however, and what was of greater concern to department stores, was Max Factor's widespread practice of discounting the Halston fragrance to mass marketers at the same time it was promoting it to department stores as a prestige fragrance. "Max Factor was doing that to itself," says Paul Wilmot. "It was the cause of great consternation among people inside the company. The fragrances were being sourced and made internationally and brought back into the United States by our own company."

"I wouldn't do it again for one reason," Mahoney says today of the JCPenney arrangement. "Because we didn't have approval over design, production or shipping. That was all done by the bureaucrats over at JCPenney. From a logistics point of view, it was a shambles. They had great distribution and if we had put NSI people in there to help with the distribution, it would have been a different story. They also had a committee Halston had to work with. They were approving his looks and this infuriated him. It's a good formula if you're making towels or sheets, but not fashion."

On June 6, 1983, the day before the JCPenney collection was launched, David Mahoney led a leveraged buyout of NSI, offering to take the corporation private at twenty-nine dollars per share in cash and preferred stock for all of the company's outstanding 25 million shares. On June 27, 1983, Esmark, Inc. made a bid of $925 million to buy NSI, which Mahoney accepted. Practically before the ink on that contract was dry, in May 1984, Esmark was acquired by Beatrice Foods for $2.8 billion. Halston Enterprises along with Max Factor and Orlane were made a division of its International Playtex Inc. division. In just over a year, Halston had been managed by three different parent companies with as many CEOs.

With these corporate maneuverings, Halston lost the protection and understanding of his friend David Mahoney, and became part of a corporate culture that saw only the red and black on a ledger sheet, but not the many shades of gray in which a designer-artist needed to function.

Carl Epstein, a former president of the Danskin division of International Playtex, was first brought in to spend several months "doctoring" the company, but was named managing director in September 1983. It was like mixing oil and water. It is clear from the way Carl Epstein today explains the reasons why the arrangement did not work that their two approaches had little ground on which to meet.

"Halston and I had a very close relationship until the first time I had to say no to him," says Epstein. "He was brilliant, absolutely brilliant. He would grasp and really understand the most complex issues, but to implement things outside of the three areas he felt comfortable in—fashion, gracious entertaining, and the lifestyle he pursued—there was something that scared him. Many geniuses have in many ways been immature outside of their arena."

Halston the name was on the verge of becoming a trademark and not a personality, says Epstein, which would have been the secret to its future success.

"It was a stage in the development of the business, and the only way it could grow to become like a Pierre Cardin, a $5 billion business around the world, was to organize it as a business and not a fiefdom. That was the essential point we were at."

The more corporate control that was exercised, the more Halston rejected and resisted it. The Olympic Tower showroom became a battleground for control of Halston Enterprises and there really was no question who would win. In August 1984, acting on the advice of his attorney, Halston's two-week vacation turned into one of several months while, says Attorney Malcolm Lewin, a claim was being prepared against Playtex. Lewin remembers that, finally, there was a standoff because Playtex would not allow Halston to exercise his contractual right to shared control over design. So it was mutually agreed that Halston's role in Halston Enterprises would be in name only, but that he would continue to receive his contracted salary of over $1 million a year. In October 1983, Halston's original ten-year contract

with NSI expired, but his $1 million plus per year salary was extended until June 30, 1988.

The last full collection Halston designed was for the Spring 1984 season. Under the design direction of John Ridge, the Halston Design Studio continued to design the JCPenney and licensed collections, and, for a short time, small made-to-order collections.

Halston never gave up the fight to buy back his company. "I'm the ultimate optimist. It's part of my great WASPy background. And I'm a Taurus so I'm a fighter. I just keep on," said Halston.

Lewin says that in 1984 Halston created the RHF (Roy Halston Frowick) Corporation, and that he both published and copyrighted a logo he designed that was a scripted version of the name Halston. He intended to design and launch a new line of streetwear based on dancewear, the proceeds of which would have gone to the Martha Graham Dance Company. When Halston could not guarantee the dance company's board members that there would be no litigation from Playtex, Graham and Halston agreed it would be best not to go forward with the idea.

In October 1984, Halston signed a letter of intent with Playtex Inc. to regain ownership of his made-to-order and ready-to-wear businesses, leaving the fragrances and the JCPenney contract in the hands of Beatrice Foods. The press reported that, at one point, JCPenney joined the bidding to purchase Halston Enterprises because, said president David Miller, he wanted to see that Halston was able to work "in a stable environment" and that "their interest was in seeing that the Halston III line reflected the genius of Halston."

Malcolm Lewin says that part of JCPenney's agreement with NSI involved an option to buy the Halston III company and that throughout Halston's negotiations with Playtex, JCPenney was kept informed. "We came close to cutting a deal where Halston would take back a big chunk of his business," says Lewin. The deal involved Halston having his own company and complete control of the higher-priced product lines and a dual ownership with JCPenney of the lower-priced line, which JCPenney would then license back to Playtex.

As part of this proposed arrangement, Halston negotiated a consulting agreement where he would work ten days a year for JCPenney and ten days a year for Playtex, receiving a $750,000-a-year salary and 6 percent profits on the JCPenney line. Neither of these agreements were ever consummated. The reason, says Lewin, is that Playtex was secretly negotiating to sell Halston Fragrances to Revlon and wanted to be able to offer the cosmetics company a package deal that included the Halston Enterprises apparel lines.

In 1986, Revlon Group Inc., headed by Ron Perelman, purchased Halston Enterprises, Halston fragrances and cosmetics, Max Factor and Almay from Beatrice Foods for, according to one source, $345 million in cash.

OPPOSITE:
Halston relaxing at Montauk, Long Island, house rented from Andy Warhol.

BELOW:
The Savage bathing suit on cover of Time *magazine, March 22, 1976.*

ABOVE:
Sunset on Montauk, Long Island.
OPPOSITE:
Andy Warhol's painting of Halston used in an ad, 1974.

Halston Fragrances became a division of Prestige Fragrances Ltd. Whatever Halston apparel and accessories licenses remained were allowed to lapse.

"I'm sorry I'm not contributing more now," Halston told *W* in November 1985. "I have to work out what I wish to do. I built such a big business and it's frustrating that I'm not able to work. I like business to be creative, stimulating and fun. I guess I'm a ham."

Never one to dwell on the past, Halston moved forward, designing costumes for Liza Minnelli and the Martha Graham Dance Company while continuing to work with his lawyers to find a way for him to design again under his own name. When his former design assistant Bill Dugan presented his first collection in April 1988, Halston sat in the front row and thanked Faye Robeson for attending and showing her support for Bill.

During the summer of 1988, while her new apartment was being renovated, Karen Bjornson Macdonald and her daughters, Maggie, then two years old, and Laura, then six, moved into one of the small houses on Halston's rented property in Montauk. She remembers that Halston had windup toys—a pig that would wiggle and a dog that would jump—that he would bring out to amuse the girls. One day while tying a bow for Laura, Bjornson casually suggested, "Halston should really be tying your bow." Her daughter protested, "No, Mommy. You should tie it. You can tie a bow better than Halston." Bjornson mildly corrected, "Well, actually, honey, Halston ties a better bow."

When Revlon purchased Halston Enterprises, Halston was hopeful that he might finally succeed with Perelman, a man who understood style and fashion, where he could not with the previous owners.

In November 1988, just when his negotiations with Revlon seemed as though they might succeed, Halston was diagnosed with AIDS. Lewin says a final draft of an agreement with Revlon had been prepared in early 1989, but Halson dropped out of the negotiations because he did not want to make a commitment that he could not fulfill.

In 1989, Halston was hospitalized twice with pneumonia and late that year moved to California to be close to his family. In December, his town house was sold. Although the press reported that Halston was going to live in San Francisco and that he was going to build a house on mountaintop acreage he had purchased in Santa Rosa, the truth was that he had moved into the Santa Rosa house of his sister, Sue.

When he moved to California, Halston had purchased a Rolls-Royce Corniche so his sister could take him for drives along the coast highway. One of his last requests was to have the proceeds of the sale of the car donated to AIDS research,

90 percent of it going to the San Francisco Medical Research Institute for AIDS research, the remainder going to ARCS, a Connecticut organization dedicated to educating adolescents about the disease. With his name on it, the car sold for much more than the two hundred thousand dollars he paid for it.

Liza Minnelli didn't know Halston was ill until very close to the end. "It wasn't discussed. I'd talk to him and he would say, 'I'm buying a car, and this and this and this.' He was always so vital and eventually you stop asking, 'Are you OK?'" She got the call that he was in a coma one minute before the Academy Awards were to go on in New York.

"He was in denial, I think, for a long time," his sister, Sue, told A&E's *Biography*: "I have pictures of him from the first part of January 1989, laughing and having a wonderful time. It was all sort of, 'this too shall pass.'"

Sue recalled that Halston would take some sun in the backyard, and lying on a chaise lounge, would call his New York friends and tell them how wonderful the weather was and that he was having a wonderful time.

In March, Halston entered Pacific Presbyterian Medical Center in San Francisco for the last time. He died in his sleep on March 26, 1990, at the age of fifty-seven.

In addition to the small family ceremony held right after his death, Liza Minnelli organized an invitation-only memorial service for Halston held in Alice Tully Hall at Lincoln Center. It was attended by family, friends, customers, clients and New York City's Mayor David Dinkins. Speakers included Katherine Graham, David Mahoney, Elsa Peretti, Marisa Berenson and the *Los Angeles Times*'s fashion editor, Marylou Luther. Martha Graham attended, but her address was on videotape.

Just two months later, Revlon announced it was closing the Halston apparel design operations as of the end of August, but would retain the more lucrative fragrance business. The *New York Times* sadly reported that "the Halston name in women's apparel, once the most glamorous designer label in America, will soon disappear entirely from sales racks in this country."

HALSTON
33 EAST 68TH STREET, NEW YORK, N.Y. 10021 U.S.A.

Eula 73.
Halston fits Bacall.

FASHIONABLE PEOPLE

Fashion is a living art requiring people to acknowledge, validate and breathe life into it. That is the single hypothesis around which Halston's fashion philosophy was formed.

Many designers create a look and then find customers that appreciate their point of view. One of the keys to Halston's success is that he took an opposite approach. First he studied and analyzed fashionable and modern women—how they live, their daily activities, the variety of body types, then he designed fashions that fulfilled, rather than dictated, their fashion needs.

While he was designing hats for the rarefied, carriage trade clients at Bergdorf Goodman, women's lives were changing, becoming more active and varied. Halston deduced that a different type of clothing was needed to accommodate newly liberated and working women. His often repeated mottoes, "Fashion is made by fashionable people, designers only suggest," and "You are only as good as the people you dress," were already formulated.

"Fashion is not made by designer and pencil in the seclusion of an atelier," Halston told *WWD* in 1964. "Fashion is made by people. It has to be on somebody's back to come alive. Even the most beautiful Balenciaga is not fashion until it's selected and worn by a woman. Actually, different social groups have made and will continue to make fashion though we single out their leaders."

From the start, Halston was perched at the perfect vantage point to observe the rituals of the rich and famous who were society's fashion leaders. As a young milliner in Chicago, he interfaced with the movie stars and socialites who were coifed at André Basil's Ambassador Hotel hair salon. Working under the tutelage of Lilly Daché, the reigning queen of millinery, Halston met and worked with many of his future clients. At Bergdorf Goodman, the crossroads for all fashionable ladies visiting or living in New York, he perfected and refined his selling and networking skills. When he opened his own business, those years of informal study were put to the test.

OPPOSITE:
Joe Eula's illustration of Halston fitting Lauren Bacall in long cashmere dress with Peretti's rattlesnake belt, 1973.
BELOW:
People *magazine cover, June 20, 1977. Photograph by Harry Benson.*

Never awed by position, wealth or beauty, Halston felt free to be casual in situations and with people that might intimidate others.

"People have preconceived ideas about noted people or people in the public eye, but people are people," Halston remarked. "There are good people, happy people, sad people, all kinds of people. I've always considered that, you know, we're all in the American scheme of things and we're all created equal and that, you know, there are just the good guys and bad guys and the mediocre guys."

Rather than a designer-to-client diatribe, Halston encouraged a dialogue that opened the doors to an insider's view and understanding of what his ladies wanted to hear and wear.

"They help you help yourself. They make you fashionable. You don't do it yourself," Halston once said. "It's a very complicated analysis of what their needs are. Then you try and solve the problem. The client very quickly tells you what they like or what they don't like. And they either buy it or they don't."

Bill Dugan remembers Babe Paley describing to Halston a tunic or vest that she particularly liked, "and the next thing you know, we would be making vests or tunics not unlike hers."

Halston both appropriated and appreciated Paley's natural style. "When I did the asymmetrical neckline, I wanted her to wear it first," he said. "She has great style. When she wears a shirt, it looks different than on anybody else."

A sketch of Paley appeared on the front page of *WWD*, "striding down Madison Avenue . . . scooting over to Halston Ltd., in her high boots, her fur-lined raincoat. She ordered Halston's black ciré midi raincoat and to wear underneath, the dark red wool jersey CityPants with a white crepe turtleneck shirt and jersey vest. Babe's taking her fashion casually these days."

Halston's physical attractiveness and personality should not be undervalued for its appeal to female clients. "The designer with the sleek hair and perfect smile of an old-fangled matinee idol, and green eyes as shiny or unreadable as the glass eyes of a doll, or of the camera lenses in whose glare they seemed forever caught" is how Anthony Haden-Guest described him in his book about Studio 54, *The Last Party*.

Halston was charm and elegance personified. With a perfectly erect, regal posture, striking good looks and a witty, quicksilver mind, he developed his own brand of public relations—part European, part Midwestern and all uniquely Halston. Clients were treated to an ever-changing recipe of playfulness, friendliness, reverence and respect, always retaining an aura of authority.

ABOVE:
Katherine Graham, chairman of the board and CEO of the Washington Post *wearing a Halston jersey shirt dress in 1980.*
OPPOSITE:
Joe Eula's illustration of Babe Paley wearing a Halston, 1973.

the
Beautiful Babe
in a Pretty
beautiful
white
chiffon Choir
shirt
Drop waist
chiffon Pants.

Eula 73

"He was the key to his own success. I don't think it worked as well when he got bigger and there were more layers of people there," said Katherine Graham. "Once in a while I've ordered clothes while he's been away. Somehow they never seem to work as well without his personal touch."

"Everything he touched was an example of his taste level," says Polly Mellen. "And without that taste and touch, it wasn't Halston. It's not just a matter of lending your name. He stayed with every product. And I think he had to."

As much by proximity as by purpose, the cues of what were considered both gauche and grand became second nature to Halston.

"For me, there are four different clients," Halston explained. "One needs pretty, ladylike clothes—she may be the corporate wife or the leader in her community. The second likes the extremes—she wants clothes that will be talked about. The third woman is the woman with discerning taste—she has her own style, she ultimately makes fashion. There is the other client, a theater client, like Liza Minnelli or Elizabeth Taylor or Lauren Bacall. They want to be noticed."

"The first thing I see in a woman is her grooming," Halston also stated. "Sophisticated people don't want those 'sock-it-to-me' numbers. They want to fall into the background."

"Almost every chic client I have wears pants all day," Halston proclaimed. "And women don't wear precious jewelry the way they used to, no public display of wealth. It's considered bad taste. For evening, they want pretty things. Men live pretty much in a gray world, and they want to see the woman across the dinner table dressed prettily. My clients like evening clothes that are very comfortable, simple rather than complicated, lightweight rather than heavy."

No one was exempt from becoming part of Halston's personal focus group and sounding board—models, friends, clients, the habitués at Studio 54. His inquiring mind was always probing to understand women and their fashions. When Bill and Nancy Dugan spent weekends with Halston at his Montauk, Long Island, house, the conversation would inevitably turn to clothes.

"He lived for fashion. He loved it, all the time," remembers Bill. "There was always a lot of critiquing going on, especially about current events, who wore what to the Oscars, who looked good and bad."

"He always wanted to know why you would like something, where would you wear it," says Nancy. "He would ask me what was in my wardrobe that I couldn't live without, what would I need, what would I look for."

He did not speak "fashionese," says Grace Mirabella. "You did not have a conversation with him about skirts being shorter or longer, or shoulders being bigger. He talked about style. He talked about looking better."

Halston used the famed disco Studio 54 as a fashion observatory for the trendier set. He could usually be found sitting in a corner, glass in one hand, cigarette in the other, watching the goings on and intermittently chatting with his friends.

One night at Studio 54, a young advertising executive, momentarily separated from her date, was sitting alone at the bar when Halston sidled toward her. He had apparently been eyeing the million-dollar emerald and diamond necklace that had been loaned to her for the evening.

"He was subtle, but he was trying to get a better look at the necklace," remembers Patricia Beegle. "Halston came over and sat down and said, 'If I didn't know better, I'd think they were real. I've never seen stones that color.' I said, 'What makes you think they're not?'"

Although Beegle was aware of with whom she was speaking, about halfway through the conversation, Halston introduced himself. They chatted about jew-

Halston and Bianca Jagger at Metropolitan Museum of Art's annual Costume Institute dinner, December 1977.

elry, colored stones and their depth of color. "What amazed me was the realness of the person," says Beegle. "I never saw the image. It was a real conversation, not 'I'm a famous fashion designer who wants information about the necklace.' There was an intrigue in the piece that he wanted to pursue and he did it in a very tasteful way."

During the "youthquake" of the 1960s and 1970s, when many designers forgot they had customers over the age of twenty-one, Halston's vision of fashion was age-less and timeless.

"I don't make an old-lady dress and a young-lady dress. The dress is of no particular age," he said. "A young woman can reveal more, of course, than say Martha Graham, who recently bought a chiffon like Betty Ford's (a thirty-year difference in age, but not in style). Though in Martha's case, because she's crippled with arthritis, you cover up with more fabric. You have to design for what people are, not what you'd like them to be. A wise designer has many silhouettes to offer."

One's profession and regular activities were always in the forefront of Halston's creations. For First Lady Betty Ford, who was always in the public eye, Halston knew she needed clothes that "are easy to maintain and look good at public functions. For instance, it's unwise to wear a two-piece dress because a picture might be snapped just when the blouse starts creeping out. And for night life, Mrs. Ford needs dresses that will look neat whether she's standing or sitting. You have to have articulate, stationary clothes that don't become unruly or call attention," the designer continued.

"Fashion is serious business, long range, for all age groups," he said. "Those who become obsessed with youth end up by making caricatures of themselves. There's no reason today for any woman not to look young while still being a woman. Most people don't realize that the youth movement stemmed from the image the Kennedy regime was to the world. Fashion subconsciously swerved towards youth, and some went overboard."

Like any artist, Halston loved to be surrounded by beautiful things and beautiful people. But he never lost sight of the fact that he was designing for real people, with assets that should be emphasized and flaws that needed to be camouflaged. He democratically dressed everyone, the ducklings and the swans.

"In the wholesale business, you dress an abstract public you don't necessarily know. But they're tall and they're short and they're medium and they're fat and they're pretty and not so pretty and they're busty and they're hippy and they've got a good figure and everything else. And you have to try your best to make them all look attractive in all kinds of different social situations."

As the bromide goes, the legs are the last thing to go, so Halston often emphasized and alluringly revealed them in his designs. Contrarily, upper arms, often the

OPPOSITE TOP:
Pat Ast wearing hand-painted caftan,
1972.
OPPOSITE BOTTOM:
Barbara Walters in one-shoulder lamé
gown accompanied by Alan Greenspan,
December 1977.

first to succumb to gravity, were often obscured with feminine and flowing sheer sleeves or overlayers.

"I think designers should get more into the store syndrome, go around the country and see, really see, what the needs are, rather than just anticipate what they are from a showroom," Halston stated. "It's a fascinating exercise to analyze all of this and to try and make a suggestion for everyone."

Hiring friend Pat Ast, the rotund Andy Warhol character actress, to work in his boutique was a typical, client-conscious stroke of genius. She was someone with whom his larger-sized customers could identify. Portly Pat automatically made customers feel two sizes smaller by comparison. Wearing specially sized dresses and caftans, Pat was the very first plus-size model, gracing his runway, popping out of cakes and performing skits to show off his Fieldcrest sheets. When she left Halston's employ, *WWD* asked, "Who's going to make Jackie O laugh anymore when she comes in to buy?"

First on East Sixty-eighth Street, and later at the Olympic Tower, Halston built showrooms that made clients of all ages and types feel pampered but not smothered, comfortable but chic. There was a warm and cozy, club-like atmosphere on Sixty-eighth Street, surrounded by Donghia's batik prints and, later, Ultrasuede coverings. The Olympic Tower showcase was a dauntingly theatrical and luxurious stage set, stark and modern, spacious and light, with an unbeatable view. In both places, you would always find vases overflowing with fresh orchids (the "sexiest" of all flowers), contemporary music playing over stereo speakers and a sensuous aroma of Rigaud- or Halston-scented candles in the air. It felt as though you were entering someone's home, not a commercial space.

The so-called ladies who lunch made up a large part of Halston's clientele, and invitations to his intimate, in-house fares were as sought after as ones to the White House. Although he told *WWD* that he rarely invited his clients to luncheon, only friends, it was difficult to tell one from the other.

"I remember dropping in one day and Mr. and Mrs. Onassis were sitting in there alone with him having lunch," remembers Joanne Creveling.

"There's never a hurried feeling when you go into Halston's," newscaster Barbara Walters told *People* magazine. "It's always, 'Sit down, have a cup of tea. What's your problem? You're going on a trip? Well, let's see.' You come away soothed by him and by the clothes you've bought."

The glamour and ambiance was enticing and exhilarating, but what truly seduced clients was their trust in Halston's unquestionable good taste and unswerving devotion to service. Despite bottomless wardrobe budgets, they knew he would not take advantage of them, and would not allow them to walk out of his salon or boutique with unsuitable or unneeded items. A traveling gallery of his artistry, he knew that if they looked good, he would look good.

A typical fashion conference with Halston was anonymously recounted as going something like this: "You'll tell him exactly what you need for a specific thing and he'll say, 'Oh, you don't need anything; anyhow, I don't have anything.' And then he'll start talking aimlessly, and I'll listen for a while before I get up to leave. Then he's doodling on a pad and presenting me with the ideal outfit. Some of my friends say he behaves the same way with them, but we all put up with it because in the end we all look so goddamn beautiful."

"He made efforts for you," says Grace Mirabella, "I used to go to him to work out my European wardrobe. I always felt that he had a thought, a plot, a plan. He didn't just sort of lay it on you and say, here, this is what you have to do. It had more to do with knowing you a bit."

"When I'd make my plans for going to the couture in Paris, Halston would sit me down and make a list of what I had and what I needed, then show me swatches and sketch out a plan for my trip, and about ten days later, I would have a perfectly planned, perfectly fitted complete wardrobe, simple and compact enough to fit in one suitcase," said Mirabella in her autobiography, *In and Out of Vogue*.

"He would force you to look at yourself. He had tremendous respect for all ages," confirms Polly Mellen. "There is nothing more exciting, I would think, for a designer than to take a woman who is not a model, not a perfect size, not perfect in every way, and make them feel youthful. That was his aim and that is what he did."

"You always felt like you were dressed when you put on his clothes," says Catherine De Natale. "Maybe you would add a pin or a pair of earrings, but you never felt like you had to fight to get dressed in the morning. It was a pleasure."

It was a matter of course for Halston to offer unconditional personal service, the kind that had only been seen before in the finest Parisian couture salons and, perhaps, at Bergdorf Goodman. Adamant about the customer always being right, a salesgirl in his boutique was tearfully fired when she did not recognize the wife of a well-known diplomat. "I cannot stand mistakes like that," Halston said. "I train my employees to recognize and acknowledge my customers with grace."

Assistant Carola Polakov had to write a letter of apology to a client who had arrived late. Halston had a fit when told that Polakov asked the latecomer to wait a moment while she finished up with another, on-time, client.

Whatever was necessary to make his clients feel welcome, Halston was willing to do. The *New York Times* reported that "he once got down on his hands and knees to comfort publisher Katherine Graham's squalling granddaughters. After tickling them into a good mood, he rose, flushed and dimpled, and announced, 'You know what? I really should have been a nanny.'"

Halston with Elizabeth Taylor, May 9, 1976.

LEFT:
*Margaux Hemingway on steps
of Ernest Hemingway's home on
Key West wearing components of
Halston's travel wardrobe, as seen in*
Town and Country *magazine, 1975.*
BELOW:
*Pamela and Averell Harriman. She is
wearing a chiffon caftan embellished
with rows of gold-plated teiki sequins,
November 1981.*

The designer was possessive about certain clients—Liza, Elizabeth, Lauren Bacall and Katherine Graham—and always worked with them personally. When invited to one of Halston's infamous parties, there was always an assistant assigned to cater to their every whim, to make sure they had their favorite drink, did not have to fight off crowds of admirers and had a secluded hiding place, if that is what they wished.

Halston would be present for fittings with such notables as Jackie Onassis and Pamela Harriman, but it was left to Sassy Johnson Connor and her colleagues to cater to most of the made-to-order and boutique clients.

"I must have talked to Jennifer Jones (Mrs. Norton Simon) every day of my life for ten years," Sassy remembers. "I did fittings on her in California or in Washington. I would fly there in the morning, do the fitting and fly back that afternoon. I bought lipstick for Katherine Graham to match a certain dress. We tried to do as much as we possibly could for each client, work out the shoes, the pantyhose or the handbags."

A particularly dramatic mission involved the wife of a colonel who had recently been released after an abduction by the Red Brigade. He was in Washington awaiting a White House reception and Halston's brother Robert, a chief NATO officer, asked his sibling to provide the colonel's wife with a gown for the event.

"We found out her measurements and it turned out she was close to my size, so I was sent to Washington," says Sassy. "At eleven P.M., the Secret Service took me to a Navy safe house. The colonel, now partially deaf, was asleep and snoring in one single bed. We (the wife and I) were standing on the other bed, trying to look in a mirror over the chest of drawers, trying to adjust the hem. I left at twelve-thirty A.M. and she had a new wardrobe."

If several clients were attending the same event, which was a usual occurrence, Halston would take care that his ladies would not see their mirror image somewhere else in the room. "If we ever found there was [a duplication], we would let one of them borrow a dress so they wouldn't be wearing the same thing. It was very important," says Sassy.

Yet wearing the exact same dress sometimes carried a status of its own. The Ultrasuede shirtdress became a uniform for the Upper East Side set. And after Babe Paley wore one of his tie-dyed chiffons to a museum opening, a dozen ladies came in to buy what she had been seen wearing in a newspaper photo.

A press agent's dream, the magazines and newspapers often wrote about Halston's coterie of loyal fans, which included an impressive array of beautiful people, theater people, executive and private people. Like the daily stock market results, the publications printed lists of their names and collectively called them his "Sweetiecakes" or the "Cat Packers."

Halston cultivated and landscaped his covey of clients as a gardener would a conservatory. "I work at it and work very hard," Halston said. "You just don't get a group of chic clients; you have to develop them. I've been working with private clients for fifteen years, so I know what they want."

But Michael Marsh remembers that it wasn't always that way. When Halston first opened his Sixty-eighth Street showroom, Marsh was sent out to the street to collect clients.

"He would look out the window on Sixty-eighth Street and see some ladies on the street that were potential customers, and he told me to go downstairs and get them," says Marsh. "He charmed them and served them tea. He was a natural about who he had to make clothes for in three days and those who could wait three weeks."

Mothers brought daughters, sisters brought siblings, and friends brought friends to be touched by Halston's fashion magic. His clients showed a fierce loyalty that few fashion designers ever know. The ultimate status symbol was having your own dress form waiting at the ready in the workroom.

For fourteen years, "he literally dressed me totally," says Katherine Graham. "I felt I looked better than I ever had. When he stopped, I didn't know where to go. For two years, I did nothing, because I was so totally dependent upon him."

Her daughter, Lally Weymouth, was first taken by her mother to Halston's Sixty-eighth Street showroom. "I think he was clever. He would figure out what was good for you. He went to the trouble to know you pretty well, asking where you were going, this and that. My grandmother used to go to Mainbocher; this was a more modern version of it. People still say to me, 'I can remember you wearing those jumpsuits, that dress, that suit.'"

Those were dressier times, says Weymouth, when there were many black-tie occasions where you could wear Halston's glamour clothes. A favorite outfit of hers was a romantic red chiffon shirt with big puffy sleeves and a black velvet skirt.

Weymouth's first appearance in a Halston, in 1972, was in a "long brown dress slit down the front, and it was very sexy, very glamorous," she recalls. "Every head turned and not just because of me! Halston invented nudity. He gave it to American women."

Jackie O wearing Halston's strapless chiffon gown at Take a Giant Step benefit, March 1977.

"He made clothes for Americans, for those of us who didn't want to pretend we're French," Weymouth says today. "He really had a major touch. You just see people like that only every once in a while."

When Halston opened his Madison Avenue boutique without any advertising, he counted on his loyal flocks to come, and they did not disappoint. Many of his made-to-order clients couldn't resist the less expensive items in the boutique from his Seventh Avenue collection.

Polly Mellen went to the boutique at least once a week. "You bought Halston in multiples. If you had a turtleneck sweater in black, you wanted it in white, in a color. Clothes you can count on. Clothes you know you look good in."

During a fitting at Bill Blass, Pamela Harriman reminisced with former Halston patternmaker Yutaka Hasegawa about the blouses she had purchased fifteen years before. She had purchased every color of one style Halston blouse and was still wearing them.

The *New York Times Magazine* reported that Jackie Onassis was in the boutique while a customer was trying on a green cashmere sweater set. She came up behind the woman and whispered to her, "You should take them. They go with your eyes." The customer immediately purchased the items. Later Mrs. Onassis asked Halston, "Is that all it takes to sell clothes? Just a tiny suggestion?"

After the initial jolt, it became commonplace for Halston's employees to see the famous and celebrated wandering the halls. "I tried not to gush like an idiot," says Jim Siewert of his first encounter with Lucille Ball and her daughter. The second time he saw her, she asked him to attend the fittings. "He scares me," said Lucy about Halston. "Can't you come in here with me?"

One day Crawford Mills got off the elevator and ran into Jackie O standing in her unmentionables. He did a fast turnaround.

Once when Suzanne Chenevas was doing a fitting alone with Jackie Onassis, Halston popped in to show her a dress he had been making for someone else that he thought she would like. When he left, Jackie asked Chenevas to return it to Halston, because, she said, "I don't like it and I don't have the guts to tell him."

Naeem Khan, whose family's business in India created Halston's beadwork fantasies, remembers Andy Warhol standing over his shoulder, teaching him how to draw with a loose, flowing hand. At a party, he met Hollywood fashion designer Edith Head and, at Halston's prodding, was kissed by Elizabeth Taylor. As a nineteen-year-old straight from Bombay, he took it all in stride, but today Khan is in awe of these star-studded encounters.

"The first made-to-order client I saw was Sylvana Mangano, the Italian actress," remembers Akira Maki, an assistant and patternmaker from 1975 to 1981. "For all the Italians in the workroom, she was their Marilyn Monroe." Another highlight was Princess Grace of Monaco's visit to the Olympic Tower showroom.

OPPOSITE:
Jacqueline Onassis in Halston's bias-cut lamé pantsuit with hidden snap closure, at opening of International Center of Photography exhibit, November 1978, speaking with Bill Swing, coordinator of the exhibit.
ABOVE:
Halston fitting actress Carol Channing at the Sixty-eighth Street showroom, 1977.

Halston's greatest knack was intuitively knowing what each woman wanted, even when she didn't know it herself. Each customer believed every outfit was conceived especially for her, although many were mainly variations on the season's theme. He may have dressed a disparate range of personality and body types including Betty Ford, Pat Nixon, Grace Kelly, Raquel Welch, Candice Bergen and Elizabeth Taylor, but he never compromised his style.

"I once had dinner at the White House, where I was photographed with President and Mrs. Ford," actress Marlo Thomas recalled. "I sent the picture to Halston with the inscription, 'I can take you anywhere!' And that sums up the way I feel about his clothes—I can wear them anywhere."

For an event at the Iranian embassy, Katherine Graham was wearing a brilliant blue chiffon dress with a low back and ruffles. "It was very unlike what I usually wore and what he designed. I thought it was kind of ghastly, but I wore it. As we went into dinner, Henry Kissinger's head Secret Service man was at the door and he whispered to me, 'Mrs. Graham, that dress is dynamite.' What a wonderful compliment."

RIGHT:
Halston's ladies, June 1973. Left to right: Betsy Theodoracopulus in a red leather wrap coat, Elsa Peretti in a rust cashmere sweater dress, Berry Berenson in gray zip-front sweater jacket and dress, Kitty Hawks in a short belted black leather jacket over sweater and skirt, and Sandy Kirkland in a beige cashmere ribbed cardigan and sweater dress.

OPPOSITE LEFT:
Candice Bergen in Newsweek *article, August 21, 1972, wearing red giraffe-neck cashmere sweater dress.*

OPPOSITE CENTER TOP:
Lauren Hutton in one-shoulder gown. Photograph Francesco Scavullo

OPPOSITE CENTER BOTTOM:
Christina Ferrare in plunging décolleté halter dress. Photograph Francesco Scavullo

OPPOSITE RIGHT:
Raquel Welch in Newsweek *article, August 21, 1972, wearing a black silk jersey cutout dress.*

Bridal wardrobes were not a special forté, but Halston made wedding outfits for Margaux Hemingway, Hillie Mahoney, Barbara Sinatra, Liza Minnelli and Sly Stone.

Hillie Mahoney, a former Miss Reingold, had become a customer of Halston's just months before her husband, David, acquired the company for Norton Simon. "I was amazed when David told me he was interviewing him. And once David bought Halston, I never wore anything else. The beauty of his clothes was that I could wear most anything."

Her Halston wedding dress was in pale pink, a chiffon shell worn over a full-skirted and belted dress that was bare shouldered except for very fine spaghetti straps. It was designed to be worn again as a dance dress.

For Liza's wedding to Jack Haley Jr. in 1974, Halston designed a yellow cardigan pantsuit with a yellow chiffon blouse and scarf; yellow because "it is good luck for her and a color she wears for special occasions," and pants "because she will have to travel an hour out of Los Angeles for the ceremony and she wants to be comfortable."

Madison Square Garden wedding of Sly Stewart (Sly and the Family Stone) and Kathy Silva. Both Halston outfits are covered with 3-D gold sequins, June 1974.

The rest of the Halston-designed bridal wardrobe included a yellow silk jersey caftan to be worn at the private reception held at Liza's father's home and a strapless black velvet dress with a small train for a big party at Ciro's restaurant given by Sammy Davis Jr.

All of Liza's wedding outfits were accessorized with Beth Levine's custom-made shoes, simple high-heeled pumps entirely pavéed with red stones, styled like the ruby slippers Liza's mother, Judy Garland, wore in the film *The Wizard of Oz*. Levine says that Liza so trusted Halston, she never saw the shoes until she put them on her feet at the wedding.

Halston also coordinated a sixty-piece trousseau for Liza, consisting of interchangeable pieces that included cashmere sweaters and skirts, a black velvet coat, navy sequined pajamas and a powder pink sequined dress from his collection.

Halston's most unusual bridal request came from Sly (Stone) Stewart, the rock music star. He asked Halston to dress not only he and his wife, Kathy Silva, but the entire wedding party including the orchestra and Sly's backup singers. At the televised ceremony and rock concert held on June 5, 1974, at Madison Square Garden, Halston outfitted the couple in head-to-toe glittery gold.

Rod McKuen and Marlo Thomas in Halston's sequin halter gown, presenting the Oscar for original score for the film Barry Lyndon *to Leonard Rosenman, March 1976.*

Socializing with clients was usually restricted to charity affairs and events that doubled as publicity vehicles. "You never heard about him going to Mr. and Mrs. William Buckley's dinner parties. If he was invited, he didn't go, so he ended up never being invited again. Once in a while he would go out with Oscar de la Renta, when he was married to Françoise, who wore Halston," remembers Joanne Creveling.

But in a very few cases, the line between clients and friends was blurred.

Halston met Elizabeth Taylor when, in 1976, an Academy Awards executive asked him to design her gown for an awards presentation. It was to be a strapless number that showed off her shapely shoulders and ample décolletage. Halston ended up escorting Elizabeth to the ceremony.

Secretary Faye Robeson intercepted the now-legendary phone call when Taylor asked, "Is this really Halston?" and he quickly replied, "Is this really Elizabeth Taylor?"

"We have such rapport. We're made for each other. I'm in love with her," Halston said.

"I wanted to take all the fancy stuff off her," he told *People* magazine. "Her overpowering clothes made her look bigger than she was. I promise you, she has the smallest waist and hips, wonderful legs, and what every man and woman likes—big ba-zooms. Of course, when Elizabeth is happy she puts on a few pounds. Elizabeth Taylor really needs a new dress every time she does a personal appearance, and she does it almost every night."

"Halston designed my evening dresses and clothes to go with my jewels," Elizabeth Taylor remembers. "He would put me in something green when I would wear my emeralds, or red for a night on the town in rubies."

Many of those dresses were worn to fund-raisers such as those held at the American Ballet Theater at the John F. Kennedy Center for the Performing Arts in Washington, D.C. For a benefit for Wolf Trap, the open-air theater and cultural center near Washington, Halston provided ninety-five tablecloths and tents made from rose-patterned Fieldcrest sheets, and two dresses for Taylor—layers of red chiffon for early evening, and a blue dress for her thank-you speech.

"I adored him and loved to play with him," says Taylor. "He was a wonderful and fun man and I still miss him deeply. People perceived him to be a snob—the way he always wore that trademark white scarf and held his cigarette holder—but he was one of the most real and down-to-earth men I have ever met."

"When we get together, it's giggles, this-that-and-everything," said Halston. "Liz loves Liza; Liza loves Liz. I love them both, and I think they like me."

When Liza Minnelli was twenty years old, her godmother, Kay Thompson, introduced her to Halston at Bergdorf Goodman. Shortly after Halston began designing clothes, "Kay sent me a note that said, 'Saw a pantsuit I thought you might like,' and this Halston pantsuit arrived. It was a perfect fit," Minnelli remembers. It was argyle with a tunic-length, buttonless jacket.

"As soon as I started earning money, I dressed in Halston all the time," says Minnelli. "But he got around things when I didn't have any money. That's how these [two silver Elsa Peretti cuff bracelets] came about. Halston said, 'Well, you can't buy diamonds and you can't buy gold for yourself, so we're going to use silver.'"

After being photographed with the Baron Alexis de Redé, he invited Minnelli to France. Not realizing the importance of the event, she remembers saying to Halston, "He invited me to that, um, horse place." Halston asked, "Deauville?" "And it was for the opening of the uhh . . ." Halston guessed, "The casino and horse show?"

"Halston then asked, 'When do you have to be there? What is your luggage situation? How many pieces can you afford?' At that point, I could only afford half of what I needed so he bought me the rest. And he filled them. I went, and the next year I was on the Best Dressed Women's list."

Before beginning to design Minnelli's wardrobe, Halston asked her what she wanted to look like. "I remember he said, 'I'm not saying you don't look like anything. I just want to know what you want to look like.' I said, 'I want to look like a female Fred Astaire during the daytime and a movie star at night.' That's all I ever told him and he went from there."

That meant many pantsuits for day, and matte jersey and beadwork for evening. "It was just what I wanted," says Minnelli. "When he found the company in India to do sequins on chiffon, then we were off and running, we really had a time. His whole point was to sculpt a woman's body so if there was a part she didn't like, he could hide it, and the parts she liked, he showed. For me, he liked my shoulders, so he would hang everything from them."

Halston became Minnelli's mentor in all things related to style. "I didn't know how

to do anything," she frankly admits. "I hadn't come up through the ranks. I hadn't really learned how to pack, let alone set a table, let alone know what linen to buy, let alone how to give a party. I wasn't brought up that way. People thought, well, you know, the servants would do it. We didn't have servants. We were lucky if we could pay the bills most of the time."

"I think we gave her confidence, made her realize how attractive and womanly she was," said Halston. He made all of Minnelli's clothes, including theatrical costumes for films and live concerts. "Every show I did, I performed in his living room first," Liza told *WWD*.

"Whenever we'd do a new show, he'd make tons of stuff. It was constant," she says. Without a word from her, "every six months, six pairs of black pants would arrive because he knew I needed them at that point, because I wore them for working and traveling. He did everything. He designed the jewelry I wore, the shoes. He literally created a look and a style and not only for me. It worked for a lot of different American women."

Today, Minnelli's wardrobe of Halston originals is carefully maintained and archived. A prized notebook that Halston prepared specially for her contains draw-

Grace Kelly wearing silk charmeuse caftan. Photograph Francesco Scavullo

ings and color illustrations of each of her Halston outfits, everything from bathing suits and suits to evening wear and theatrical costumes, many with detailed instructions on how to accessorize them.

"You felt so good when you wore his clothes," says Minnelli. "It felt like you had a friend. His clothes seemed to caress you that way. Everything he made for me just sort of did what I did, went along with me."

Minnelli still opens and closes almost every show wearing a Halston iridescent beaded chiffon cardigan and pants, and also often performs in a red crepe trapeze-shaped cardigan and skirt. Other of her favorite Halston outfits include a bias rainbow-striped, one-shoulder, one-piece dress that fastens with a single hook; a Kandinsky-inspired print jacket; and a jacket and top sequined in an ombré of shades of gray to black, which was worn for a Carnegie Hall concert.

Over the years, Liza returned her friendship and appreciation to Halston by modeling in his fashion shows, performing in the French-American fashion gala at Versailles and giving him continuing moral support after he was ousted from his business.

Halston set out and succeeded in proving that clothes must reflect the wearer's personality and that designers only offer the means for them to do so. There is no doubt that he also consciously appraised and exploited the publicity value of his well-known clients, always with an eye on the bottom line.

"What am I doing?" he asked. "I'm giving women what they want. Women want to be comfortable and they want to look sexy. It's as simple as that. People aren't interested in fashion the way they used to be. Now everybody is into creating different lifestyles and I'm interested in creating clothes to adjust. I honestly believe that women, and this includes the shopgirl and the socialite, can be turned on to the same thing if it's pretty and easy to wear."

Halston, Elizabeth Taylor and Liza Minnelli at a celebration for The Little Foxes, *1981.*

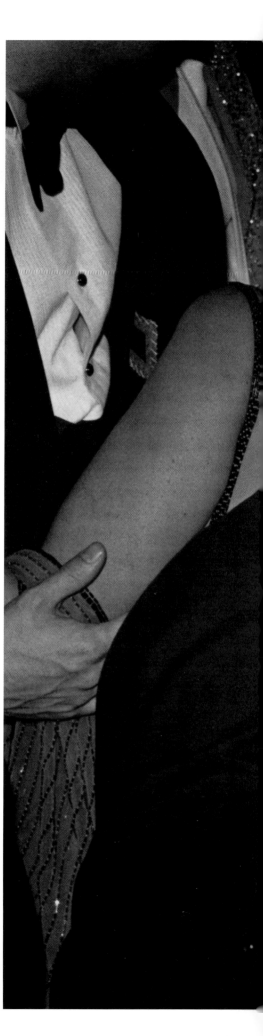

HARPER'S

BAZAAR

FULL
REPORT
ON
PARIS-
AMERICAN
COLLECTIONS

LETTERS
OF
D. H. LAWRENCE

SEPTEMBER 1961
60 CENTS

MASTER MILLINER

Halston's childhood fascination with hats was not an unusual one considering the era in which he grew up. During his formative fashion years, the 1930s to the 1950s, millinery was the focal point of every woman's wardrobe. From housewives to society matrons, in big cities and small towns, for formal and everyday activities, no self-respecting woman, or man, for that matter, would venture out in public without something covering her or his head. Women often owned more hats than dresses, and choosing the most perfect, most fashionable hat was so important, they were often purchased first, worrying later about finding something to wear them with.

There were few name apparel designers in those days, but millinery was a relatively easy way for fashion hopefuls to become local celebrities. Many notable designers—Coco Chanel, Claire McCardell, Charles James, Adolfo—took their first steps into fashion as milliners.

As early as age seven, Halston was intrigued by hats. Roy was so enamored of his grandmother's hat wardrobe that he would climb into her lap and tug at the veils and the brims, "as if he were trying to figure out what made the hat tick," his mother, Hallie May, said. It was such an obsession that she started hiding her hats from him.

Flowers picked from neighbors' gardens were transformed into hats for his mother, which she would obligingly model. On Easter Sunday, 1945, his family was quite surprised when thirteen-year-old Roy presented his mother with a homemade red hat and veil decorated with a gold metal pot-scrubbing sponge. "We all wondered how and why he did it," recalled his brother Robert. "But it was a smash and really flattered my mother."

It was not until Halston moved to Chicago that millinery became anything more than a hobby. In his spare time, in between night classes in illustration and days dressing windows at a department store, Fro made hats on a used sewing machine in his small apartment.

His mentor and lover, André Basil, the preeminent hairdresser at the ritzy Ambassador Hotel, encouraged Fro's talents. The move into Basil's luxurious Astor Street apartment gave him his first workroom, the spare bedroom.

Sophia Loren about to be crowned with a Halston hat by the designer, September 1961.

In the fifties, the Ambassador Hotel was a home away from home for celebrities passing through Chicago, and they relied on Basil's basement salon to keep them primped and proper. It seemed only logical that, after being coiffed, the ladies might be interested in a new hat to finish off their look. Basil not only paid for Halston's hat supplies but in 1956 set up a small space near the front of his hair salon to display his friend's handmade creations. The hats were made at home and delivered to clients at the hotel.

Before a client rose from Basil's chair, the possibility of a new hat was suggested, and they were escorted over to the hat stand. At first, Fro was too timid to do this himself, but he soon got over his shyness and adopted the gestures, the walk and the self-confidence of a fashion sophisticate.

Halston admitted to *WWD* in 1968 that his first millinery attempts were "just terrible," but he and his hats were an instant success. Lucia Perrigo, the well-connected and powerful director of publicity for the Ambassador, befriended Halston and took every opportunity to introduce him and his creations to those who passed through. Fran Allison, then star of the highly popular television show, *Kukla, Fran & Ollie*, was his very first customer. She bought three of the four hats he made for her, and they were featured on the pages of the *Chicago Daily News*. A week later she came back with a friend, the wife of the president of RCA Whirlpool, who ordered four hats. Through the power of word of mouth, Fro's hats soon donned the heads of such notables as Deborah Kerr, Gloria Swanson, Joan Crawford, Perle Mesta, Kim Novak, June Allyson and that most famous of all hat connoisseurs, Hedda Hopper.

Perrigo also made sure that the local press learned about Halston.

"Lucia was in the salon when I was there having my hair done, and she said she wanted me to meet someone," remembers Peg Zwecker, then the fashion reporter for the *Chicago Daily News*. "He was sitting there, like old-fashioned dressmakers used to sit, cross-legged on the floor with the materials all around him, making hats while others were having their hair done. He got up, a real gentleman. He was charming."

Zwecker began writing about him in her column, "Fashionably Speaking," and it was she who first suggested that he use his distinctive middle name, Halston, as his fashion moniker. She also introduced him to designer Charles James, the son of a Chicago-born heiress and a British colonel, who Zwecker believes introduced Halston to some of the "important" people in the city.

After an introduction by Zwecker, Florence Sewell, a wealthy Chicago socialite, became a regular Halston customer. "He was just like your little brother," she remembers. "You laughed and you cried with him. He was just great fun. And, oh, my, how he loved chic women!"

Across from the nearby Drake Hotel, Benjamin Benedict Greenfield, better known as Bes-Ben, had been the hatter to Chicago society for generations. He now had some worthy competition.

"We had Bes-Ben, one of the great hatmakers of all times, who made little tiny jeweled hats," says Sewell. "Halston didn't do that. He made more feathery hats, that made you feel feminine but not all jeweled to death. He had those hats with a little veil that came down just over your nose. It was so flattering. I felt so spiffy in them." Sewell still has boxes of Halston's hats stored away in her Chicago home.

By observing Basil, Halston soon knew what to say and do to please such discriminating customers. "Whenever we'd go in there, we'd practically stay the whole day and then go out to cocktails," says Sewell. "He'd let us try on everything, and he'd tell you if he didn't like what you were wearing. He could pick up a scarf and do something with it like nobody else could do. We'd sit there and laugh, and we always walked out with a package."

It was never just hats for Halston, says Zwecker. "He was interested in the look as a whole—the lengths, the purse. Halston would suggest to people to simplify what they wore. He would teach them about how clothes should suit the person, the face, the height, the age."

Chicago Daily News *fashion editor, Peg Zwecker, wearing a Halston hat, with the designer, circa 1956.*

"If you didn't like your hat after you wore it for a few days, he would say bring it back and he wouldn't charge anything extra," says Sewell. "We talked about fashion all the time. So-and-so has a new such-and-such, talked about lengths. He could tell you what everyone would wear next year."

With Halston's success, Basil decided they needed more space, so on February 18, 1957, together they moved to larger quarters, on the third floor at 900 North Michigan Avenue. When *Women's Wear Daily* covered the press opening of the new locale and his Boulevard Collection, Halston received his first national press coverage.

WWD reported that Halston's hats sold for between twenty-five and thirty dollars. And they included "intricate manipulations with silks that soften jaunty profile hats and add dimension to domes and cloches. This designer considers silk an ideal medium for off-side profiles. He covers one with bright pink floral silk balanced by a self bow, and contrasts a white straw body with a yellow polka-dot chiffon scarf. Taffeta, plain and moiré, is worked as 'petals' draped in layers for oversized dome and rounded muffin shapes. Scarves match other silk hats, one in a mauve to peacock print that swirled to a peak. Veiling trims many hats, with veils drawn from under the chin to tie in a huge bow on the wide brim of a polka dot silk cartwheel. A white toyo profile has a heavy net veil that draped under the chin."

Zwecker had appointed herself Halston's personal press agent, and got him to participate in the city's many charity fashion shows. She was close friends with world-renowned milliner Lilly Daché, who would often visit Chicago to promote her books or her hats. Zwecker wrote to Daché, recommending she meet Halston, and arranged an in-person visit.

Daché wanted to meet Halston casually, without him knowing she might be interested in employing him, so she and Zwecker concocted a ruse. "Lilly was going to a formal ball and told him that she was trying to figure out what to wear around her neck," says Zwecker. "She had an antique jewel and she asked him to make something for her, a choker. Then they got to talking about millinery."

"The first time I saw Halston he was a baby. Innocent. He was wearing a navy blue sailor jacket in the cellar in the hotel in Chicago where there was a beauty salon," Daché said. "Halston was just hanging around there. It was the first year Wallis Simpson came to the United States after marrying Edward and she was wearing a beanie. Everyone started wearing a beanie and there was Halston in the cellar making beanies in his little blue suit. He offered to come to my suite to sew for me."

Daché was so impressed that she offered him a job in New York, which he accepted several months later. Halston met two of her key criteria.

"She had an instinctual magnet for recognizing people that had potential," says Daché's daughter, Suzanne. "And she loved having good-looking men in the showroom." Counted among Daché's protégées were Arnold Scassi (then Isaacs),

Melanandri and hairstylist Kenneth. In fact, when Halston arrived in New York, Kenneth's hair salon was already in place on the first two floors of Daché's Fifty-sixth Street town house, where she both worked and lived.

Through Daché, Halston had firsthand exposure to what was needed to build a successful fashion empire. "She was a strong lady who knew what she wanted and ran her business with an iron fist," says Kenneth. "She very much believed in having young people around. She was trying to have an empire. She realized that hats weren't going to be as popular as they had been, so she opened a beauty parlor, then went into makeup, skin care and started selling to stores around the country."

Halston's arrival in New York to work for Daché should have been noted as an omen of what the city was to have in store for him. A mix-up with his reservation at the Waldorf-Astoria Hotel landed him a luxurious suite, rather than a simple room. Without skipping a beat, he called a press conference, alerting every fashion editor he knew in New York that he was moving to the Big Apple.

Like a thirsty sponge, young Halston soaked up the atmosphere of the city and all the knowledge that Daché had to offer. At the time, she and Mr. John were the country's most important trend-setting milliners, catering to the most fashionable and wealthy women in the city, such as Greta Garbo and Marilyn Monroe, many of whom, including Jacqueline Bouvier, would become Halston's future customers.

"I learned more in one year about fashion and fashion shows than anyone could imagine," Halston told Zwecker about his days at Daché. Among his duties was helping to stage fashion shows, where models languidly promenaded down a dramatic spiral staircase that became a Daché signature.

Over the years, Halston never forgot the woman who discovered him in Chicago. Whenever he would visit the windy city, he always contacted Zwecker. In March 1976, when he opened the Water Tower Place boutique and launched his new perfume, the two reminisced over lunch at the Ritz, and then went together by limousine to his alma mater, the Art Institute, where he spoke to the students. When Zwecker retired from journalism in 1978, Halston sent her an Elsa Peretti–designed diamond pendant from Tiffany's.

T he frenzied, stimulating pace of New York City quickly became home to Halston. And after a year with Daché, he was ready to take on more responsibility and independence. Thanks to a fateful meeting, he got that chance. During lunch with Charles James at La Côte Basque in 1958, Jessica Daubé, better known as Miss Jessica, the head of Bergdorf Goodman's millinery department, was seated at the next table.

"I was doing the John Mills wedding, one of the society events that year, and Jessica had wanted Bergdorf Goodman to get the entire wedding party," Halston explained. "Instead, they were doing the bridal dress and I was doing the bridal

"When I first came to America in 1965 and began working on Seventh Avenue, he used to do all my hats. He was the most influential designer of the seventies and he remains an inspiration to American designers today."

—OSCAR DE LA RENTA

headpiece. Miss Jessica felt I must be something special because I was doing this social plum. So she leaned across the table and said to me, 'If you're ever going to make a change—come and talk to me.'"

Halston talked and Daché obviously listened. In 1959, he started working in the custom millinery salon at Bergdorf Goodman, the beginning of what would be a nine-year, career-changing experience. Halston filled a position vacated by the Cuban milliner Adolfo, who resigned because the store would not allow his name to be placed on the label of the hats he designed. The two were destined to have their careers follow a very parallel course.

"I always felt that millinery was an exciting career at that time," says Adolfo, who first met Halston when he was working for Daché. "Affluent women would buy hats, discard their hats, give them to their maid, and come back and get another one. To make hats the way we did was a very intricate occupation, not an easy thing to do. It takes a great deal of patience."

Miss Jessica tried to alienate the two milliners, but without success. "We often had dinner together and laughed and compared the problems I previously had with the ones he was having. Just the idiosyncrasies of department stores. Every cent and dollar had to be written down. Too many people to make decisions for you. It is very tiresome to go through all of this when you are an artist."

Bergdorf's had the largest custom millinery workroom in the United States (Sophie Gimbel's department at Saks Fifth Avenue was the only other serious competition) and it was responsible for a significant part of the store's revenues. Adolfo remembers forty ladies sewing only hats, twelve working specifically for him, with the others dispersed between the two other designers. At its peak, Halston's custom millinery department employed 150 full-time custom milliners, twelve salesladies and sixteen assistants.

"There wasn't any type of hair gadget they couldn't do more perfectly than anyone else," says Leonard Hankin, the stock boy who climbed the ladder to become the executive vice president of Bergdorf Goodman. "I used to take much pride in taking people around the millinery workroom."

The custom salon, for both clothing and hats, was located on the second floor, with the millinery workroom located in the back. The apparel workroom was on the eighth floor, which today displays home furnishings. Behind-the-scene elevators went directly from the workroom to the first and second floors, constantly carrying hats up and down. There were small private fitting rooms where tailors from the suit and coat, dress or fur ateliers, would come to take customers' measurements. The millinery designers overlapped with all of the other designers, creating coordinated hats.

"Couture was something very special to all those ladies," remembers Elieth Roux, who worked next door to Halston in the custom apparel salon. "We used to open at ten A.M., and the ladies would be there at nine, ready for their fittings. Everything was flamboyant, lots of money, chauffeurs."

"In those days, instead of going to a psychotherapist, women came to the millinery department," says Hankin. "They spent their time and money having their egos massaged."

Halston's ambition was obvious from the start, and his creativity and personal flair was finally given the room and resources to flourish. "When you are surrounded by all these beautiful things, you get stimulated. You learn how things are made. It is in the atmosphere," explains Adolfo.

With Ethel Frankau, the head of the custom salon, Halston regularly went to view the European collections in Paris, Italy and London. In Paris alone, they saw seventeen complete couture collections plus five solely devoted to hats. They went armed with a budget to purchase the rights to several hundred original hat and fash-

*Halston helps Italian actress
Virna Lisi select a hat at Bergdorf
Goodman's custom millinery salon,
May 1964.*

Katherine Graham with Truman Capote, wearing Halston-designed mask at Black and White Ball Capote gave in her honor, November 1966.

ion designs that would be copied using the designer's name, or adapted for their own custom collections. At Balenciaga, one of the biggest sellers at Bergdorf's, Halston would purchase a minimum of fifteen styles per season. The custom salons were so Europeanized that Roux remembers they used to buy thread, fabrics, buttons and shoes from France.

"We went to all the milliners, had dinner in their penthouse apartments. He took me to parties every night," says Tom Fallon, Halston's assistant from 1966 to 1968, who accompanied Halston on one of his last trips to Europe for the store. "He took me to every show with him, I sat with him in the front row. He introduced me to Chanel, Givenchy, Cardin, Balmain, everyone."

This is how Halston not only became acquainted with fashion at its finest, but was also able to see how each couturier's work progressed from season to season.

"I had the advantage of the terrific schooling of a young man sitting in the front row, being one of the youngest persons in the fashion business," Halston admitted. A few years earlier, Halston stated, "I learned about fashion at Bergdorf Goodman's. At the time it was the largest retail outlet for European couture in the country. I got to know Mmes. Grès and Schiaparelli. I absorbed lines, proportion and fabric. Such dedication and thought went into every stitch of those haute couture clothes."

Halston never copied those designs, except when specifically asked to for a customer that wanted the exact hat she saw on the runway, but he was certainly inspired by the taste of the French couture.

To be a milliner in the 1950s and 1960s involved being part craftsman, part artist and part psychologist. The goal was to achieve a balance between the client, the couturier's design and the milliner's vision. By the time Elieth Roux had arrived at Bergdorf Goodman in 1966, Halston had already achieved that goal. He knew everybody and she saw him work his charm on whoever entered the custom salon. "I remember that Halston was quite sick with hepatitis at one point. You should have seen the trees of flowers that the ladies sent to him."

Andrew Goodman, president of the store, was not always Halston's greatest supporter, more because of Halston's aggressiveness and ego than his obvious talents. But even he had to admit that Bergdorf's customers adored him: "Mrs. Paley and the Duchess of Windsor would lunch at the Colony and then they'd spend the afternoon at Bergdorf's trying on hats. Halston got to know them and the Ford sisters and Mrs. Charles Engelhard. He'd talk to them about fashion and they respected his taste. They listened to him."

Katherine Graham was one of the Bergdorf Goodman customers who would remain loyal throughout Halston's career. He made the mask that she wore to the Black and White Ball that Truman Capote gave in her honor in 1966, what she called her "midlife debutante party." The mask was made to match a Balmain dress that had been copied at Bergdorf's.

"The only direction I gave Halston was to remind him that I was five feet, nine inches tall and didn't want something that would stick up too far," said Graham. "I also told him that Truman and I would be receiving the partygoers, so I couldn't have a mask on a stick that had to be held."

Halston's influence could be seen everywhere you turned at the ball. He made a mask of white feathers for Mrs. Charles Wrightsman, one in black velvet for Mr. and Mrs. Alfred Gwynne Vanderbilt, and for Mrs. William Paley a mask containing jewels from one of two ruby necklaces. The necklaces were purchased with her gown, which was a simple, sleeveless, form-fitting, floor-length sheath in white zibeline, slit up the front and lined with cardinal red zibeline.

Fallon recalls that Halston made three masks for Paley, and after the fitting she said she couldn't decide which one she preferred and bought all three. The night of the ball, Fallon and his friends stood outside the Plaza Hotel as though it was Oscar night, waiting for the luminaries to arrive. He saw Mrs. Paley wearing a mask he did not recognize as one of Halston's. "She had extraordinary eyes and bone structure and didn't want to shield her eyes, so she had Adolfo cover a huge over-sized pair of sunglasses with the zibeline from the dress, but she was too much of a lady to say anything to Halston."

The who's who of the world was always in and out of Bergdorf in those days," Halston told *Esquire* in August 1975. "First of all, that gives you all the good contacts that one needs. My background is with people. I mean, I really know Jacqueline Onassis and I know what she can wear and what she can't or what she might like."

The turning point in Halston's career at Bergdorf's came in 1961 when he designed the pillbox hat that Jacqueline Kennedy wore to her husband's presidential inauguration. The Hollywood costume designer Adrian first popularized the pillbox hat worn by Greta Garbo in the 1932 film *As You Desire Me*. Halston reshaped and enlarged it in proportion with the First Lady–to-be's large head size and hair style. Jackie, who did not like to wear hats, had been taken to task for not doing so during Senator Kennedy's campaign. Halston thought this would be a simple, easy-to-wear shape that she could endure and would quiet her detractors.

As with anything the model-like First Lady wore, the pillbox was instantly copied by Jackie wannabes all over the country. The hat also became a bone of contention between Halston and designer Oleg Cassini. Cassini, who was designing Mrs. Kennedy's wardrobe, also took credit for the hat. But others in the know, including Kenneth, Mrs. Kennedy's hairdresser since 1950, confirm that Halston was the hat's one and true creator. Jackie did, however, add an unplanned touch of her own: she wore it pushed back on her head, instead of letting it sit squarely on top.

Jackie and Halston shared a physical trait that often came in handy during the course of their professional relationship—they had the same head size. So Halston was able to try on and fit her hats, even when she was traveling. "We made about 120 hats for her—everyone from the famous ones she wore to India to the hats for christening ships," Halston told *WWD* in 1968. Halston also made the bow that she wore when she married Aristotle Onassis on the Greek island of Scorpios.

Halston's illustrator, Audrey Schiltz, who sketched Jackie's hats, remembers Jackie "never wanted to try the hats on because she never wanted to mess up her hair."

Halston's admiration and respect for Jackie continued throughout his career: "She's the most interesting, good-looking public figure we've had in this century. She's got everything and handles it discreetly. She doesn't seek publicity. Perhaps that's why each time she makes a public appearance, it's news."

"Mrs. John Kennedy is very natural when she's out of the public eye. She's charming and kind to people. In my lifetime, she's been the most influential woman in fashion," he reiterated to *WWD* in 1968.

Fallon remembers a more somber Kennedy occasion, when Rose Kennedy visited Halston at Bergdorf Goodman to purchase an outfit and hat for the funeral of her son Bobby. "It was heartbreaking to see her. I still remember that scratchy Boston voice saying she wanted a chiffon veiling, that she needed to be seen but still be perceived as in mourning, negotiating how many layers of chiffon the veil should have."

After she left, Fallon told Halston he was stunned that, under the circumstances, Mrs. Kennedy was able to function so coolly. Halston's reply showed how well he understood his clients and was able to rise to any occasion with which a custom milliner may be faced. "She's totally in shock," he explained. "She understands her role. People have to see the face of the stricken mother."

Jacqueline Kennedy wearing Halston's pillbox hat at inauguration of John F. Kennedy as president of the United States, January 20, 1961.

BELOW:
Black coq feather "wig" hat by
Halston for Bergdorf Goodman,
October 1962.
BOTTOM:
Ciré turban by Halston for
Bergdorf Goodman, August 1962.
OPPOSITE:
Oversized sun hat, March 1967.
© Neal Barr

Following the pillbox sensation, Halston's hats began appearing regularly on the covers and inside fashion pages of *Harper's Bazaar* and *Vogue* magazines, rarely fewer than half a dozen items per issue. *WWD* called him "the Hoosier with a head for hats" and Bergdorf Goodman's executives became aware of his drive and ambition.

"He always wanted to be talked and thought about," says Hankin. "I don't know at what stage he started to think about going on his own, but he used everything on the way to bring him closer to that point. He used his relationship with the magazines extensively and often, and at the expense of Bergdorf Goodman."

Frances Stein, then executive fashion editor of *Vogue*, explained why Halston was so popular with the editors. "You could always count on him. If a tweed turban was needed to go with a tweed suit that was going to be photographed at Avedon's at eleven A.M., Halston would get it there by eleven A.M., and it would be perfection."

"His hats were completely enchanting fantasies. They were very provocative and beautiful," remembers Polly Mellen, who worked with Diana Vreeland as an editor at *Harper's Bazaar*. She remembers doing a shoot with Richard Avedon and said that "Halston would show up at the photo session with a box full of ideas, such as the Elizabeth Taylor cover for which he produced an extraordinary hat with feathers curving under her throat."

Halston approached millinery as a hands-on, highly creative and individualistic undertaking. He often fit the hats on his own head, says Fallon. "He would put the hat on his head because he could feel what the hat was doing, the weight, the height. He would look at it from 360 degrees."

"He had beautiful hands, and he would sculpt the hat, pulling it this way and that. His hands were so huge, he could engulf the entire hat. In a way he was a sculptor," recalls Audrey Saltzman Schiltz. "He knew what he wanted. No doubt, very sure. A clear vision. He liked everything simple."

Halston described the part he felt millinery played in the total fashion picture: "A hat is a head covering which is supposed to make you glamorous, exciting and more interesting than anyone else. Nobody really needs or wants a hat, but it's one of the most inventive parts of the fashion business today."

Halston especially proved his inventiveness in the way he conceived hats to coordinate with specific outfits. It was typical for Bergdorf's custom milliners to be given an extra half-yard or so of fabric used in suits, dresses, coats or furs and to be asked to create a harmonious chapeau for a customer or for photography.

A keen eye for proportions allowed Halston to analyze and exploit a garment's shape and details with complementary, not matching, hats. A coat with an extra-large collar would be topped with a tiny headpiece, so as not to distract from the garment's design. A rounded skirt on a suit would be paired with a tall, slim, cylindrical hat, a play on geometric shapes. The shape of a flounced hem on a chemise dress would be mimicked in a hat with a bell-shaped brim. A wide, draped cowl neck was topped with a huge white linen roller, the brim folded back

in the opposite direction to the collar—so that the wearer's face became the focal point, not the dress or hat. The large circles in a Japanese-inspired print would be exaggerated and softened into a circular, puffy, cloud-like hat of white organdy.

True to his philosophy, the majority of Halston's hat designs were elegant and wearable. But when the editors called, he knew how to make the extravagant, larger-than-life styles that were needed for photography. There were Egyptian crowns in white Bali with big pink grosgrain bows at the forehead, looking like an upside-down bucket. In 1967, he created a huge circle hat so wide, a real-life wearer

APRIL 1963   *HARPER'S*   *60¢*

BAZAAR

HEAD
OVER
HEELS
IN LOVE
WITH
FASHION
BEAUTY
CONVERSATION

HOW TO
EXERCISE
WITHOUT
REALLY TRYING

Layered hat of white silk organza by Halston for Bergdorf Goodman, April 1963.

would not be able to fit through a doorway without turning sideways. In 1966, Avedon photographed a wildly extravagant feathered hat worn by Maya Plisetskaya. And as *Harper's Bazaar*'s April Fools' joke in 1963, photographer Richard Avedon snapped a truly elegant poodle wearing a black and white bias check beret and matching scarf, all by Halston.

"He was probably the greatest hatmaker in the world," proclaimed Diana Vreeland, former editor of *Vogue*. "I'd say to him, 'Halston, I had a dream about a hat last night,' and I'd go about describing it, and then, by God, he'd give it to me, line for line. Once he made me twelve snoods in the twinkling of an eye. He was an absolute magician with his hands."

At lunch with Joel Schumacher at La Grenouille, Halston saw two ladies across the room who were from *Harper's Bazaar*. "He took his napkin and fashioned this incredible hat out of it and sent it over to the ladies. It showed what ingenuity and talent he had."

In 1962, Halston was rewarded for that magic when he received his first Coty Award, a special award for his innovations in millinery. In 1964, Halston's hats were featured in Barbra Streisand's first television special, called "Barbra," which was shot at Bergdorf Goodman. In one scene filmed in the custom millinery salon, she sings and dances around the room going from one mirrored dressing table to the other, trying on a different Halston hat at each stop.

When other milliners were adding froufrou and trims, Halston was taking it off. He turned the mundane into chic. Familiar shapes were pulled a bit here, angled a little bit there, and made uniquely his own. No matter how tailored or structured the shape, it was always softened and feminized by a bow, an ostrich plume or a scarf draped or tied around the crown.

Leather and fur were among his favorite mediums. "If a woman can have only one hat, she should own a mink," Halston told *WWD* in 1963. "It goes with everything. It's become what a black velvet hat used to be."

Halston worked closely with Bergdorf Goodman's fur designer, Emeric Partos, to create original looks in mink, chinchilla, sable and sealskin. Among the most popular were one-piece scarf-and-cap styles that draped on top of the head and around the neck. For younger fur wearers, aviator-like helmets fastened or tied snugly around the head and under the neck. In 1966, to coordinate with hair calf coats stenciled in stripes and giraffe-skin patterns, Halston concocted two modern headwear options—huge, tent-shaped pullover hoods with a cutout for the face and triangle scarves that were tied babushka-style behind the neck.

Sable hat by Halston for Bergdorf Goodman worn by actress Elsa Martinelli, December 1962.

Leathers were sculpted into mannish fedoras. He manipulated and pleated the skins as though they were fabric, looking like the channels of a mushroom on the underside of a wide brim. White kidskin was fashioned into a cloche, or a square-shaped hat was decorated with leather-covered cubes around the lower edge.

Scarf hats were one of Halston's greatest millinery successes. In nun-like simplicity, heads were tightly wrapped with scarves and then covered with big brimmed hats.

Toward the end of his hatmaking days at Bergdorf Goodman, Halston stylized and cleaned up versions of ethnically inspired shapes, such as sombreros, gauchos and Australian safari hats. Around the same time, he reacted to the new craze for active sportswear by creating luxurious and sophisticated visors in plastic, fabric or fur, with or without an attached cap. Other casual headwear looks included snug jersey hoods, head wraps and ski caps. In 1965, Halston made headlines with wind socks; they were big, soft, elongated and exaggerated berets that looked as though the wind had blown and permanently fixed the fabric toward the back of the head.

Viewed in retrospect, some of Halston's hats bore indications of some of the apparel designs that were to surface much later. A narrow drape of jewel-studded fishnet veils tumbled from the top of the head to below the nose, with a rhinestone at each intersection of the net. Huge, floppy-brimmed sun hats were not unlike the ones he made years later for the Halstonettes to wear during the Braniff junket to Acapulco. Like the floaty chiffon shells and caftans that were yet to come, overlayers of transparent gilded silk fell from a stiffened net dome, or were worn with a medieval-style rhinestone-dotted cap underneath. Creating an effect similar to his "flying saucer" skirt concept, contrast colored circles of organdy were sewn together at the circumference and pulled up in soft drapes into a soft crown.

It might be an exaggeration to say that Halston single-handedly kept Bergdorf Goodman's custom millinery salon alive, but he was such an important draw that he did what Adolfo could not—have his name appear on the label of Bergdorf Goodman's hats. Adolfo believes the store's executives probably acquiesced to his request, fearing Halston might have taken his talents elsewhere, just as he had.

This was also the "swinging sixties," when fashion formalities, including hats, were no longer an everyday necessity, but hair and hatlessness were the news. A 1963 *Newsweek* article about Bergdorf Goodman reported, "High fashion is a losing proposition these days. The custom dress department chalked up a net loss last year, and of the luxury operations only the fur department ran at a profit."

"It was an area that belonged to a period of time and the world was moving away from that kind of thing," Hankin remembers.

Halston saw the writing on the wall and used his star status as leverage to move his career into its next phase. He convinced Goodman to allow him to design a small apparel collection that would be sold in a special

Halston boutique. "He fought very hard for that clothing collection," remembers Audrey Schiltz. "I think he wanted to grow a lot faster than Andrew Goodman was allowing. I remember slamming doors and Halston being upset after meetings. But I don't think Andrew wanted him to leave."

"Making hats is tremendously good training for being a dress designer," Halston told *Esquire* in August 1975. "You learn to think in three dimensions so your dresses have a sculptural quality. Also you think in terms of small details."

Ever the perfectionist, Halston was at the store at 7 A.M. on the morning of his first apparel show, there to make sure the chairs were properly lined up. The promise of a new fashion talent attracted a standing-room-only crowd. In the two collections Halston designed for Bergdorf's, the focus was still on hats, with clothes to go with them. The clothes were young and futuristic, perhaps too big a change for the store's stalwart carriage trade customers, and they were not as successful as he had hoped.

"Halston wanted to be what Yves St. Laurent was, not to copy his clothes, but to be where YSL stood in the fashion world. He wanted to be on the top," says Berkley Johnson, the salesgirl Halston transformed into his house model who then went on to be a cover girl.

With the intention of redirecting his fashion career into apparel, Halston left Bergdorf Goodman in 1968. But he would never completely abandon his first fashion love. While building a profitable new apparel company, he supported himself by making hats and wigs. One of the first things he did was sign a license with the Lin-Mac Hat Co., one of the country's largest producers of popular-priced millinery, to design a line of hats that would be sold at hat bars in department stores. Called Halston USA, it was aimed at a younger customer, with retail prices in the fifteen- to thirty-five-dollar range. In the first six weeks of business, he sold over two hundred thousand dollars wholesale.

At the same time, he was making expensive hats in his own workroom under the Halston Ltd. label, priced up to six to seven hundred dollars retail for sable furs. In May 1968, after he got his first order for three hundred hats priced at a minimum of ninety-five dollars each from Bonwit Teller, he told *WWD*, "It's the largest order I've ever had since I started in the hat business. I guess people are richer, they're buying extravagant mink hats, three or four pelts. Nothing is more flattering than Russian lynx and women are discovering them."

Also selling well were hood-style hats in natural ranch mink. "The average customer has been able to relate to them.

OPPOSITE TOP:
Transparent plastic hat from Halston's first apparel collection for Bergdorf Goodman, 1967.
OPPOSITE BOTTOM:
Scarf hats by Halston for Bergdorf Goodman, August 1966.
© *Gösta Peterson*
BELOW:
Pale green oversized beret by Halston for Bergdorf Goodman, March 1962.

They don't have the rich lady connotation anymore. Women can buy them at any price."

At a time when doom and gloom characterized most of the millinery business, the Halston USA and Halston Ltd. lines were selling so well that both Bloomingdale's and Neiman Marcus credited them with generating new excitement and sales volume for their stores.

Another licensing agreement was signed in 1968 with the Hat Corp. of America to produce fur hats and collars for men. Halston described it as "a simple, classical collection. There are toques and shakos, nothing far out. We are doing them in all kinds of furs—Persian lamb, mink, sable, nutria, African lamb. We hope that it will be a whole other market."

Another line of less expensive hats, to retail under ten dollars and to be called Halston Americana, was planned but never produced.

In the 1960s, as hairpieces became part of the general fashion scene, wigs and hairdressers began replacing hats and milliners. In 1962, *Newsweek* estimated that half a million women in the United States were wearing wigs as part of their regular fashion regime. *WWD* reported that $1 billion worth of wigs were sold in 1969, which meant that two out of three women in the United States owned one.

As the popularity mounted, name designers were called upon to add their special touch and credibility to wigs. Halston and Adolfo were the first designers asked to design modacrylic wig collections for a company called Abbot Tresses in 1968.

When the offer was first made, Halston called Adolfo and learned that he, too, had been asked to design a wig collection. Adolfo warned him, "You know everyone's going to be upset in the millinery world. Ladies will buy wigs, not hats."

Halston's wig collection was so successful, he claimed that "if he had thousands of those $30 synthetic wigs, he could sell them even in Iceland." In 1970, Bloomingdale's sold the wigs in four separate places within the store, and Bergdorf Goodman had opened a separate wig department that was selling at least four hundred wigs per week.

Halston continued to design wig collections for many years, at least through 1975, for Designer Collections, Inc., the company that acquired Abbott Tresses.

Halston was so closely identified with hats, it was noted by *WWD* at the showing of his Fall 1970 collection that it was the first time his clothes were shown completely bare-headed. "Neither of us made hats; we became so involved with clothes, that hats took second place," says Adolfo. It was a sign of changes that were taking place in fashion that "the clothes looked better without hats. It looked too dressed up."

After that, hats would appear from time to time in Halston's apparel collections, and when a photo of his Ultrasuede hat appeared on the cover of *Newsweek* magazine, the orders came pouring in. In his Fall 1974 collection, *WWD* noted hats as the standout accessories, including puffy, stitched and snood-like berets. In 1976, he would license Commodore Hat Co., a sister company of Designer Collections, Inc., which marketed the Halston wigs, to manufacture and distribute a popularly priced, department store hat line that debuted at Saks Fifth Avenue.

When Halston left Bergdorf Goodman to start his own business, he took with him two of his expert milliners, Brenda Bogart and Natalie Ostrander. Although few hats came down the runway with his minimalist clothes, Halston kept the two milliners on the payroll until he himself was squeezed out of Halston Enterprises in 1984. They were mainly kept busy making headpieces for the Martha Graham Dance Company costumes that preoccupied his later designing years, but the ladies were also kept employed as one of Halston's few nods to nostalgia.

Even when he was king of his Olympic Tower empire, he always held a soft spot for his early days. One day, in a fit of temper, he lashed out at Brenda and Natalie. He held the elderly lady milliners, and their art, in such esteem and felt so badly about the outburst that he was seen sauntering into the millinery workroom, where he sat down with the two and began making a hat. It was his way of apologizing, a gesture they understood, without any words being exchanged.

Halston with his creations. Left: pale blue straw hat trimmed with flowers and ribbon streamers; right: pale flowers on bed of green velvet.

FASHION'S FIRST MINIMALIST

Before ever once putting scissors to fabric to make a garment, Halston had a mental image of what he knew women's fashions should be.

"If I were to design clothes, and yes, I'd love to, and maybe someday I will, they'd have to be snappy, all function and ease," he told *WWD* in 1964, two years before he designed his first apparel collection for Bergdorf Goodman. "For day, simple action clothes that women can breathe in, work in, play in. Nights, that's different. Time to splurge, live the dream that's fashion. And let's face it, dresses are not going to have feathers and fuss in the future. No tricks for me, though fashion is tricky. I can understand them in things like jewelry, never clothes. We'll go on simplifying, everything uncluttered. This is a tailor's world, not a dressmaker's world."

From the first of his designing days to the last, he never swerved from that uncomplicated formula—simple by day, simply extravagant by night. But he offered more than just a talent for designing attractive clothes. Halston proselytized a theory about how people should live and dress that was vastly different from the mode of the day.

"Evolution, that's what keeps fashion in flux today. Revolution is out," Halston's theory went. "Life's too active to be pinned down by one revolution or another. Too often, revolution means going back to things past."

Halston believed that all clothes should be as comfortable and easy to wear as sportswear, but elegant at the same time. Almost more important than the way they looked was how they felt on the body. That theory set the precedent from which modern, minimalist fashion was derived.

Looking back, the first two apparel collections Halston designed for Bergdorf Goodman in 1966 proved he had the right stuff to move beyond hats into clothing, but they were mainly experimental. Contained within the Bergdorf collections were few hints of the look for which he would become famous. The fashions were clean and neat in a somewhat futuristic, space-age way and very different from the haughty refinement that Bergdorf Goodman was known for.

"I remember one dress that stuck with me forever," says Audrey Schiltz. "It was navy and white A-line with white cuffs and collar. Very French schoolgirl. It was really new looking. Nobody had done it at that time. At Bergdorf Goodman I was

Karen Bjornson wearing hammered silk satin spiral cut strapless gown, 1976. Photograph Francesco Scavullo

BELOW LEFT:
Hooded doublefaced wool pullover
tunic and body suit from Halston's
first apparel collection for Bergdorf
Goodman, 1967.
BELOW RIGHT:
Contrast color-pieced jersey dress
from Halston's first apparel collection
for Bergdorf Goodman, 1967, modeled
by Marisa Berenson.

used to seeing couture clothes and old ladies. This to me was something I couldn't afford but I could wear."

The shapes were modern but less fluid than what would eventually become the Halston look. The bold graphics of the period were interpreted in jersey dresses pieced in colorful contrasting bands and boxes. Pullover jumpers and tunics were worn over bodysuits and tights. For evening, there were layered chiffons and floor-length dresses also color blocked in harlequin-like diamonds. Clear plastic accessories ran throughout the day wear portion of the collection, including see-through bubble hats and leg-hugging boot stockings with plastic ball heels.

"I really don't understand beads and ball gowns anymore. And I really don't want the collection to look like couture," Halston told *WWD* prior to unveiling his first Halston Ltd. collection. Clearly, he knew what he did not want, but the general concept of what he did want needed to be refined and better defined. His original think tank, especially Frances Stein, worked with him to distill the essence of the simplicity he sought.

"Frances had a brilliant eye," says Joanne Creveling of the former fashion editor. "She convinced Halston that women really didn't want to be wearing heavy, constructed clothes and that women really didn't want snaps, zippers and buttons. He always loved a lot of jewelry, until Frances decided he'd better start thinking about scarves."

With his carriage trade background and his only moderately successful apparel efforts at Bergdorf Goodman, the fashion press and retailers were prepared for Halston Ltd.'s first collection to be some variation on old-world couture. They were instead surprised with pared down, simplified fashion that was all pure shape and style.

"No one who ever worked in fashion at that time will ever forget his first show," said Grace Mirabella. "We were all taken aback because down the runway came a whole new way of dressing for daytime; he called it pajama dressing, but it was more than that. The style was simple, the line uncomplicated, the fabrics interesting and unexpected. Tops and pants were cut on the bias—unusual for made-to-order clothes, so they were very narrow. He used tie-dyed fabrics and chiffon for small tops and see-through pants; he did pants in matte jersey for daytime, and in black charmeuse for evening. The clothes had immense impact without being overdesigned."

"They were soft, functional clothes that you could roll up in a ball and throw in a suitcase, but not inexpensive," Creveling confirms.

Halston Ltd.'s first collection, shown in December 1968, consisted of twenty-five coordinated pieces, "all the parts that the stores and customers can have fun putting together," the designer told *WWD*. And in what was probably the very first quick response* effort, he planned to add a small group of twelve things every six to eight weeks. The collection was an instant success, selling to such prestigious specialty stores as Sakowitz in Houston, I. Magnin in Los Angeles and Stanley Korshak in Chicago, retailers that knew Halston from his millinery.

Harlequin evening gown from Halston's first apparel collection for Bergdorf Goodman, 1967.

* A fashion industry term that only became widely used in the mid-1980s. It refers to the need for manufacturers and retailers to respond quickly to consumer demands and fashion changes by replenishing stocks of merchandise based upon what has sold, and by frequently offering new merchandise.

BELOW:
*One-of-a-kind tie-dyed chiffon
tunic and pants, 1970.*
OPPOSITE LEFT:
*Jacquard coat and knit trousers
from Spring 1970 collection.*
OPPOSITE TOP RIGHT:
*Wrap jacket of shiny, supple ciré cloth
with black ciré scarf and snakeskin
belt, March 1969.*
OPPOSITE BOTTOM RIGHT:
*Argyle jacquard knit pantsuit from
first Halston Ltd. collection, 1969.*

By 1969, just a year after going out on his own, most of the looks that would become Halston signatures were already firmly in place in his collection. Most notable were pants ensembles with long cardigan jackets or coats, chemise dresses, fluid separates, one-shoulder dresses, knits and long A-line dresses with high armholes. Though retailer response confirmed that the look was right, Halston, ever the perfectionist, felt there was something missing.

"I'm tired of flat, skin-tight clothes and of everybody looking alike. I want more shape," Halston told the *New York Post* when announcing he hired the acclaimed designer Charles James as a technical consultant.

Halston had known James for many years, first meeting him in Chicago. Despite James's cantankerous and volatile personality, Halston greatly admired and respected James's unquestionable skill. So much so that in 1969, Halston and Mrs. Henry Kaiser sponsored a retrospective show of clothes that James produced between 1929 and 1963, at the Electric Circus, a popular New York City disco. The forty dollars per couple tickets benefited the engineering, not fashion, students at Pratt Institute.

"James has always been one of my heroes," explained Halston when asked why he undertook to sponsor the event. After the show, James's clothes were donated to the Smithsonian Institution and his drawings were given to the Chicago Historical Society and the Arizona Costume Institute; but not before Halston bought a number of James's sketch books and erotic drawings for himself.

"He's an engineer of fashion and will help engineer the mechanics of our fashions, such as putting in pockets or working out the wraparound trousers," explained Halston to *WWD*. Halston was helping himself and James at the same time, because James was in serious financial debt.

"He wanted his expertise, because it was something he was new at, but I'm convinced that he also wanted to help James," remembers Bernadine Morris, a big Halston fan, and then fashion editor of the *New York Times*.

"I am sure it was very complex," says Joel Schumacher. "But Halston was the most generous person I have ever known. It probably disturbed him that someone of James's talents was that destitute."

James was a sculptor of fashion who would spend months, even years, perfecting the cut and shape of a single garment part. Halston referred to him as the Leonardo da Vinci of fashion because he was more interested in the construction technique than what was seen on the surface. Like Halston, James strove for perfection. But where Halston wanted soft, flowing, comfortable garments, James's were so structured that they could stand up on their own. No wonder Seventh Avenue referred to them as the "odd couple" and *WWD* questioned their alliance, asking, "In the soft 70s, who wants engineered clothes?"

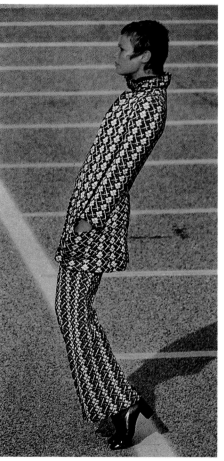

James worked in the top floor of Halston's Sixty-eighth Street studio, which Bernadine Morris described as "a cross between a doctor's office and an artist's workroom with anatomical drawings on the walls, some headless forms of the human body and a surgical white decor."

"He helped shape the collection, like Balenciaga helped Givenchy," explained Halston to the *New York Times*. He worked out the basic shapes that could then be varied and quickly produced for mass production.

But Halston got more shape, and more chaos, than he bargained for. Only one collection resulted from the collaboration, and even that one was never completed, reportedly because of James's refusal to compromise perfection to meet the deadline. The collaborative collection was an incoherent mixture of Jamesian and Halstonian designs and there was no problem determining which was which.

Halston openly acknowledged that some of James's 1930s landmark shapes were updated and incorporated into the "Halston shaped by Charles James" collection. These included: wraparound trousers with pleated hips; wide, cropped suede tops that rested on the hip; a sloping no-shoulder cut; a circle scarf that James invented for Elizabeth Arden; gently flared evening skirt-pants; and ponchos slanted over one shoulder like shawls. "A long satin skirt . . . is straight from Charles James's fabulous ball gowns," said Eugenia Sheppard in the *New York Post*. "It's a little like watching Shakespeare in modern dress."

Both to congratulate and interview the designers, Morris went backstage after the show and was immediately grabbed by Charles James, who had a vest in his hand made of 250 pieces that was only half finished. "He won't show this," James complained, referring to Halston. "When I saw Halston he told me, 'Charley wanted me to show this vest and it was only half finished. I couldn't. While it may have been a terrific vest, it couldn't be done commercially.'" Morris says.

Shortly after the show, the two had a final falling out and James left Halston's employ.

"Both were sure they were the best. It was like putting two bulls in the ring together, and they locked horns," says shoe designer Beth Levine, who knew them both well.

With the knowledge Halston acquired from James and his own innate taste and talents, in some ways the student soon surpassed the teacher. Halston never copied James, or anyone else, but he used details of James's designs as a starting point for creating his own brand of comfortable, modern shapes without complex inner construction. It is certain that Halston's bias tube dresses were inspired by James's

OPPOSITE:
Charles James's sketch made in 1967 used in collaborative Halston collection shown in 1969.
BELOW:
Halston and models at Brooklyn Museum exhibit, "The Genius of Charles James," viewing mannequin in a James dress, October 1982.

"taxi" dress, with its seam and zipper that spun around the torso. Halston's ongoing attempts to eliminate armholes and seams were also surely derivative of James's inventive cuts. And Halston's elliptically shaped shoulders were a modification of James's concave and convex arc shapes.

As a way of thanking James, in 1982, four years after James's death, Halston Enterprises underwrote a retrospective exhibit of James's work at the Brooklyn Museum called "The Genius of Charles James" and took charge of restoring the garments. The exhibit traveled to the Chicago Historical Society's Costume Gallery, where Halston's old friend Peg Zwecker chaired the benefit gala.

Halston declared his independence from designers who made fashion complex and restrictive. He singularly focused on simplicity and ease, reshaping a sleeve, resizing a neckline or reformulating the construction within his familiar forms. He ceaselessly tweaked, manipulated and perfected his designs, impossibly always finding one more way to update them. While staying within his overall simplistic framework, each season he gave his collection a new edge and excitement, but never outdated himself.

"Everybody in the fashion business is looking for something to excite the customers, to encourage them to buy new clothes. Halston has found the way, without

One of two ads featuring the American flag and ruffled garments, 1981.

HALSTON 81

any tricks, without seeming as if he were trying," Bernadine Morris remarked.

Before Halston, American designers looked to Europe for directional cues to follow. After Halston, they needed to look no farther than their own backyard. Immediately after leaving Bergdorf Goodman, Halston made several research trips to Europe, but once he opened Halston Ltd. his traveling days were temporarily over. "When everybody else was running over there every four minutes, Halston would sit and study old *Vogues* and *Bazaars* from the 1930s," says Joanne Creveling.

The inventor of the first truly American style of high fashion, he was proud of his Midwestern heritage and verbally waved the flag at every given opportunity.

"I think we ought to have American pride and back it up. I want American tables, American rugs, American things," Halston told the *RAM Report* in 1978. "Fabrics come from everywhere, but I don't want to go to Europe to buy them. I like the food and flowers in France, but if they want to sell me their fabrics, they have to come here."

In 1973, before any other American designer was even thinking about going global, he pronounced that "the American look in fashion is coming to the fore. The modern way of life is American and it has to work for the world market. All of a sudden the American designer, if he has an original point of view and a product, has an opportunity he never had."

Halston ad for U.S. bicentennial, 1976.

It was inevitable that Halston would be compared to other designers, especially the Europeans who were considered the fashion leaders. Fashion editors meant well when they made comparisons.

"Halston is doing for fashion in the 1970s what Rudi Gernreich did in the 1960s. Or what Mainbocher did in the 1930s. . . . In the midst of the era when fashion was one big costume party, he saw the handwriting on the wall," Bernadine Morris wrote in the *New York Times*. "Halston and Mainbocher are at the same end of the scale in different eras. . . . In fact, a couple of women viewing the Halston Resort and Spring [1973] collection said it made them want to pull their old Mainbochers out of the closet."

"Halston could be called the American counterpart of Givenchy, and his customers and fans, too, are worldwide. Like Givenchy, he also knows well how to make movie star clothes for celebrities—clothes that have all the flash but none of the sleaze," Carrie Donovan, then fashion editor of the *New York Times Magazine*, wrote in 1980.

"The shadow of Balenciaga hovers over the Halston collection. . . . It's not that Halston is making line-for-line Balenciaga copies, but he recaptures the spirit of elegance, and then appropriately relaxes it," the *New York Times* stated of the Spring 1979 made-to-order collection.

But any comparison was a stretch because his designs were different from anything that had come before. He offered homegrown elegance, glamour and class—something that Seventh Avenue was just becoming aware of.

"His look was as different as Pucci's was when he came on the scene. What he had, no one else had. No one," says Guido De Natale, a partner in Halston Originals.

Great as these designers are, Halston rightfully considered himself an original and did not like being compared to them, though when asked, he sung their praises: "Balenciaga was really the great one. You would [see his collection and] say, 'I don't believe it.' What this man has done. He has done clothes for everybody in the world market."

"Balenciaga and Givenchy are the fathers of world fashion," Halston stated a decade earlier. "St. Laurent is the most avant-garde designer in the world."

And in 1971, Halston explained, "I'm not putting everyone on Seventh Avenue down, but I've never known a silhouette to come from there. They come from people like Chanel, Givenchy, Balenciaga and St. Laurent can pull it together, too. The American fashion industry is basically a copyist industry . . . great technicians who can take something from the couture and adjust it to the public."

On the morning of September 1, 1976, Akira Maki, one of Halston's assistants and patternmakers, was called into Halston's office. The designer pointed to the front page of *W* magazine that featured two large photos, one of Yves St. Laurent's new Russian peasant designs next to one of Halston's champagne-colored, hammered silk, one-piece, strapless evening dresses. "Are you clear about what I'm trying to do?" Akira was asked.

W magazine pitted the two designers against each other, pointing out the drastic contrast between Halston's "Mr. Clean" designs, and Yves St. Laurent's "Monsieur Fantasy" creations. What the comparison affirmed, however, was that Halston was equally capable of producing fantasy and romantic clothing, only without gimmicks.

Halston never stood for the kind of fashion that is synonymous with trends and change; rather, he epitomized a kind of style that endures. Style is, in Halston's own words, "the way they arrange their flowers, or the way they serve their wine. This is true from the White House on down. Men care about the clothes their wives wear. If they give a party, it has to be the right party . . ."

"People have become more conservative. They're buying more quality and not so many things," Halston also said. "I think women are more interested in entertaining at home. The charity ball is dead. Dinner parties have certainly become more important. People want their homes to be pretty. They want flowers, lovely linens, beautiful bedrooms and luxury bathrooms."

From season to season, year to year, Halston's fashions changed slowly and

deliberately, not dramatically. He ignored the standard seasonal fashion clock and set his own pace for change.

"I never give up a good idea, but I don't always show them to the press because sometimes the good ideas are plain and maybe people will be bored by them," Halston told the *RAM Report* in April 1978.

"You may not find Halston inventing a brand new silhouette," said June Weir, then fashion editor of *WWD*, "but the question is whether women want a new silhouette today. They buy for comfort and sex appeal and Halston can do both and keep it young."

Front page of W magazine, September 3, 1976, contrasting Halston's and Yves St. Laurent's designs.

He had to digest every idea, to make it his own, remembers Akira Maki: "He would put these ideas on his working table, meaning he would look at it the day after, week after, month after. He may use the idea, but only after he digested and made it his own."

"To me, this is the most interesting part—to invent new cuts and new points of view in fashion," Halston told *Vogue* magazine in June 1980. "And how that happens isn't that a light bulb goes on and click! You have it. You have to pull it out of yourself—and pull and pull and pull until it comes. As Martha [Graham] says, 'It's like giving birth to a cube.'"

Like a zealot, Halston was aware of other ideologies but believed in only one, the doctrine of simplicity, femininity and comfort. His fashion bible preached slow evolution, not seasonal revolution, simple glamour, not unnecessary excess, and functional luxury, not practical dowdiness.

"Fashion is dull because too many designers don't believe in what's theirs," said Halston. "I say designers are doing their best to make women conform. If it were up to them, they'd all look like cookie cutters. . . . What we lack is something new, exciting in real clothes to be worn by real people on the streets. A shape. What Charlie James would have given us in his heyday."

"He always had a knack for making news with his collection even though they were repetitive and long," says Bernadine Morris. "And I think that was intuitive."

"I remember saying to myself, 'Another Ultrasuede shirtdress?' But they were always slightly different," adds Bill Dugan.

What was always newsworthy was Halston's genius for detail and cut, construction and finishing. Such subtleties were often lost by those used to seeing fashions see-saw from one obvious and dramatic look to the next. The more successful he became with his simple formula, the more others doubted his originality, calling him a stylist who repeatedly made the same uniforms, not a couturier. The critics were both jealous and perplexed about how he could be so successful designing such simple clothes.

"About the only objections competitors are able to raise about Halston's clothes is that 'there's nothing to them.' That happens to be what makes them work," said Bernadine Morris. "It would be quite difficult for a woman in a Halston outfit to look 'done up' no matter how many of Elsa Peretti's ivory and silver bracelets she added."

"Many fashion authorities feel that Halston's impact has been exaggerated and even his admirers say he's no radical," said a *New York Times Magazine* article in 1973. Some of the comments received included: "He's no Pierre Cardin." "His clothes can only be worn by young women with beautiful bodies." "Halston makes no-clothes clothes" (designer Anne Klein). "You couldn't call him an original" (Blair Sobol, fashion columnist for the *Village Voice*). Even St. Laurent was quoted as saying, "Halston does nice things, but he is no designer."

What they did not understand is that it is much more difficult to make apparently simple things than blatantly complex ones. Often there were no buttons, zippers, darts, seams or trimmings—nothing to detract from the fabric and shape.

"Simplicity in design is never easy. Usually we cover things with buttons and bows to hide our mistakes. When design is simple is when it is most difficult," confirms designer Stan Herman.

Even those involved in creating the garments were in awe of the final results. "It was so simple that after it was explained you would say, why didn't I think of that," says Marie Levine, director of administration for Halston for nine years.

"Once you understood the pattern, his ideas were very easy ones. But at first, when you are making all those patterns, it is not like you have a regular neckline, shoulder, or armhole," says Akira.

Polly Mellen was a great Halston supporter and customer who did understand. "Someone who says they do not understand Halston has not worn Halston. There are designers whose clothes you have to wear. To wear a Chanel jacket is an experience. Like wearing a Halston jacket or sweater."

Norman Norell made one of many personal appearances at Martha's Palm Beach store in 1971 when she also happened to be displaying a long jersey Halston shirtdress. "Over all these years, Norman never even looked into the stockroom to see what others were doing," remembers Lynn Manulis, the store's owner. "This time he asked me if I would mind if his model tried on that Halston shirtdress. I was absolutely stunned. When they were finished I asked Norman what he thought. He said, 'I wouldn't pass my students at Parsons if they handed me a dress made like this, but it has a goddamn good shape.'"

The Halston garments that seemed the simplest and purest were deceiving in that they were the most complex to conceive. The bias cuts that dominated every collection were rarely attempted by other designers because of the difficulties involved with cutting, fitting and sewing.

To fully understand the bias concept, one needs to know that fabrics are woven with a grain which runs vertically and horizontally. Generally, the top-to-bottom direction of a garment runs in one of those directions, because they are the more stable and stronger. But garments may be cut so that the top-to-bottom runs diagonally, or at a 45-degree angle to the grain. This makes the fabric very stretchy, but also allows it to drape more closely, and softly, around body contours. This is what Halston chose to do, and this is what made average-size bodies seem taller and thinner than they actually were when in Halston's bias cuts.

"I just think bias is more sexy," Halston explained. "I keep cutting straight-grained clothes and they all look too familiar somehow. The bias gives you a plus. The theory is that you can cut everything on the straight and then throw it on the bias but that really doesn't work. The fabric in a funny way tells you what it's going to do. And since we are into such a sexy night period . . . for day, everyone is in sweaters, shirts and skirts. . . . I just find the bias cut the perfect answer. At night I think you want to be turned on and there is nothing more of a turn-on than a fabric which hits the body the way the bias does. It adds another dimension of softness."

The cut that Halston consequently called a "tube" construction first appeared in his Spring 1974 collection, and was the basis of many of Halston's most successful and famous trademark looks. It allowed a garment to be made completely on the bias, all in one piece, by spiraling a single seam around the body. Most garments rely on side seams to create a shape. Without side seams, the shape has to totally rely on the drape of the fabric itself, a much more difficult task.

The bias tube concept was used in caftans, dresses, skirts and tops that would hang softly and sensually on the body. One of the most famous strapless styles closed only with self-fabric ends that were knotted at the bust. The only add-on that might be allowed was a hand-sewn hook and eye at the neck opening and perhaps a small button, but only if it was finessed to the inside of the garment so it would not be visible.

"His incredible spiral seam! You just dropped it on the body and you were the best-looking girl in the room," remembers Polly Mellen.

"He liked the bias cut because it is simple," says Yutaka Hasegawa, a Halston patternmaker from 1977 to 1982. "The bias tube skirt looks like nothing; it looks like a straight skirt. But if we made one mistake, a calculation slightly too small or big, we had to start all over again."

The construction technique also had implications, both good and bad, for the type of fabrics that could be used. Because these bias cuts required using a very long single-ply length of fabric, "we would have to wait until everybody left the office to cut the fabrics," remembers Maki. On Sixty-eighth Street, they would use the floor of the main showroom, and at Olympic Tower, "we used the floor of the fitting rooms, because that was the only place big enough to cut the dresses."

"The pattern looked so strange, but it allowed you to use a smaller piece of fabric to make a big dress," says Sal Marano, one of Halston's assistants and patternmakers.

All types of four-season fabrics were cut on the bias—cotton, silk chiffon, silk crepe—but "very few manufacturers made silk in the wide widths that [Halston's] designs required," Akira continues. "The only fabric I could find that was wide enough was chiffon, which is the reason he used a lot of chiffon. He started to buy from Italian mills because they had wider fabrics, and by the end we were using specially made 118-inch-wide silk from Mantero. Producing these fabrics cost a fortune."

For a long, sweeping gown cut in 360 degrees with one seam, the only mill that could develop a ninety-nine-inch-wide silk crepe de chine was an Italian upholstery

BELOW:
Halston's original sketch for the tie-front strapless one-piece dress.

RIGHT:
Lee Radziwill wearing the tie-front strapless one-piece dress, May 1976.

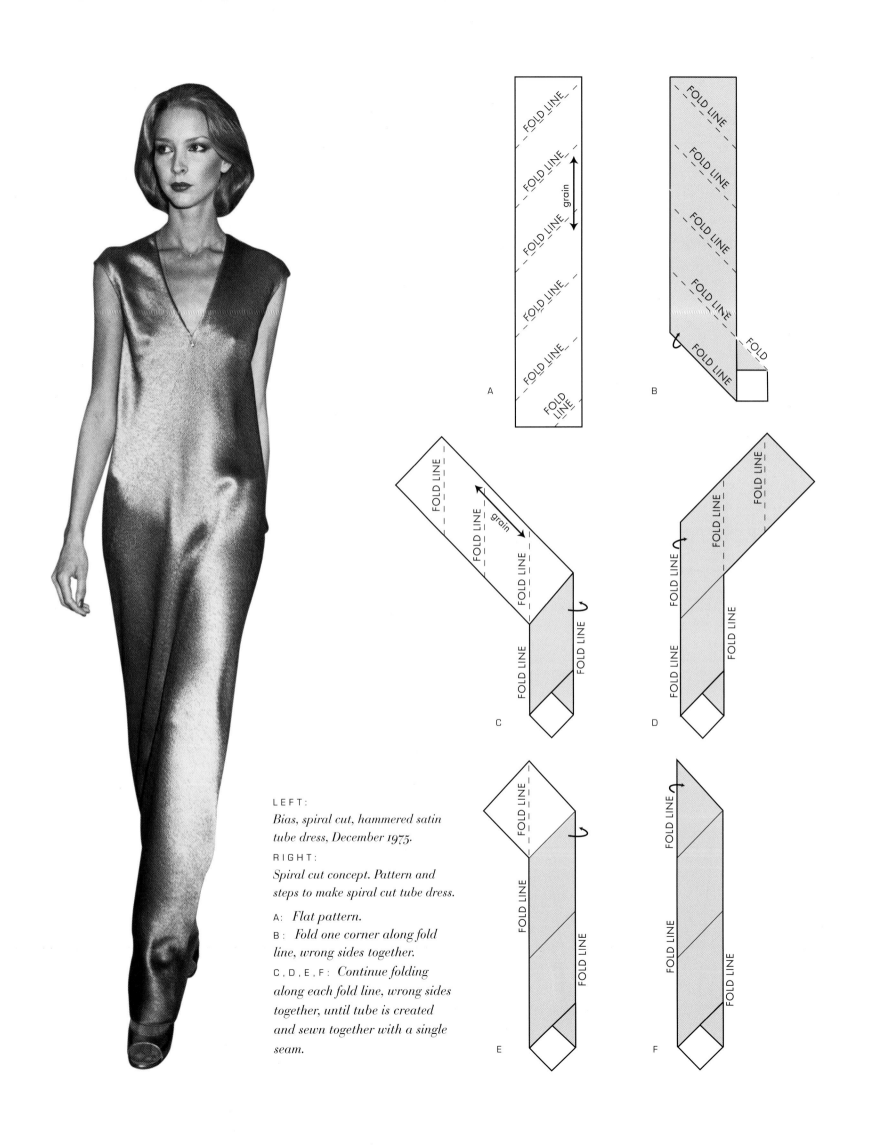

LEFT:

Bias, spiral cut, hammered satin tube dress, December 1975.

RIGHT:

Spiral cut concept. Pattern and steps to make spiral cut tube dress.

A: *Flat pattern.*

B: *Fold one corner along fold line, wrong sides together.*

C, D, E, F: *Continue folding along each fold line, wrong sides together, until tube is created and sewn together with a single seam.*

A

FOLD LINE
FOLD LINE
FOLD LINE
grain
FOLD LINE
FOLD LINE
FOLD LINE
FOLD LINE

B

FOLD LINE
FOLD LINE
FOLD LINE
FOLD LINE
FOLD

C

FOLD LINE
FOLD LINE
grain
FOLD LINE
FOLD LINE
FOLD LINE

D

FOLD LINE
FOLD LINE
FOLD LINE
FOLD LINE

E

FOLD LINE
FOLD LINE

F

FOLD LINE
FOLD LINE

mill. Including the research and development costs, the fabric ended up costing about two hundred and eighty dollars a yard, according to Peter Eng.

When these dresses were replicated in mass production, to prevent stretching and rippling, they were stitched on paper that was then torn away. Many styles then needed to hang for several days to allow the fabric to "grow" before they were hemmed, says Guido De Natale.

"The dresses always looked so simple, but I can tell you from experience, they were very intricate clothes," agrees Sassy Johnson Connor, who was responsible for fitting those dresses on made-to-order customers. Of the bias and tube dresses she says, "To alter and fit that was extremely difficult. On very thin models, the dresses would just fall. But on women with a body, I would find the complexities of those dresses enormous. To alter and adjust something that's on the bias and is one strip of fabric, you have to do it in small increments or it begins to pull and get out of shape."

Just as Coco Chanel took highly constructed clothing one step closer to softness, with his bias and tube cuts, Halston pared fashion down to yet another simpler level.

"Halston would make form-fitting, slinky clothes and women had to take off those bras to wear them. We would build them in, if need be," remembers Sassy.

The goal for each of Halston's designs was to eliminate all unnecessary closures and trims and to have as few seams as possible. Except in some tailored suits and coats, traditional set-in armholes were forsaken for a dropped or dolman style, or, ideally, were cut in one with the body of the garment. In order to do that, many garments were made out of a single piece of fabric, an architectural feat that few, if any, have been able to replicate with equal success.

"The lines would always continue from front to back without any breaking-off points on the side or center back," remembers Rita Malfitani, a Halston dressmaker for thirteen years.

No garment or accessory escaped his quest for seamlessness. For the custom-made clothes, Halston insisted on making long sash belts that wrapped around the waist twice, without any seams, which meant using, and wasting, a lot of fabric. "The two or three yards of fabric needed for a single belt might cost $200 alone," says Hasegawa.

A single layer of fabric cut into an elongated rectangle was folded like an envelope and, with just three folds, created a boxy pajama top with a pointed hem. A caftan was created from a trapezoid-shaped piece of fabric that was folded on the bias and seamed into a box shape, with a hole and a slash in the center front or back for the head. If cut on the grain, the result would have been stiff and boardy, but the bias cut allowed it to fall in soft drapes.

The pattern for a long-sleeved, one-piece dress looked much like a flattened pinwheel. But when folded in half along the shoulder line, and stitched together with only two continuous side seams, it produced a sinuous, sexy shape.

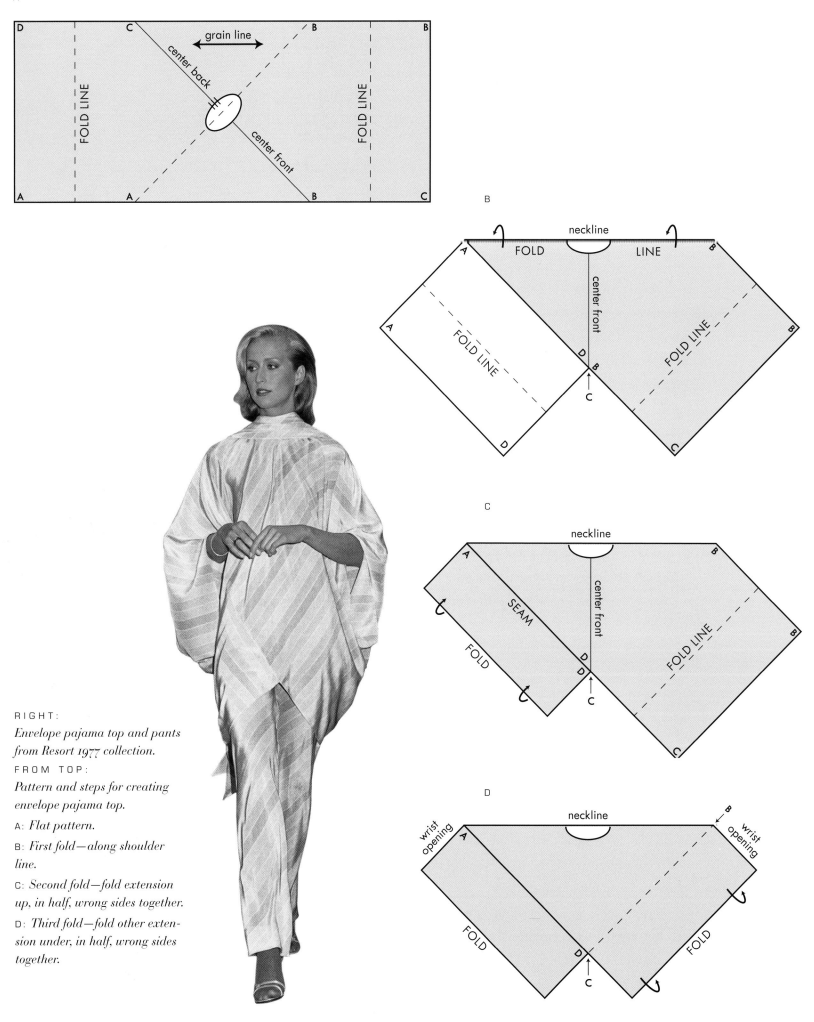

A

D C B B
center back
grain line
center front
FOLD LINE
FOLD LINE
A A B C

B

neckline
A FOLD LINE B
A B
center front
FOLD LINE
FOLD LINE
D
B
C
D

C

neckline
A B
SEAM
center front
FOLD
FOLD LINE
D
D
B
C
C

D

neckline
wrist opening
A B
wrist opening
FOLD
FOLD
D
C

RIGHT:

Envelope pajama top and pants from Resort 1977 collection.

FROM TOP:

Pattern and steps for creating envelope pajama top.

A: *Flat pattern.*

B: *First fold—along shoulder line.*

C: *Second fold—fold extension up, in half, wrong sides together.*

D: *Third fold—fold other extension under, in half, wrong sides together.*

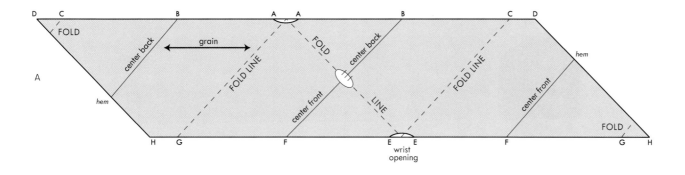

A

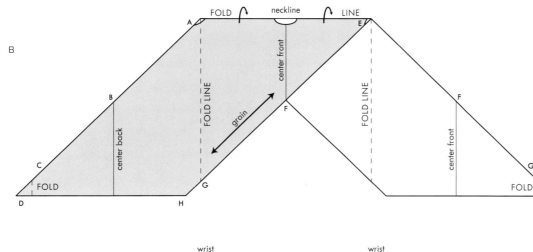

B

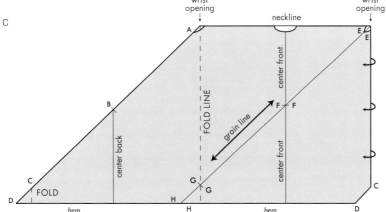

C

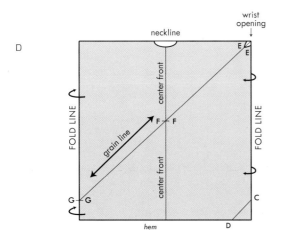

D

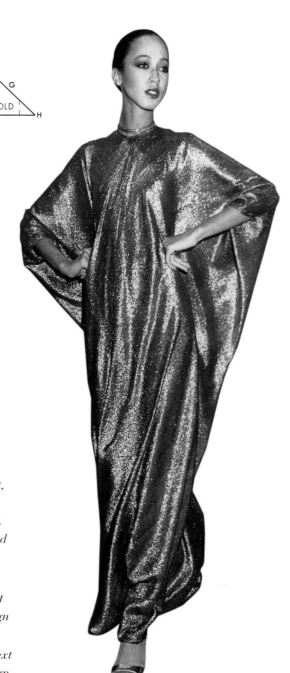

RIGHT:

Lamé spiral cut one-piece caftan worn by model Pat Cleveland.

FROM TOP:

Patterns and steps to make spiral cut, one-piece caftan.

A: *Flat pattern with cut out for head. Center front or back would be slashed for head opening.*

B: *Fold in half along shoulder line.*

C: *Fold right extension up along next fold line, wrong sides together, to align center fronts.*

D: *Fold left extension under along next fold line, wrong sides together, to align center backs.*

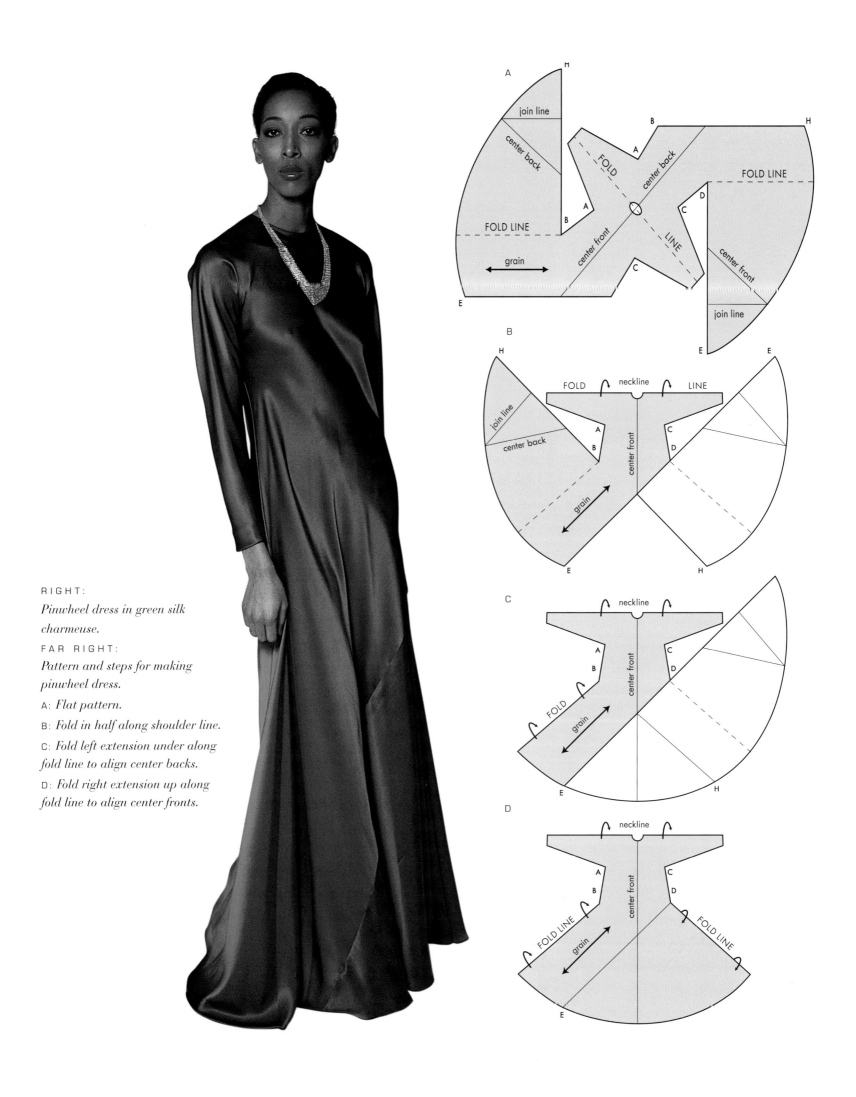

RIGHT:

Pinwheel dress in green silk charmeuse.

FAR RIGHT:

Pattern and steps for making pinwheel dress.

A: *Flat pattern.*

B: *Fold in half along shoulder line.*

C: *Fold left extension under along fold line to align center backs.*

D: *Fold right extension up along fold line to align center fronts.*

Some of Halston's "simple" clothes caused some problems and funny incidents with customers, so much so that they often came with written instructions on how to wear them. One time Ethel Kennedy had ordered a dress that she sent back because she could not figure out how to put it on. The top of the dress twisted and wrapped around and then tied in the front. Rita Malfitani remembers pinning notes to each spot of the dress—"left side," "right side," "center back," "center front," "tuck under here"—and then returning it to Mrs. Kennedy.

On another occasion, Mrs. Kennedy stipulated that she would not buy one of Halston's complex, multilayered dresses to wear to a dinner honoring her late husband unless Sassy Johnson Connor agreed to go to the Waldorf-Astoria Hotel on the night of the event to help her get dressed.

Jacqueline Onassis called Sassy after wearing a Halston dress and complained that it had not been correctly fitted. It turned out she was wearing it backward. This was a common faux pas when putting on Halston's dresses, so much so that the Seventh Avenue collection eventually sewed labels marking the front into their garments.

Malfitani remembers an incident where someone wore a dress with a deep décolleté neckline when being presented to royalty. When she curtseyed, her bosoms fell out. The client was going to sue Halston, but he calmed her down enough to have her bring the dress in. It turned out that she, too, had worn the dress backward.

For every detail and design Halston attempted, his greatest satisfaction came from making it better and differently than anyone else. Like his hero Charles James, his joy was in the creation.

"It has everything," said Halston of designing. "It's difficult, it's hard work, it's harassing, it's full of drama. I don't quite know where I got my ambition but I have it. I go into things with an optimistic point of view and I look at it straight and try to make it the biggest and best success I can. But the thing that holds my interest always is more, what's next, what's going to be the next exciting thing."

Instead of cutting shapes and then seaming together two different-colored fabrics to make blocks of contrasting colors, Halston devised a more complicated, but also more clever and attractive, technique for the "flying saucer" garments in his Spring 1978 made-to-order collection. Two different-colored circles were seamed together around their circumferences and then pulled apart. Depending on where the circular opening for the waist and the shaped opening for the hem were placed within each circle, the colors would form different shapes—bands running horizontally around the body, or diagonal bands angled either across the body or dipping toward the front or back.

OVERLEAF:
Easy opulence in lamé and silk from Holiday 1978 collection.
© Harry Benson.

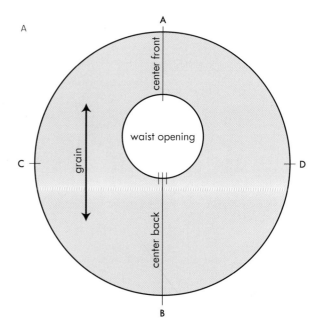

A

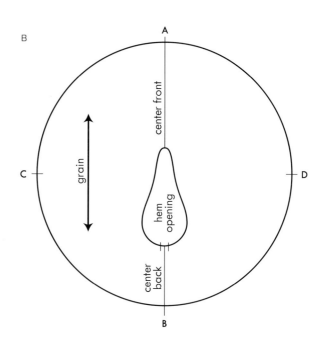

B

RIGHT:

Bicolor peach and white silk charmeuse "flying saucer" dress from Spring 1978 made-to-order collection.

ABOVE:

Pattern for "flying saucer" skirt where bands of color dip towards the back.

A: *Top circle—shorter in front than in back due to placement of waist cutout.*

B: *Bottom circle—longer in front than in back due to placement of hem cutout.*

See page 121 for more details.

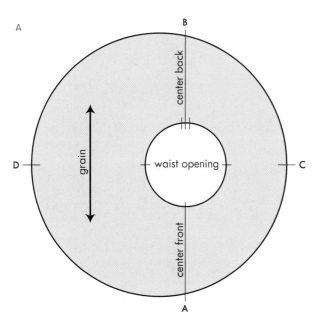

A

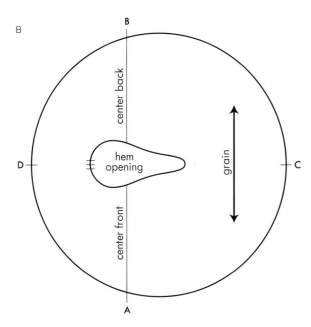

B

LEFT:

"Flying saucer" one-shoulder dress from Summer 1978 made-to-order collection, the first one shown at Olympic Tower.

ABOVE:

Pattern for "flying saucer" skirt where bands run diagonally across the body.

A: *Top circle—shorter on right side of body than on left side due to placement of waist cutout.*

B: *Bottom circle—shorter on left side of body than on right side due to placement of hem cutout.*

See page 121 for more details.

In the late 1970s through early 1980s, Halston went through his ruffle period. It was something of a departure for him, but one that offered an engineering challenge. Although other designers, notably Oscar de la Renta, had become well known for their feminine ruffles, Halston was determined to find a way to do it better. How the ruffle evolved was typical of how Halston developed any cut or concept—first slowly and purposefully, testing the waters, and finally building to a crescendo of unprecedented technique and beauty of design. Eventually all his lines at every price level, from made-to-order to lingerie and blouse licensees, featured some version of his ruffles.

"This was a time when everyone was talking about luxury," remembers Akira Maki. "Halston said, 'If that's the way people want to dress, then I will make it. But I'm not going to make a ruffle like Oscar's. I'm going to make much more artistic ones.'"

The first few small ruffles appeared in 1974 in a big-topped pajama with ruffled cuffs and bra top. They were rarely seen again until the Resort 1976 collection, in which a subtle ruffle was seen only once, in a silk chiffon pajama, on the bottom of pants worn with a one-shoulder top.

"The ruffles are on the bias and rather spare. They're cut to make you look 10 feet tall," Halston told *WWD* on September 16, 1976.

It wasn't until the Summer 1980 collection that Halston was in full ruffled splendor. That was the year *WWD* gave Halston a new nickname, "Mr. Ruffle," seeing them in his collections "winding sinuously down the sleeve, perching on a shoulder, wreathing about the neck and shooting straight from the hip—for day and night."

Double and triple layers of silk organza ruffles gently undulated around the face of a blouse collar, dubbed the "calla lily collar," and it was important to have the same petal collar repeated on the matching suit jackets. Ruffles also sprouted on swimsuits, along the hipline and, jabot-like, along the V-neck front.

The next season (Fall 1980), Halston perfected his ruffle technique. *WWD* called it a paradox because, "while virtually every piece of clothing sports some sort of flourish or ruffle, the best of these also possess a cleanly sculpted feel."

"It was probably the most beautiful made-to-order collection he ever did, and it probably sold better than any collection we ever had," says Sassy Johnson Connor.

"I love the idea of a ruffle that seems to come from nothing. I like things that look sculptural and yet are soft," said Halston.

What he was referring to was his original construction technique in which the ruffles and body of the garment were created from one piece of fabric. There were a number of variations on this technique, one more elaborate than the next.

At its extreme, evening jackets were totally covered with row upon row of ruffles that, in silk gazar, fluttered like swan feathers when the models slid down the runway. Pants had ruffles running up and down the side of the leg, and each leg, front and back, hem to hem, including the ruffle, were cut in one piece. These were worn with a companion "dinosaur" ruffled blouse or jacket that had layers of ruffles running along the shoulder and down the length of the sleeve. In a "fantail pigeon look," a white organza, slim evening dress had a cascade of ruffles running down the back. A ruffled shawl was also produced with this seamless technique.

One ruffled dress that stands out in Akira's memory was "made out of very wide iridescent silk taffeta with only one seam and one tie. The ruffle was continuous from one corner to the other."

When some of these ruffled dresses were taken on the World Tour trip, they were so big that they each required their own suitcase. And at each city where a fashion show was being given, they all had to be pressed, indelibly etched in the memory of one of the backstage pressers, Akira.

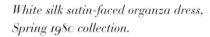

White silk satin-faced organza dress, Spring 1980 collection.

RIGHT:

Pattern for long-sleeved version of ruffled blouse.

A: *Front*

B: *Back*

BELOW:

Silk organza short-sleeve blouse with cut-in-one ruffles, Spring 1981 collection. Several layers of ruffles cut in minimally graduated widths to create a soft, fluttery look.

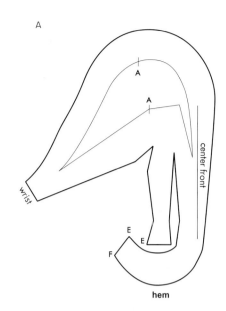

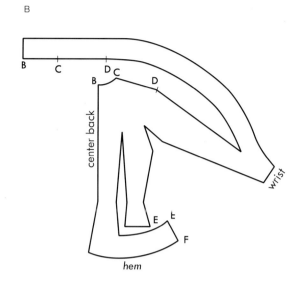

ABOVE:
Waterfall of translucent tiers of rose pink silk gazar in jacket from Resort 1980 collection.
LEFT:
White organza dress with cascade of fan-tail ruffles from made-to-order collection for Spring 1981.

Black faille cancan skirts with bright organza built-in panties and petticoats from Halston Sportswear collection, Fall 1979. © Rico Puhlmann

LEFT TO RIGHT:
Matte jersey draped and tied Empire halter dress, May 1975; hammered satin, bias, spiral cut halter dress from Fall 1976 collection; halter dress with body baring cutouts, November 1976.

Wrapping, draping and tying was another Halston signature technique that enabled him to further pursue his crusade for the trimless, buttonless and zipperless garment. Fabrics were draped and folded into feminine softness, not stiffly constructed to hold their shape. With the use of his trademark obi sash belt, and variations thereof, dresses could be adjusted to the body that was wearing them.

"Halston has introduced a whole new generation of women to the joys of strapless dressing, without the bones and wires of the Brenda Frazier era," said Bernadine Morris. "Halston just knots and twists and the dresses seem to stay up." In fact, many of them had sewn-in bras, but not the wired or boned kind, just a piece of chiffon to keep everything under control. In 1976, Halston dressed Elizabeth Taylor, Marlo Thomas and Marisa Berenson for the Academy Awards presentations, all in strapless Halston sarongs.

"It's every man's fantasy—a dress that's like a Christmas package. You just pull the pretty bow and the beautiful wrapping slips right off," said Halston in *WWD* on August 11, 1982.

True to type, Halston hunted for and found every possible way to wrap, tie and drape a garment, causing *WWD* to call his Spring 1983 collection a "wrap session—dresses that wrap any number of ways around the body and might require an assembly kit to put on."

Shoulder-baring Empire-waist dresses wrapped around the front leaving lots of leg showing. Waist-wrapped silk dresses were cut high on the thigh. Torso-wrapped evening looks in bias-cut pink lamé wrapped around like a sarong. The Savage bathing suit, the only swimsuit in the Summer 1976 collection, wrapped and tied like a high-fashion diaper. Apron-like wrap dresses opened flat and could be easily packed. Silk evening jackets wrapped around the body in enveloping cocoon shapes.

Halston's famous tulip skirt, seen both for day and evening, was made from a single layer of fabric, shaped something like an isosceles triangle that was then attached to a waistband. The entire piece was wrapped around the body, the edges meeting off center and with the point falling at the center back hem.

A skirt that ended up looking something like a sarong was actually made from one piece of fabric with extensions that were shirred in both horizontal and vertical directions to create the draped and tied effect.

Probably the most dramatic of his draped dresses were inspired by Grecian togas, with drawstrings creating deep

Silk gazar wrap "petal" pants and silk wrap blouse from Spring–Summer 1981 collection.

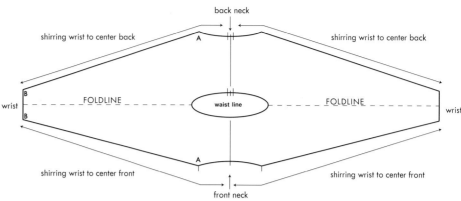

shirrs and folds of fabric. Halston devised his own, more interesting construction technique to achieve that look for tops and dresses. The bodice of a dress was created from a single piece of fabric, its longest dimension running from wrist to wrist, widening in the center to accommodate both the front and back lengths and an oval opening for the waist. The piece was folded in half lengthwise, bringing the only two raw edges together to be seamed and shirred, forming the shoulder and sleeve, with an opening in between for the head. The channel for the drawstring and the cord used was tight enough that even on slippery fabric, the draping stayed in place. It was seamless from the waistline and along the underarm. A one-shoulder dress version was shirred from the neck shoulder point to the opposite underarm, with the drapes on the side of the body, again, without any seam. Made from fine sheer matte jersey fabric, incredibly soft, full and luxurious folds resulted.

TOP LEFT:
Shirred matte jersey drawstring dress, August 1980.
TOP RIGHT:
Pattern for shirred top.
ABOVE:
Shirred bathing suits from the Halston retrospective exhibit at Museum at FIT.
OPPOSITE:
Shirred matte jersey dresses.

In 1976, Halston introduced an asymmetrical neckline that continued to evolve through the last collection he designed, in 1984. First, a V-shaped neckline was skewed off to one side in long and short bias-cut dresses and tunic tops, either in hammered satin, matte jersey, fine cotton knits, glamorous chiffons or silk charmeuse. Both baring and concealing at the same time, the width of the V was varied, sometimes a collar was added and sometimes the V was placed on the back. Asymmetric necklines were often shown with an Elsa Peretti pin at the base of the V to emphasize the shape. Halston continued to reangle, reshape and reproportion the asymmetry until it became a single lapel on suits, blouses and coats.

Hemlines were also cut in asymmetrical angles and shapes—slanted in profile from front to back, up to thirty-five yards of chiffon fabric cut in six to twelve separate layers of graduated lengths that flirted when you walked. Floral-shaped pants inspired by Lana Turner in the film *The Postman Always Rings Twice* were made in sheer silk gazar worked in bias folds across the front and back to give movement. And the ultimate in Halston asymmetry was the signature one-shoulder dress or top.

Left to right: Black rayon velvet wrap jacket and slim pants; bark-textured silk crepe de chine dinner dress with asymmetrical neckline; bias cut black rayon velvet strapless dress worn with Elsa Peretti's diamonds by the yard; single-breasted natural black opal mink coat with casual feeling by Ben Kahn, 1976.

LEFT:
*Spiral cut tunic with asymmetric
neckline, bias cut pants and
scarf from Spring 1977 made-
to-order collection.*

RIGHT:
*Burn out velvet pajama top
with asymmetrical neckline
and hem with chiffon pants,
from Fall 1976 collection.*

OPPOSITE:
*Asymmetric neckline bathing
suit, March 1977.*

RIGHT:
*Faille arc sleeve jacket and silk
tulip wrap skirt from Spring 1979
made-to-order collection.*
OPPOSITE:
*Halston fitting ruffled dress on model
Chris Royer, October 1980.*

In the late 1970s and early 1980s, when football-player shoulders became an important fashion trend, Halston did not avoid the shoulder issue, he merely skirted around it. When everyone else was deciding on the thickness and shape of their shoulder pads, Halston found a way to create a more shouldered shape without using any extra or uncomfortable inserts or devices other than the cut of the cloth. He created melon-shaped sleeves that curved outward from the shoulder to the elbow. He also gave width and roundness to the shoulders by using a yoke that extended into a sleeve, with a giant, softly folded pinch pleat where the sleeve cap would have been.

Halston never had formal or technical fashion training, never learned how to make a pattern, but was an expert at draping, learned from millinery. Something else Halston had, however, could not be learned in school—an instinctive sense of fit and proportion and a finely tuned eye for color. Halston's talented assistants, tailors and patternmakers may have been the technicians who erected the incredible structures he conceived, but they always credited Halston with being the architect who provided them with the blueprints. There were group design sessions with the key assistants where each could offer ideas and express opinions to the master, but there was no question that the final ideas were Halston's, and Halston's alone.

"There were so many changes every season. He had thousands of ideas. Never without ideas," says Salvatore Cardello, Halston's assistant and patternmaker for more than ten years. Cardello remembers having a drink with Joe Eula and Halston the night before a collection fashion show, and Halston was already talking about ideas for the next season's collection.

"One thing that is always interesting to a designer like myself is what is yet to be done," Halston said. "It's always the next thing. The thing that holds your interest is what you're going to do next month, next year, projecting your think-

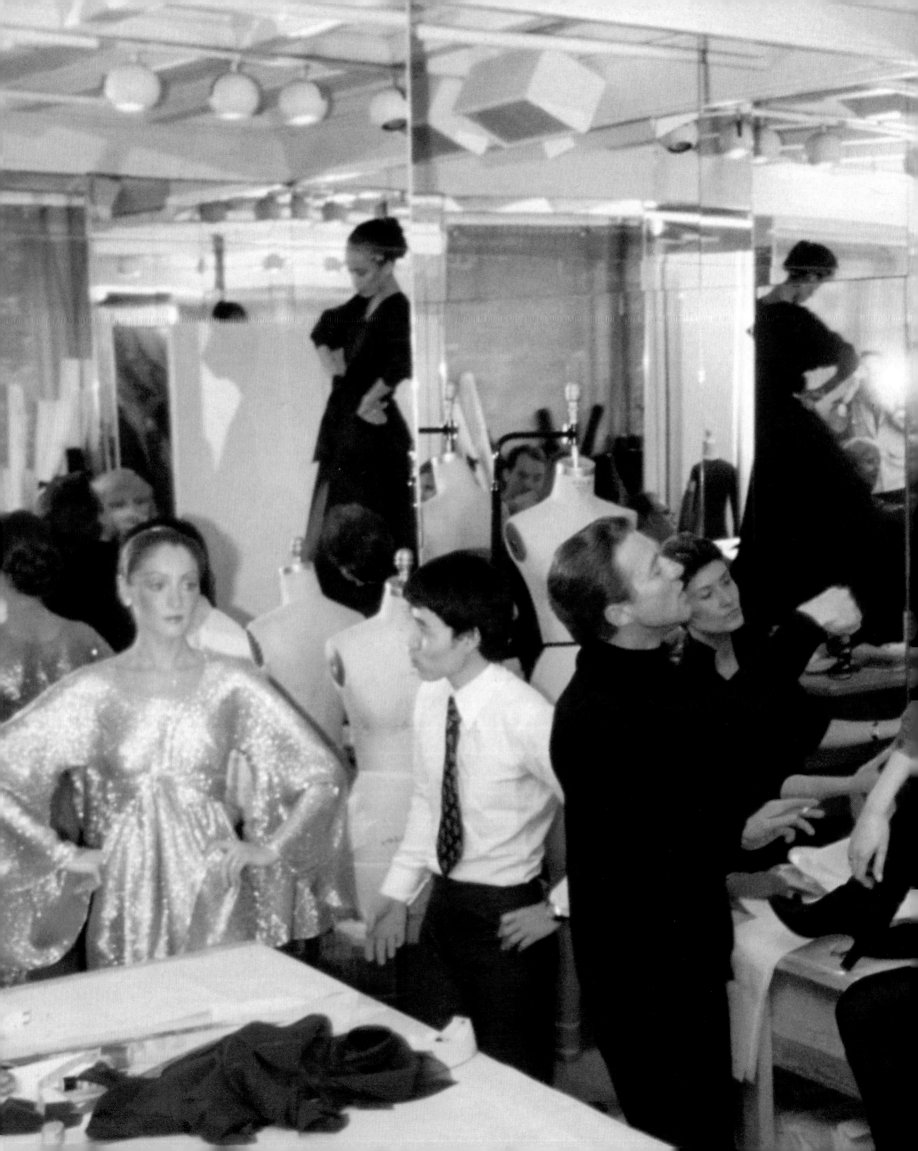

Halston and his team in the Sixty-eighth Street custom workroom, April 1977. Left to right: House model Shirley Ferro, assistant/patternmaker Akira Maki, Halston, Pat Mori, model Chris Royer sitting, model Pat Cleveland standing on table, assistant/pattern-maker Salvatore Cardello, model Kyle. Pat Cleveland wears hothouse red satin body stocking under paper-taffeta dress and red satin boots.

ing into a year or two away. It's always the next experiment. . . . You know, I'm privileged in order to be able to do that kind of thing. It makes me happy."

"He knew everything. He couldn't do it himself, but he knew what he wanted. He was a natural artist," says Cardello. "Halston did not copy. That I can swear. He didn't copy anybody. He concentrated on trying to develop new things."

A "Halston" was immediately identifiable, not only because it was zipperless, buttonless, unlined or had elasticized waists, but because this lack of construction was paired with a unique look and fit. A Halston T-shirt was never just a T-shirt; the neckline would be wider, the armhole lower. But those who didn't wear or examine the garment would just see a familiar shape. A caftan can be elegant or heavy, the trick to making it sexy is in the draping and molding. "It's art, not a formula," says Halston dressmaker and assistant Suzanne Chenevas.

"Today in designing there are many things in the public domain," Halston told *WWD.* "The trench coat, for instance. St. Laurent does it his way, Bill Blass does it his way and I do it in my way. I make my own thing. I don't go to Europe, buy a coat and knock it off. That's plagiarism."

The first Halston Originals collection, June 1972
Left to right: Black mohair jersey cardigan coat; Ultrasuede pantsuit; jersey suit with wrap skirt; short silk jersey evening dress; silk and cashmere giraffe-neck sweater and skirt; angora cape coat with skinny sleeves and full skirt over matching halter neck dress.

Sketching was not one of Halston's greatest talents, although he briefly studied fashion illustration at the Chicago Art Institute. It was, however, the method he preferred for conveying his design ideas to customers and the workroom. He sketched constantly, while he was on the phone, while he was talking to someone. "He'd come in the morning with a batch of sketches under his arm," says Faye Robeson. "He said to me one day, 'I have a million sketches up here [in the office].' And I'm sure he did."

When his simple, straightforward sketches could not convey some of the more intricate cuts he had devised, Halston would borrow from Japanese origami and fold pieces of paper to show his concepts. This was the method used for the bias tube configuration.

The visuals were supplemented with detailed and colorful verbal descriptions. Rita Malfitani remembers Halston describing a wrap skirt as being like a tulip, and a tiered skirt as being like a carnation. He would have everyone scrambling for the flowers to get the exact look and shape he wanted.

When finer and more artful sketches were required for the workroom or for publication, Halston had some of the best fashion illustrators working at his side to interpret his concepts—Audrey Saltzman Schiltz at Bergdorf Goodman, Stephen Sprouse during the early days at Halston Ltd. and then the famous artists Joe Eula and Kenneth Paul Block.

"Halston was very articulate and very knowing," says Kenneth Paul Block, who worked for the designer for many years. "Many designers can't tell you in language what they meant to do and where they were going, but he could."

When it came to the softer dresses and knit garments, especially chiffons, Halston often draped what he wanted on a mannequin and then turned them over to the technicians. This became considerably easier when he started to employ a small army of half-sized mannequins.

When an assistant purchased one of these mannequins from Wolf Forms Company, Marie Levine decided it was something that Halston might like and presented him with a single mannequin. Halston loved the idea and asked to order a dozen with legs and a dozen without. Unfortunately, the company only made them without legs, to which Halston replied, "I'm a fancy designer. I'm sure they'll do it for me." And so they did. He draped half of the Spring 1980 collection on these mannequins and continued to use them sporadically. For some reason that was never explained, he refused to have a photo taken with them, saying that he didn't want anyone to know he was designing this way.

Many times Halston could also be found on the floor, cutting right into a very expensive piece of fabric. If it didn't work, he'd get back on the floor, retrim it, redraw the chalk marks to get the shape right. "It came down to cutting into the fabric, no muslins," says Bill Dugan. "He said if you're going to make a jersey dress, you have to use jersey to drape it, regardless of the cost of the fabrics. As soon as a fabric would come in, he would rush to cut into it."

Halston's eye was so finely tuned that he could see if a hem was even a quarter of an inch off and would have his assistants redo it, even if it was noticed late the night before a fashion show and there were many more obvious things needing attention. He would never compromise in even the smallest way and challenged his already proficient technicians to go even further. The fact that his name was on the office door and on the label of every garment was something he took very seriously.

"To get the exact look he wanted was very difficult. You had to sweat it out, but in the end, once you got it, constructing and finishing the garments wasn't that much work," says dressmaker Mallitani.

Long-hair alpaca wrap coat, 1977.

"He could see when something didn't fit, and he would say, 'Go back and fix it, I know you can do it,'" remembers Sal Marano, assistant and patternmaker. Like the jacket that Marano knew had been made according to the pattern, but Halston insisted was too small. The pattern was checked and found to be correct. Marano's sleuthing finally detected what Halston—but no one else—could see: the garment had been pressed so much that the fabric had shrunk.

Many times he would approve a garment in the evening, and then in the morning, change his mind. Or in the morning, the tailors would find a small mannequin that Halston had draped himself sitting on the workroom table to show how he wanted things done.

"There were so many experimental dresses," remembers Akira. "I don't think he ever stopped dreaming. He would go from one possibility to hundreds or thousands, until he would round out the idea. Season after season, he would do the same things, but in a more advanced stage."

He was such a perfectionist that even though he used the same eight models, time and time again, he insisted on fitting every single garment on them for a show. "If you know the guy or girl for so many years, you pretty much know how to fit them, make the hem, everything else, so you could fit on the girl in half an hour. He never liked that. Sometimes he made even the most expensive girls stay all night long," says Akira.

It was this perfectionism that usually triggered Halston's famous temperament, a combination of "insecurity and fear of things not turning out exactly the way he liked it," says Bill Dugan. "He wanted it to be the best it could be, and he had a fear that those who were working for him didn't know as well as he did what the end result should be."

His attention to detail was so acute that when weights needed to be inserted into hems to anchor jackets that had no interfacing, though they would not be visible, he insisted on using jeweler's sterling silver chains, not silver-colored ones, for the samples and custom garments. He was also very specific about how he wanted things finished. All the made-to-order garments were completely handmade, including endless hours spent hand rolling chiffon hems.

"I have to be involved in every aspect, because it's interesting and it's fun. And I want the success, not just for my own ego. It's big business, you know, and the livelihoods of thousands and thousands of people depend on your productivity. You have to be serious about it," the designer insisted.

There was great mutual respect between Halston and those in his workroom. He appreciated their skills and their ability to give life to his ideas. They appreciated his creativity and generosity, and so did all they could to please him. The feelings were so strong that during interviews for this book, tears were shed by several of his longtime employees. "I forgot I was a little dressmaker because it was a very glamorous job, glamorous surroundings, glamorous boss and glamorous treatment of the workers," says Malfitani of her days at the Olympic Tower.

And there are many kindnesses that are fondly remembered. The first Christmas after he bought his town house, Halston invited the entire staff to his home for a party. When a snowstorm was forecasted two days before a show, the whole workroom was put up in a hotel, each person with their own private room. "He supplied us with shopping bags with a toothbrush, a nightgown and money for breakfast the next morning," Malfitani reminisces.

He never had to be asked twice about giving clothes to models, tailors, patternmakers and assistants, and Elsa Peretti's silver pieces and diamonds by the yard were often given as gifts.

Suzanne Chenevas was allowed to bring her poodle, Bingo, to work, although he was not fond of the cleaning people or their brooms. The company mascot once bit a janitor's ankle, and when the man complained to Halston, the designer dryly quipped, "Bite him back."

"We were like a big family. We worked hard but laughed a lot, too," says Chenevas.

"At collection times, it got more serious, but in between it was fun," says Bill Dugan. "Individual projects would come along and we treated it like an exercise in creativity."

Between his charm and own drive, Halston knew how to squeeze the proverbial juice from the orange. "There was no greater energy on the planet than what was going on in that company," says Marie Levine, who often gave midnight birthday parties for those working until two or three in the morning.

"You never had your own life, but you loved to do it. I think once in your life you have to have that kind of passion," philosophizes Akira.

The night before every show, and there were fourteen shows per year when Halston was at his busiest (two for made-to-order, four for ready-to-wear, two for menswear, two for furs, two for sportswear, plus two for special design projects), everyone stayed up all night to finish the collection, usually to finish hand rolling the chiffon hems. There would be only brief breaks to return home, shower, change clothes and come back for more.

"If you counted all the hours, we didn't work one year but two years," jokes Sal Marano.

And during such crunch periods, there was no money spared, remembers assistant Naeem Khan. "When we were waiting for beadwork to arrive from India, and it was late, he told me to go as far as getting a private jet to have the beads flown to New York in order to have it for his show, even though I told him it would cost about forty thousand dollars." It turned out not to be necessary, but contingency plans were made.

Even during the years when it was assumed that Halston spent every night, and all night, out at Studio 54 or some other trendy club, when it came to show time, Halston was there working.

"At two A.M. he would come into the workroom and thank everyone. He would always say, 'Thank you ladies. Your dresses are beautiful.' Someone would always reply, 'No, *your* dresses are beautiful.' He would counter, 'No, *your* dresses,'" recalls Malfitani.

"One night I was with him working late. When we left, he asked where I was going, and he had a car drive me home, all the way out to Long Island," says Sal Marano.

Once things became corporate, Halston was pressured to hire seamstresses only when they were needed rather than keep them on the payroll full-time. He refused, because "if I don't keep them here and pay them, I won't later be able to find them again," Halston told Marano. Besides, there were so many collections that the sample hands were always busy and the custom dressmakers never had a lull of more than a few days.

After a time, his assistants and fitters learned the tricks of the Halston fit and could anticipate what he would want.

"You really learned fashion from him when you were in a fitting," says Khan. "I used to say to myself, let's see what Halston is going to say about this. You prejudged him to understand his mind and that's how you learned."

"The balance of the garment was important to him," says Salvatore Cardello. "To make straight clothes, the balance is very important."

Classic easy spring pantsuit.

"A fat woman looked slim in his clothes because he didn't accentuate that square look. His clothes had a shape that would cut her body." says Guido De Natale.

A narrow shoulder, a narrow but comfortable front and higher armholes were what made Halston's fit look small but also be very comfortable and allow for easy movement. To compensate for the narrow shoulder, there was ease added around the circumference of the sleeve cap.

Sometimes the shoulders were slightly widened, dropped a bit and tilted slightly toward the back. Most of his jackets and tops were made about a half inch longer in back than in front, so they would sit more firmly on the shoulders. One front of a jacket was cut slightly wider than the other near the clavicle, so there would be an underlap preventing the jacket from gaping when the wearer moved.

In 1970, when the industry was debating what role pants would play in a woman's wardrobe, Halston already considered them a wardrobe staple, "like pantyhose. I see them continuing forever. They give a woman a freedom she's never had before and she is not about to give it up."

That comfort and freedom could mean anything from the simplest elastic waist pull-ons in cashmere or lightweight silks, to complex and dressy wrapped pant-skirt hybrids "from which legs emerged like parts of a flower." What made them special was their cut and how they bottomed out the total outfit.

"When you wore Halston's pajamas to a dinner party in New York, heads would turn. Seas of short, poofy skirts would part to consider your soft, bias-cut pants. You'd be treated like someone uniquely in-the-know. And you'd be the most comfortable woman around. A modern woman, feeling fantastically feminine, in her pants . . . the Halston woman—comfortable, dashing, supremely self-confident." said Grace Mirabella.

RIGHT:
Silk paper-taffeta knee-length coat with matching pants and scarf from Spring 1979 made-to-order collection.

OPPOSITE LEFT:
Unlined cashmere cardigan, cashmere sweater and wool flannel pants, Fall 1973 collection.

OPPOSITE RIGHT:
Pantsuit with soft inverted pleats on jacket and pant waist, worn with soft wrap blouse, from Spring 1980 collection.

Halston also completely changed how women thought about jumpsuits, taking them out of the realm of mechanics and ski outfits, transforming them into practical, comfortable evening glamour. Jumpsuits had been in Halston's line since 1971, paired with matching stoles nonchalantly tossed over the shoulder, or matching cardigans covering up the more revealing numbers. The cashmere knits clung like glorified union suits. Some were practically open to the waist or bared with halter bodices. Others were so feminine and flowing only the wearer knew they were not a dress.

BELOW:
Cotton voile halter neck short jump-suit with side seam ruffle from Spring 1980 made-to-order collections.
RIGHT:
Ultrasuede jumpsuit from Fall 1975 collection.
OPPOSITE LEFT:
Crystal beaded cardigan jacket and jumpsuit from Summer 1981 collection.
OPPOSITE RIGHT:
Engineered stripe cotton jersey jumpsuit and matching cardigan.

BELOW LEFT TO RIGHT:
Long, ribbed top, cashmere knit dress with ribbed, zippered cardigan; cashmere polo dress with cardigan wrapped waist, November 1972; tank top sweater set and Ultrasuede skirt, November 1973.
OPPOSITE:
Halston reshapes and revives the sweater set, March 1973. © Neal Barr
OVERLEAF:
Halston's cashmere separates worn with Elsa Peretti's cuff bracelet, necklace and horseshoe buckled belt, March 1972. © Gösta Peterson

Clearly, it is impossible to pick out one of Halston's many signature looks as being the most memorable, but certainly his way with knits is near the top of the list. He reinvented the sweater set in substantial four-to-eight-ply cashmere, adding casual zippers and hoods. He took the British schoolboy look of tying a cashmere cardigan over the shoulders and made it a symbol for rejecting showier clothes in favor of simpler, softer, more contemporary ones. Cashmere knits in general were transformed from a dowdy British commodity to a must-have fashion item. Wool, rayon, silk and cashmere knits were glorified into versatile pieces "to take a lady from the dentist and having her hair done to shopping" and on into the night, depending upon what they were worn with.

"His success could be judged by the number of women who copied the gesture he made famous and wore their cardigan sweaters knotted around their neck. It was

*Cashmere knit dress, zippered
cardigan and shawl worn with Elsa
Peretti's silver buckled belt, Spring
1977; cashmere knit, zip-front, hooded
sweatshirt and pants with fringed
cashmere scarf, June 1975; long
cashmere dress and cardigan coat,
September 1972.*

as prevalent as the girdle-hitch in the days of the two-way stretch. . . . Halston is still knotting sweaters around the neck, though occasionally he makes them floor length and just hangs them on the shoulders. And sometimes he has the mannequin tie her sweater around her waist. He's also still making coat dresses, pushing up the shirt-sleeves and adding the sweater for decor—and very little else," Bernadine Morris wrote in the *New York Times*.

When she was named the editor of American *Vogue* in 1971, Grace Mirabella went to the Paris couture for the first time wearing a wardrobe of Halston separates that the designer planned carefully and made in his custom-order department months in advance.

Her wardrobe consisted of three V-neck cashmere pullover sweaters, one in white, one in beige and one in black; a beige woven cashmere trouser and a gray cashmere trouser; a pair of black matte jersey pants for day, and for night, a pajama made up of a black, bias-cut, charmeuse shaped T-shirt with bias-cut black charmeuse pants

and another very simple, unstructured, thin, black charmeuse top with a very simple, unstructured gold lamé jacket that wrapped and tied with a sash. It added up to sets of pajamas that would vary just in the degree of dressing. "If I wanted to be more dressed, I'd wear gold and charmeuse. If I wanted the look to be less dressed, it would be matte jersey. If I wanted it bare, I would take the jacket off and the top would be bare down the back. And if I wanted ornamentation, Halston would provide a perfect little drop of some accessory designed by Elsa Peretti. I always found this to be my core wardrobe, traveling or not. The organization carried me through everything I did."

She sat next to Hebe Dorsey, the flamboyant and unconventional fashion reporter for the *International Herald Tribune.* In her report the next day, she said that Mirabella came to the couture in a "sweater" looking "like the girl next door," and it wasn't meant to be a compliment.

What made Halston's turtleneck sweater different, according to Polly Mellen, was that "it was thin, it hugged your neck, it wasn't droopy and had a high armhole."

Knit separates from the Spring 1976 made-to-order collection. Left to right: Wool jersey wrap coat; luxe sweatshirt, pants and shawl in dove gray cashmere; slim jacket and pants in silk-striped jersey.

ABOVE:
Revealing V neckline bodysuit topped by Ultrasuede floor-length overskirt and cashmere knit shawl.

OPPOSITE:
Halston with model Pat Cleveland wearing cashmere jersey wrap dress over red cashmere body suit with red cashmere wrap, April 1977.

"Nobody had ever shown me before that you could get dressed up and look elegant in a cashmere sweater," says Ellin Saltzman.

The fit of his cashmere knits wavered from loose to stick-to-the-ribs skinny, but as with all things he put his mind to, "he went forward with his thought. His cashmere dresses to the floor were long-sleeve crew or V-neck, but they weren't just tubes; they had small armholes, were neat on top, yet very cozy and at the same time very glamorous," says Polly Mellen.

"Halston brings back woolies," said the *New York Post*'s Eugenia Sheppard when in 1977 he shook up the knitwear market by introducing the bodysuit, or as he preferred to call it, the body sweater.

"This is something I have been working on for years," said Halston. "It's going to change the pace of fashion. This is revolution fashion."

Made in wool knit, cashmere, stretch satin or stretch lace, in only five colors—brown, taupe, gray, black and hothouse red—and sized small-medium-large, some covered the feet, others stopped well above. All were surely inspired by Halston's close association with dance master Martha Graham and her company, for it was "like a dancer's exercise uniform, it gives the body complete freedom," said Sheppard in the *Post*.

Halston showed the bodysuit under everything from storm coats to taffeta gala dresses. The ribbed cashmeres had zippers, while the satins were stepped into. In his favorite head-to-toe look, they were worn with color-matched shoes and boots from licensee Garolini.

For day, a red bodysuit was worn under a black cashmere shirtdress, but the same bodysuit was shown with a black satin, knee-length wrap that easily accommodated going out to cocktails or dinner. Suitable for the dressiest of evenings was a hothouse-red bodysuit and red satin boots topped with a paper taffeta wrap dress. Bodystockings were also worn under to-the-floor sweaters.

Deemed too sexy and only for young and trim figures, in the short term, Halston's bodysuits had less than the revolutionary effect that was anticipated. Today the bodysuit is a staple in women's wardrobes.

"I think he was ahead of his time, because it's now," says Bill Dugan of the bodysuit. "It didn't sell on Seventh Avenue. They were great for the photos, but they were not knocking down the door to buy it. They were too special. Some of the bodysuits in cashmere sold in made-to-order, but not commercially."

*Bodysuits for day and evening in
black satin, black cashmere, brown
wool and hothouse red satin, May
1977. © Harry Benson*

BELOW:
Sleeveless, layered, bias-cut chiffon dress with angled hem from Summer 1978 collection.

RIGHT:
Heart print, collared halter neck, wrap dress from Summer 1978 collection.

Dresses were always special to Halston. He grew up in an era when they were the core component of a woman's wardrobe, a true mark of femininity, being one of the few thing that a man could never wear.

"I think the one-piece dress is the most useful for most people," he explained. "It's easy to get into and you always look orderly. Some women find it difficult to put several pieces together. Dresses should have a biasy-type skirt that has movement. They should be below the knee but not midcalf. The midi is for a very special person, one who wants to attract attention."

Halston's dress looks ran the gamut from his most basic upstyled shirt-dresses to full-blown evening extravaganzas. The evening looks exuded sexiness, using deep slits and angled and dipping hemlines to spotlight legs. One-shoulder and halter necklines bared shoulders. Plunging décolleté and backless cuts bared everything else that it was legal to bare. Body cutouts revealed just enough flesh to be tastefully seductive not vulgar. Nothing was sexier than the hint of the body underneath his long column dresses of cashmere or matte jersey, or his draped silk evening styles.

"Sexy sells," Halston knew, lapsing into speaking in the royal third person "we" for the *New York Times*. "Everyone should look like a movie star—feminine always—never masculine. We will be more comfortable in the daytime, but a little more extravagant in the fabric, maybe with a feather boa . . . and very high heels if we do not have to walk too far."

Those slithery, slinky siren dresses were strictly for rail-like figures. But Halston had the majority of womankind in mind when he started the caftan craze in 1970. Using dazzling, sumptuous fabrics, he single-handedly Westernized the Moroccan caftan he wore at home. An ethnic costume became a loose, comfortable, modern garment that made even large-size women feel and look glamorous. Almost every designer on Seventh Avenue followed suit. He designed them in floor-length for night, cropped above the knees for day, varied the necklines and offered them in a range of featherweight fabrics from chiffon to sheer cottons. Lauren Bacall wore one on the televised version of *Applause* in 1973. Babe Paley owned ten in different colors; she was seen wearing a black velvet flocked chiffon caftan over a chiffon bra and pants at dinner at the chic restaurant "21." Caftans filled the licensed loungewear collections for Dorian, fabricated in everything from velour to polyester jersey, printed and plain.

Bias striped one-shoulder dress from Summer 1976 collection.

OPPOSITE LEFT:
*Dot printed silk dress from
Summer 1977 collection.*

OPPOSITE RIGHT:
*Black satin-faced silk organza
halter neck wrap dress with
dipping hemline.*

RIGHT:
*Body-baring wrapped and shirred
matte jersey dresses from the Spring
1978 collection.*

ABOVE LEFT:
*Engineered multicolor-stripe silk
caftan from Spring 1976 collection.*
ABOVE RIGHT:
*Cotton seersucker caftan from
Summer 1976 collection.*

The balance and proportion in Halston's designs revolved around the importance of dresses and the fact that he was a proponent of moderate skirt and dress lengths. When other designers went from mini to maxi, fluctuating as rapidly as the Dow Jones average, Halston stayed within a prescribed range that hovered around the knee.

"Nearly everybody's wearing miniskirts these days and every designer is showing floor-sweeping coats. What's a girl to do if she wants to be noticed? Halston may have the answer: moderation," offered Bernadine Morris.

"I tried all lengths, long and short, and this one looked best to me," said Halston about the just-below-knee length (about one to two inches below) he was showing. "It's both ladylike and groovy."

One month later he boasted, "Everyone is testing my below-the-knee length, but they don't have any confidence in it yet. It's a new proportion for buyers. But my private customers have all ordered it. I showed live models in this length—some shirtdresses, some skirts with shirts—they've all ordered evenly. All my coats are below the knee and all have ordered."

Always conscious of women of all ages, Halston observed that "when a woman of a certain age wears her day skirts too long it has a tendency to make her look older. So she is probably better off wearing them just below the knee."

"Women talk with their legs," Halston added. "There is a whole sort of dialogue with men. Legs are a very important part of a woman. American women have beautiful legs and they like to show them."

Halston was beyond caring about skirt lengths themselves, only concerned about what was becoming to the wearer. He even proportioned his coats to a longer, all-purpose length that could be worn day or night. "It can make your pantsuit look new. And it looks equally well with skirts and dresses. Perhaps you add a longer scarf, a muffler. The coat should have a little bit of a fuller proportion, a little more ease."

"Without ever raising a skirt length fully above the knee, Halston has created some of the most leg-conscious, leg-flattering looks in town," said *WWD* of his Spring 1980 Halston Originals collection.

"If you're going to get people out of blue jeans and still give them the coverage they want, you've got to offer them something like this," Halston said of the longer lengths in his made-to-order collection for Fall 1973, showing his concern for women sitting on the floor or on low stools at parties.

The only exception to this self-made length rule came about in 1974. When all of Seventh Avenue was preferring below-the-knee lengths, he designed the "Skimp," a not-quite minilength three to five inches above the knee.

The story goes—although many question that this is the truth—that the Skimp was an idea hatched in collusion with John Fairchild, publisher of *WWD*. Halston and he met at Orsini's for one of their frequent lunches when Fairchild, noticing a waitress's short attire, expressed a longing for the return of the miniskirt. Halston mentioned he had been working on some short designs and practically the next day, *WWD* heralded the arrival of the Skimp for Spring 1975 on its front page.

For consistency's sake, Halston's made-to-order collection for Spring 1975 also skimped on length. "We kept shortening and shortening the proportion for this collection. The allover shorter mood here looks right . . . and younger," Halston explained. There were longer coats over Ultrasuede and sweaterdress Skimps, cotton knit Skimp dresses with matching cardigans, short and longer skirt combinations in chiffon for evening and Skimp-oriented foundations.

The Skimp was never commercially successful and lasted only one season. It did, however, prove the power of the press and Halston's influence, causing quite a brouhaha among the industry, which may have been what the scoop-seeking journalist had in mind.

"I haven't been able to get off the phone," said Halston the day after the first Skimp was publicized. "Generally, everyone loves it, particularly the tailors who are working on it and the kids who are modeling it. There are lots of young girls with great legs who are not buying long skirts, and this will inspire them to buy something other than pants."

Other designers reacted to the bold hemline change with a mix of disbelief, delight, exasperation, ecstasy, confusion and nonchalance. Donna Karan, then designer for Anne Klein, said, "My first reaction was, I don't believe it; only Halston can do it. It's totally opposite of what everyone else is doing. Halston said it perfectly—for the model woman with great legs it's an adorable change."

Pierre Bergé of YSL could only say, "I have seen the page one and I have never seen such beautiful stairs in all my life," referring to the *WWD* photo that was taken in Halston's town house.

Retailers were wary of still one more hemline change, although most agreed with Nan Duskin's Roy Witlin, who believed, "There are hard-core Halston customers who will wear anything he designs, even the Skimp. The Skimp is just an added dimension to today's way of dressing. Not for everyone. Not for every day."

Without trims or closures for design interest, fabric was pivotal in giving Halston's clothes their richness and form. Many of his signature looks were as closely dependent on the fabrics used as upon the silhouette. And the same shapes and styles were made in different fabrics that allowed them to carry over from day to night.

Halston was responsible for introducing or reintroducing a number of fabrics to the American market—hammered silk satin from the 1920s, silk charmeuse from the 1940s, cashmere knits, double-faced wool and cashmere wovens, silk and rayon matte jersey and the most famous of all, Ultrasuede.

He used only the best fabrics from the best mills. And when it came to fabrics, price was no object, says Peter Eng, who for five years was in charge of textiles for both the made-to-order and ready-to-wear lines. It was common for him to sample fabrics that cost between $80 and $140 yard, and those were 1970s dollars.

"The equivalent today, you couldn't afford. It would be like trying to build San Simeon now; the price would be prohibitive," says Eng.

Halston had the entire fabric world literally on his doorstep, but was very consistent about the types of fabrics he preferred, and so an impressive array of colors was built for each type. "When he sampled the line, very seldom did he see something new that he liked, maybe a print," remembers Guido De Natale.

"Chiffon is the most beautiful feminine fabric for women of every age. I like simple silhouettes with something that floats around," said Halston to *WWD*.

In the fabric room at the Olympic Tower offices, there were bins with dozens of rolls of chiffon in different tonalities. He would always go back to chiffons, says Eng, because they were seasonless and feminine. "He would tell us to bring all the chiffons, forty to sixty rolls, into his office and leave them for him to look at. At the end of the day he could have ninety to a hundred rolls of fabric."

This was a strong image for Eng, seeing these bolts of solid-color fabrics— chiffon, georgette, charmeuse, wool—lined up and leaning against the mirrored walls of Halston's office. "It looked like a big bouquet of flowers," he remembers.

Halston developed close relationships with certain mills, one being Jasco, a specialist in wool knits and one of the few domestic mills he frequented. "We always did whatever he asked," says Howard Silver, owner of Jasco, whose father, George, worked closely with Halston. "He would have an imagination based upon what he thought our potential was. And we did it as much for art as commerce. He always challenged us."

Today Jasco is still selling a fabric they refer to as the "Halston Crepe," a doubleknit creped on the knitting machine, not in the yarn, that was developed for the designer but that he never used.

"When Halston first started using double-faced fabrics, we bought the contractor the machine for splitting the fabric. There weren't any in this country," says Guido De Natale.

"Doublefaced fabrics had existed for a long time, but Halston really introduced it into the fashion world. He made it into a fashion statement—in long dresses, long ponchos, caftans, coats," says Dugan.

Halston's couture suits and coats were almost always doublefaced, no matter what the season. "It was so light and comfortable to wear, and so warm," says Akira. "If you had a cashmere sweater and a doublefaced cashmere coat, even in the middle of winter, it was so warm. And it felt like you weren't wearing anything."

Fabrics were also specially and exclusively developed for the less expensive and short-lived Halston Sportswear line. Upon Halston's request, marled and tweed Scottish sweater yarns were woven into coordinating fabrics. "It gave him the head-to-toe look he liked," remembers Crawford Mills, who headed the Halston Sportswear division and was responsible for developing fabrics.

"Working for Halston was an incredible high and an incredible low," says Eng. "He demanded the most and that sometimes brought you to the verge of a nervous breakdown. Three or four weeks prior to opening a line, suddenly Halston hated everything. He would go to Jerry Brown [a high-end fabric store on Fifty-seventh Street] and see something he liked. Then he would yell at us for having compromised."

Layered chiffon in asymmetric neck-line dress from Resort 1976 collection.

id Halston make Ultrasuede or did Ultrasuede make Halston? That is the question many fashion historians have asked. In the 1970s, the two were synonymous.

Halston was not the first designer to work with the imitation suede fabric, but he was the first who fully understood its potential. Halston first saw the fabric at a dinner party six months before it was distributed in the United States. Japanese designer Issey Miyake had been given a piece of Ecsaine, as it was originally called, by the Japanese mill that created it, Toray Industries, and was wearing a shirt jacket he made from it. Once the fabric arrived in the United States under the name Aquasuede, shoe designer Beth Levine had also been asked to do some early trials with the fabric. Reportedly both Calvin Klein and Bill Blass were offered the fabric before Halston.

"I flipped," Halston told the *New York Times* in 1973. "The material was so soft, so luxurious yet so utilitarian. I immediately started visualizing all the things I could design."

Although the fabric was completely machine washable, Halston incorrectly thought that it was also waterproof and so the first Aquasuede garment that appeared in a Halston collection was a raincoat, shown in January 1971 for the Spring 1971 season. It was so successful that the following season he followed it up with a classically casual shirtdress, style #704, in the fabric now called Ultrasuede by its U.S. distributor, the Skinner division of Springs Mills.

BELOW LEFT TO RIGHT:
Ultrasuede skirt suit, April 1977; three-quarter-length Ultrasuede jacket with self belt and Ultrasuede beret, June 1973; hooded Ultrasuede windbreaker jacket and pants, June 1973.

OPPOSITE LEFT:
Ultrasuede ensemble—A-line coat, skirt and hat, September 1973.

OPPOSITE RIGHT:
Ultrasuede shirtdress style #704 with cashmere cardigan tied around shoulders, August 1972.

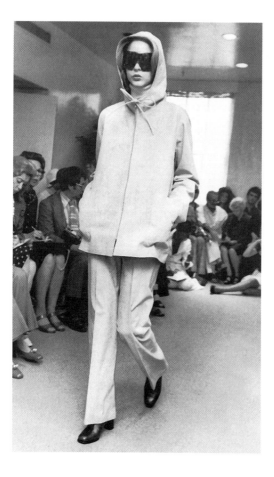

"It started as a blouse, developed into a long evening gown and ended up as a casual shirtwaist. I made over a hundred sketches before I got what I wanted," Halston said.

Little did Halston know that he had designed one of the top-selling dresses in fashion history.

Model Karen Bjornson wore the first Ultrasuede shirtdress on the *Dinah Shore Show*, and "of course, Halston wanted to demonstrate that you could throw it into a washing machine. Technically you could, but the garment would get out of shape, and it was recommended that it be dry cleaned," says Dugan. "But because it was such a big selling point, Halston said on the show that it could be machine washed and apparently there were a lot of complaints, because ladies threw their dresses in the washing machine."

Despite that initial error, Halston stuck with and finessed the fabric. And there was something about it that struck an unexpectedly resounding chord with Halston's heretofore unsporty customers. Everyone looked for reasons in its practicality and packability (it didn't wrinkle), the way it felt (as soft as real suede), the novelty (it had been used for car upholstery before) and the exquisite range of rich, beautiful colors it came in (fifty colors to the industry, twenty-seven to the home sewing market in 1976). But it was really something unexplainable in the ether that turned it into such a fashion phenomenon.

That single dress became a uniform for the Upper East Side set, as an avalanche of orders came in from his custom clientele. Suddenly, nobody seemed to care if they wore the identical dress to a luncheon; it was shared like a badge of honor.

When in the apartment of *Fashions of the Times* editor Carrie Donovan, Kenneth Paul Block remembers seeing the first Ultrasuede dress hanging in her shower after it had been washed.

"I like Ultrasuede for casual clothes, especially for pants. It also comes in such beautiful colors, you can wear it almost all year round. It's easy to pack, it doesn't wrinkle and it always hangs out. For easy care, I think it is better if it is unlined," said Nancy Kissinger.

"I remember being in Greece several years ago putting one of the little Ultrasuede dresses over a bathing suit, and then after a swim going to lunch with it wet. It dried beautifully and was ready to travel the next day," remembered Jennifer Jones Simon.

"I think Ultrasuede is one of the major fabrics of the seventies. It's durable but light. It's cool in the summer and warm in the winter. I find the Halston Ultrasuede pants, skirts and coats I own extremely practical. They're washable and they don't wrinkle. Eventually, when they wear out, I plan to buy more," said Halston customer and friend Betsy Theodoracopulus.

Halston succeeded with Ultrasuede where others failed because he treated it like real suede instead of like fabric. Because of the nature of the fabric, regular seams were bulky and could never be pressed enough to lie flat. Halston directed his samplemakers to overlap the seams and topstitch them together with two parallel rows, which made them appear paper thin. Because the fabric had a substantial amount of inherent body and weight, neither linings nor interfacing were ever used in Halston's Ultrasuede garments. Collars, plackets, cuffs and sashes were made by stitching together two identical pieces with polyester thread that would not shrink should the garment be washed.

By the time Guido De Natale became a partner in Halston Originals, in 1972, Ultrasuede comprised 80 percent of the ready-to-wear collection, with the remaining 20 percent made from matte jersey, chiffon and a few doublefaced coats. That one style, shirtdress #704, sold for six years and the company couldn't keep up with the demand.

Ultrasuede originally sold for nine dollars per yard at thirty-three inches wide, which allowed style #704 to be sold for seventy-nine dollars wholesale. That first season, "we had orders for 138 pieces and could only cut 130 because we couldn't get enough fabric," says De Natale. "Six years later, when the fabric price was raised to twenty-nine dollars per yard at forty-four inches wide, we priced the same dress at $189 wholesale. We ended up selling more than fifty thousand dresses."

The original shirtdress was a classic with a placket-and-button front and a shirt collar, and was worn with or without a self-sash. As was Halston's way, it evolved to a step-in dress with a zippered neck, and later had a standup collar or a scoop neck. The original buttoned cuff was alternated with a plain edge or no sleeves at all. There were Ultrasuede safari suits for men and women, coats with matching skirts, wrap and full skirts and culottes. Eventually silk crepe de chine and silk charmeuse fabrics were dyed to match the Ultrasuede colors for blouse and dress ensembles. For evening, Ultrasuede battle jackets teamed with long cashmere dresses in the exact same shade. A forerunner of today's sweatsuits worn as casual sportswear, the most casual Ultrasuede was a zip-front hooded windbreaker with matching pants. Ultrasuede trench coats and quilted, boxy, drop-shoulder jackets also sold well, along with the totally faux coats with Ultrasuede outside and Borg sherpa on the inside.

Although the novelty of Ultrasuede eventually wore off and became an increasingly smaller part of his collection, from his first shirtdress until he stopped designing, it was always present in Halston's Seventh Avenue collection. For the runway, Hartmann's Ultrasuede luggage was dyed to match the colors used in the collection, but was actually sold only in beiges and black. Fieldcrest's thousand-dollar Ultra-

Ultrasuede jackets—his is shirt styled, hers is collarless with matching pants.

suede bedspread also sold surprisingly well considering the high cost. Braniff Airlines' flight personnel uniforms featured coats and suits of the fabric. No masculine wardrobe was complete in the late 1970s without an Ultrasuede sport or safari jacket made by licensee J. Schoeneman.

When Bergdorf Goodman ordered and sold out two thousand pieces of style #704, De Natale invited every salesgirl and stockroom worker in the store to a party at sales director Jerry Uchin's apartment. There they were presented with 14-carat-gold pins that said "704."

Thanks to Halston, in 1976, just four years after its first appearance, the American fashion industry was using 1.5 million square yards of Ultrasuede annually, approximately $30 million wholesale. Japan had limited its production to 192,000 square yards a month, with 65 percent of that being exported, primarily to the United States. Most manufacturers were being limited to 75,000 square yards per year, but Halston always got first priority and was able to sell as much as he could get. Even so, "each month I'm 10,000 yards behind what I could use," Halston told *WWD* on March 2, 1976.

BELOW:
Silk crepe de chine jumpsuit with dyed to match Ultrasuede pea jacket

OPPOSITE:
Princess Grace of Monaco on the steps of the palace wearing a floor-length Ultrasuede dress, October 1974.

In Ultrasuede and all other fabrics, Halston's color palette was rich and full. Since mainly solid colors were used, they made an impact and statement on their own. He favored outfits that had everything matching, from head to toe, including shoes and stockings, so that the pieces of an ensemble could be broken up into interchangeable separates. Because he was using different types of fabrics (knits and wovens) and fibers (wool, silks, rayon, cotton), precisely matching them was a major dyeing challenge.

"Mostly, he wanted shoes that matched, or something that blends," says Beth Levine. "He didn't put a show on like it was a masquerade. I respected him because he was not afraid of shoes. Many designers wouldn't show a certain style unless it was already in the fashion forefront. Halston showed what he wanted and what he felt looked good with his clothes."

Halston did not have favorite colors, but in addition to camel and gray neutrals there was usually a brilliant red, coral, pink and royal blue. For spring, traditional navy-and-white and black-and-white was often used. Flowery feminine pastels in lilac, pink, green, peach and mauve variations were added for summer.

"I like all colors, for different seasons you have different colors that are just logical," he said. "In summer you wear lighter colors, in winter you wear darker colors. There's no special theme of colors in the collec-

tion, but there's a range of colors. I think there are certain guidelines and certain rules that, you know, you do instinctively."

Halston reported, "I always make a lot of red [dresses] because it's the color noticed most. I advise clients who do major appearances to wear bright red, blue or yellow. During the Olympic Games, Queen Elizabeth's seating section was in bright red and she, very wisely, chose a shocking pink dress. Superrich women, if they can change their clothes often, like bright, strange colors. Women who don't have unlimited funds tend to choose a limited palette of colors like beiges or black and add accent colors."

"His color sense was incredible and he never had enough colors," says Akira Maki. "Lilac is never the most popular color but he made it popular because the shade he brought to the market was so beautiful. He knew when a beige was from last season's collection and we could not use it again. From a whole range of beiges, he knew which one would be most flattering for a particular client. And if the lining didn't exactly match the outside jacket fabric, he would never let you finish it."

Halston was the only one who noticed that the ivory color of the Halston cosmetics cases was off, later discovered to be caused by changes in the manufacturing process. He made sure that the color reverted to the original shade. "It was ivory and it was meant to be ivory. To the untrained eye it wouldn't make any difference, but to me it did."

When he designed a wedding dress for that fashion-conscious Muppet Miss Piggy, it was accompanied with a detailed letter describing what color eye shadow the bride should be wearing so as not to clash with the green color of the groom, Kermit the Frog.

Black could be counted on in every collection, just as it was his own personal uniform. You would be more likely to sight a UFO than to see him wearing anything but a black turtleneck and pants, with, possibly, a beige or neutral jacket over them. And his assistants were instructed to do the same. The reason was not mysterious or aesthetic, but practical. Halston did not want to be distracted from the colors of the garments being fitted.

Unlike the assistants, those in the workroom could wear whatever they liked, which for the men usually meant a shirt and tie. "If we sometimes wore a loud necktie, he would tell us to take it off. When looking in the mirror during a fitting, he would see my tie and it would be distracting," says Yutaka Hasegawa.

Most other fashion designers change their color palette and look from season to season with the express purpose of forcing obsolescence. Contrarily, Halston believed in the concept of investment dressing and long-term consistency of lengths, shapes and colors so a small number of pieces could be added each year to update and build a dynamic wardrobe. As Bernadine Morris said, "A Halston follower doesn't really need a lot of clothes to keep up. She just seems to want them."

Limiting colors to make them compatible was the basis of Halston's concept for building versatile career and travel wardrobes. "With red, white and black you can't lose," he declared.

"I think the secret is to limit the colors," he said on another occasion. "That becomes quite a personal choice: blondes usually like light colors, beiges and taupes—brunettes usually like brighter colors." One of his color pointers: "Something that reflects color onto the face is always pretty, since the lights in business establishments aren't the most flattering."

Halston wanted all his garment pieces to be able to be mixed and matched, with each combination a different look: "A woman with a limited wardrobe can get at least 16 outfits by mixing the pieces of four looks. And she'll always have something for every occasion."

For the executive-level working woman who could afford his clothes, Halston devised a separates plan of interrelated jackets, pants, shirts, blouses and sweaters that could be interchanged to meet every wardrobe situation one might encounter in a ten-day period, yet could fit into one small suitcase. Essential pieces included a one-piece dress, a skirt with blouses, a suit, a separate jacket and some sweaters. Wrinkle-resistant, lightweight fabrics were the key; including singleknit and doubleknit wool jerseys, cashmere knits and wovens, velvet and, of course, a few Ultrasuede pieces.

Halston believed that "career dressing should be conservative by nature, but still feminine; it shouldn't be too high fashion, because that's off putting, and it shouldn't be too provocative. No décolletés in the daytime. But if you're going out to the theater or to dinner, you can always unbutton a couple of buttons."

Always thinking of all the things a busy woman would need, he said the essential accessories should include "comfortable shoes—not too high a heel, if you're going to wear skirts. You need one good bag for everyday that houses working materials, and a small bag that can go inside and that you can take out for evening. And I think it's nice to have a couple of special, decorative belts. A hat or two can be very practical—a little beret or a knitted hat, so that if you don't have time to go to the hairdresser, you can put it on and still look attractive across a dinner table."

For traveling ladies, in 1972 he designed a wardrobe that "a lady can pack in one suitcase with a couple of shirts and some jewelry and have enough to wear for a week's trip." His "Five Easy Pieces" included: a simple short halter dress, a skirt and jacket, a coat and pants—all in navy wool jersey from Jasco. The concept was updated in 1979 to a wardrobe for a two-week trip on a private yacht. Halston's travel essentials included: a pretty dress "for a big party at Cap Ferrat"; four pairs of pants, all white; four loose and T-shirt–like tops in different colors, for day or night; an overshirt to wear over a bathing suit; a T-shirt dress; three evening pajamas; one caftan; one long dress; four swimsuits; two or three sarong-y wraps; one sweater; one windbreaker; and one city-travel outfit "to wear on the plane."

"Halston was an American designer who didn't try to design European couture, but he also didn't just do blue jeans. He was the first one of the new generation of designers to create a true American style, and the fact that he stopped working made room for people like Calvin Klein and Ralph Lauren. He did some rather fabulous things, especially his minimalistic look. Norman Norell, for instance, was never known in Europe the way Halston was."

—KARL LAGERFELD

One does not usually associate Halston with suits, but they made up a significant portion of his collections, always ladylike, deftly cut and impeccably tailored, subtle and never overpowering. He offered suits that could be the epitome of corporate chic during work hours, but could be dressed up for after work. Dinner suits were designed to look beautiful across a table, emphasizing jacket and blouse details, often worn without a blouse underneath. Blouses would usually be ivory or fresh white or perhaps pink to add a rosiness to the complexion. Jackets were tailored with a hint of a peplum that topped the hip, or skimmed right by them, never tight fitting, in longer, boxy shapes. The necklines were varied—square, calla lily, cardigan and collarless—as were the sleeves—dolman, arced, kimono and set-in. Skirts might be wrapped, pleated or with some softly shirred-in fullness. Double tops were a favorite look, either a jacket worn over a blouse with the same collar shape, or where a jacket and blouse were tucked into a cummerbund, both pieces in the same shade. Tunics were a jacket alternative, belted in for more formality or worn loose for after hours.

OPPOSITE LEFT:
Casual pants suit with band collar, tunic-length top from Spring 1978 collection.

OPPOSITE CENTER:
Doublefaced wool pants suit from Spring 1979 made-to-order collection.

OPPOSITE RIGHT:
Doublefaced wool, easy kimono jacket from Spring 1981 made-to-order collection.

LEFT:
Matching doublefaced cashmere coat and jacket with similarly shaped collars.

BELOW:
Doublefaced wool skirtsuit with self-belted, shaped collar wrap jacket.

RIGHT:
Leather belted wool flannel pantsuit with arced shoulders on a wrap jacket.

BELOW LEFT:
Shaped collar weskit jacket from Spring 1980 collection.

BELOW RIGHT:
Double-breasted single-lapel jacket from Spring 1980 made-to-order collection.

OPPOSITE LEFT:
Self-belted wrap jacket and wrap skirt from Fall 1976 made-to-order collection.

OPPOSITE RIGHT:
Bias-cut silk, V-neck evening tunic and pants from Spring 1976 made-to-order collection.

Interchangability and wardrobe building were relatively easy because few prints and patterns were used in Halston's collections, with just a few more for spring and summer. Prints were never completely eliminated because Halston knew their value for camouflaging certain figure problems, but he leaned toward abstract and irregular patterns, such as soft washes and brushstrokes of color, rather than recognizable motifs.

His earliest collections revived argyles in a small-scale, jacquard knit, cardigan suit. Geometric Art Deco silk georgettes were printed in bias black/green/red/yellow patterns worn with matching caps and scarves that circled the throat. One of a kind tie-dyed chiffons sophisticated the hippy versions popular at the time. They were ombréd, but not in the typical tonalities of a single color; Halston's graduated from one color to a completely different one—mauve to orange, green to orange, apricot to turquoise.

Once Halston discovered a studio run by Japanese artist Reiko, she hand painted his original patterns on chiffons, replacing the tie-dyes. Dina Merrill wore a cloud painted dress to hostess the Coty Awards.

Halston's print and pattern choices were more influenced by fine arts than the fashion arts. A brief impressionistic floral period in 1974 featured hand-painted red and green peppers, cherries, pink anemones and red tulips on chiffons and crepe de chines. More in keeping with the true Halston spirit was a series of hand-painted prints on chiffon and matte jersey adapted from Jackson Pollack's drip paintings and Andy Warhol's poppies. Much later, for Summer 1979, Kandinsky-like prints—soft-edged zigzags, circles and rectangles—appeared on scarf-like dresses and slim pajamas.

Many of the hand-painted and printed designs were borrowed from natural and organic forms. Brown dogwood blossoms were splashed on white matte jersey. For evening, giant white daisies were painted on pink jersey. Bicolors and monotonalities represented waves, the sky, wind and rain, often on white or sky blue grounds.

Dots were a recurring theme, in lollipop size and larger, abstracted and stretched into ovals, twisted into hearts, and also engineered to run down the side of the body on either side of chevrons running down the front.

"Anything that was ditsy or flowery usually went by the wayside," says Bill Dugan. "We used a lot of small-scale prints for the licensees, especially Halston IV, the less expensive two-piece dress division. If there was some free time, Halston would tell the assistants to do H prints and, at some point, every assistant did. Geometric, freehand, interlocking Hs, free-flowing Hs, every which way. There was always a need for them."

"He hated stripes, plaids, anything directional because it forced his design, that's why he did a lot of multidirectional, tossed type of things," says Crawford Mills.

He may not have liked designing prints, but he certainly knew how. For one Halston Sportswear collection, Joe Eula had designed an entire line of fruits and

Halston and his Halstonettes photographed in his office at Olympic Tower, October 1981, wearing light-weight wool separates from the Spring 1982 collection. Left to right: Chris Royer, Halston, Pat Cleveland and Karen Bjornson.

vegetables—apples, oranges, bananas—all the same size, all on colored grounds, which was not diverse enough to appeal to department store buyers. Crawford then witnessed Halston, Eula and some assistants completely redesign the print line in three hours.

"It was probably one of the most exciting and incredible things I ever saw, to watch all this happen in such a very short period of time. After all these years of working with designers, I knew I had finally met someone worthy of the title, a genius. I was so excited by the experience, I walked all the way back to Seventh Avenue motored by the energy created by the event."

The only place where patterns did play an important role was in Halston's trademark beadwork for dresses, caftans and tops. Surprisingly, his first few collections had few if any evening outfits, but once Halston got gold fever he did it sexier and more spectacularly than anyone else. "So many people think I'm plain Jane. But I can do the jazziest clothes, dress the jazziest people," Halston declared to any doubters.

At Olympic Tower, he even installed special MR16 theatrical lights so the beads would sparkle aplenty on the runway. "The light reflected around the face—it's a great sign of luxury, whether it's a small embroidered scarf or a whole dress."

ABOVE:
Multicolor Jackson Pollack–inspired drip print hand painted on a matte jersey dress , May 1974.
RIGHT:
Andy Warhol's poppy painting interpreted on silk crepe de chine, May 1974.
OPPOSITE LEFT:
Black and white engineered stripes from Spring 1979 collection.
OPPOSITE RIGHT:
Burnout velvet dress, April 1977.

BELOW:
*Tropical fruit print on silk pants
ensemble from Resort 1978 collection.*

RIGHT:
*Kandinsky–inspired print on polyester
pantsuit from Summer 1979 collection.*

OPPOSITE:
*Layers of chiffon in graphic print-
over-print effect.*

Halston's first glittery pieces appeared in 1973, three-dimensional sequins applied to by-the-yard fabric for a baseball jacket and in a cardigan–halter top pajama ensemble. With few resources available that could create beadwork to Halston's design specifications and price range, for years he relied on metallic yard goods, and gave subtle shine to his hand-painted fabrics by applying clear sequins over the designs.

"He loved glamour but even his glamour was very simple in many ways, clean glamour," says Naeem Khan, whose family business created Halston's beadwork fantasies starting in 1978.

India was a mecca for embroidery and beadwork, but "Halston was the first one to actually develop Indian beadwork on a designer level," says Khan. "Before that, all the beading from India was ethnic-looking. We made it today. It was Halston's vision and our technique and the combination was beautiful."

With a resource that allowed his fertile imagination to run free, Halston soon became better known for his extravagant evening wear than for Ultrasuede. Halston's simple shapes and sophisticated beaded patterns made glitter acceptable, associating it with taste and wealth, not the circus or Las Vegas showgirls. Other designers were selling beaded dresses, but in the ten- to twenty-thousand-dollar price range. With the low labor costs in India, Halston was able to sell his for two to four thousand dollars.

"It took us a year or two to really understand how he functioned," Khan remembers. "We started with simple things and he wasted a tremendous amount of money in development. First time out we must have botched up twenty to thirty thousand dollars worth of beadwork that he never used. He used to spend sixty to eighty thousand dollars on samples."

Khan was a liaison between Halston and India. Under the designer's direction, he researched designs from art books or the Costume Institute at the Metropolitan Museum of Art, enlarging or reducing them, placing them and turning them into designs appropriate for embroidery. He drew the designs on paper, wrote the color combinations, then painted them to be sure the grading was correct. After Halston approved the design and selected the types of beads he wanted to use, Khan would note precisely where the beads were to be placed within the garment. He sent this to India, where draftsmen would do the technical layouts that are laid on top of the chiffon or organza fabrics, showing the embroiderers precisely where to stitch.

At its height, there were a minimum of eight, sometimes as many as fifteen to twenty different beaded styles per season, with eight or

OPPOSITE:
Short bugle-beaded tank dress and organza scarf from Spring 1981 collection.
BELOW:
Lamé evening pantsuit from Fall 1975 made-to-order collection.
OVERLEAF:
Lace-effect beadwork on silk organza.
© Rico Puhlmann

twelve of them selling very well. "It used to be a phenomenal business, up to $2 to $3 million a season," Khan said. "We cut three hundred to eight hundred pieces of a single style."

Each of the beaded garments were pieces of wearable art and nothing short of spectacular. The best-selling beaded silhouettes were a cardigan jacket with a slim, set-in sleeve, a short T-shirt dress that was almost shapeless and a little T-shaped jacket that topped a tank dress and was reworked every season.

One season the outlines of large roses were beaded, the inside of the petals cut out and then filled in with waves of pearls forming a mesh-like pattern. Norwegian sweater designs were interpreted mixing mirrors with teiki and bugle beads. A wave pattern was pulled from one curve in Van Gogh's painting *The Starry Night* and engineered so the wave hit just above the bust. Peacock feathers were enlarged with a rainbow of colors from copper to turquoise to royal stroked across the dress. In the archives of the Metropolitan Museum of Art, Khan found a jacket so old its sequins had melded into one solid piece of plastic; that was the inspiration for the Fourth of July fireworks series. For a fall season, Halston covered an entire dress with fringes

OPPOSITE:
Bugle-beaded, silk organza chemise with dipping hemline, August 1979. © *Rico Puhlmann*
BELOW LEFT AND RIGHT:
Explosion of colorful fireworks of sequins on black tulle from Fall 1980 collection.

of gold beads. He liked it so much, it was repeated the following season, mixing pink, blue, green and white together, appearing like strings of hanging confetti.

Certainly the most decadent of all the beaded dresses interpreted Andy Warhol's roses and poppies paintings into a group of dresses adorned with 24-carat-gold paillettes, called teiki beads, that were hand hammered in India into perfect circles. Martha Graham and Betty Ford owned these couture caftans, which were later made in gold-plated silver for the mass-produced line.

Topping off all this minimalist luxury was even more expensive luxury, the finest of furs, produced by a series of licensees that began in 1974. Ben Kahn Furs was the last, longest and most prestigious. Beginning in 1976, part of Halston's Madison Avenue boutique was devoted to a "Ben Kahn at Halston" corner, which featured all of their joint efforts.

Halston was just one designer in a series that both preceded and followed him as a Ben Kahn licensee, but one that owner Ernie Graf says stood out from the crowd. "He was like an architect," says Graf. "He would have a plan on a board and would do it. Some designers are all over the place. Not Halston."

BELOW LEFT TO RIGHT:
Hand-hammered gold-plated teiki sequins on chiffon tunic top and pants from Fall 1979 collection; bugle beads fringe an evening jacket worn with drawstring-waist pants and draped bra top from Resort 1981 collection; beaded top and floor-length cardigan coat worn with heavy silk pants and wide obi sash, from Spring 1981 made-to-order collection.

OPPOSITE LEFT:
The waves from Van Gogh's painting The Starry Night, *interpreted in beads.*

OPPOSITE RIGHT:
Gold-beaded fireworks from Fall 1980 collection.

BELOW:
Beige silk rain jacket lined in natural dark ranch mink worn with black cashmere sweater and pants, September 1973.

RIGHT:
Mink peacoat by Ben Kahn Furs from Fall 1978 collection.

Halston would sketch the fur designs and then, armed with fur experience from his millinery days, would confer with Graf about which furs to use for each look. The muslin samples, or canvases, were made in Halston's workrooms and then given to Graf to be manufactured in fur.

"In fine furs, the most important thing is the fit," says Graf. "And simple is better. It doesn't get dated. But in its simplicity, everything in the construction shows."

Halston's simple shapes were easily made into fur, and many of his fur firsts are still selling in Kahn's collection. He was the first to combine fur with fabric, such as wool jersey, mainly in fur-trimmed wraps. His shapes were sportier and more relaxed, with lower armholes. And he used colored furs, which were then brand new; a lavender one stands out in Graf's memory.

Halston did not favor particular types of fur as long as they were the best quality. He used sable, Russian lynx, ermine, broadtail and, of course, mink, which Halston recommended for executive women.

"I think the dream is always mink," Halston stated. "It's practical, it's a good investment and it goes anywhere, anytime. It doesn't have to be a coat—a jacket is always good."

"Halston had *je ne sais quoi* elegance which stood out," says Graf. "He was an elegant man and his coats also had a simple, classic elegance."

BELOW:
Fur-lined nylon raincoat.
RIGHT:
*Princess Grace of Monaco
wears a mink-edged cashmere
knit wrap and dress from Fall
1982 made-to-order collection.
Photograph Francesco Scavullo*

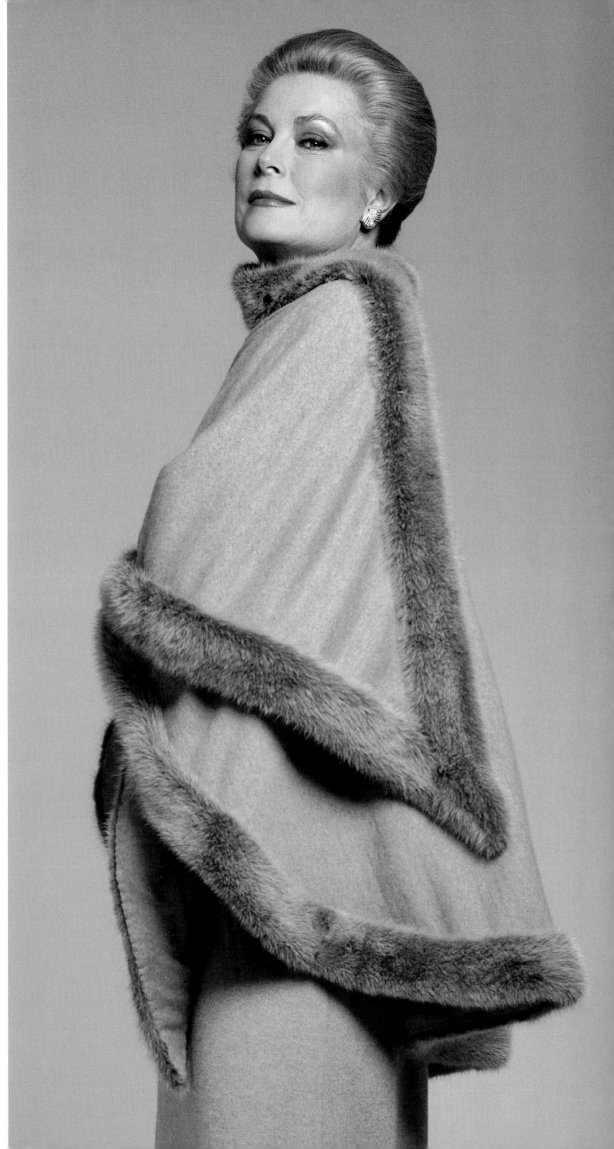

Halston purposely designed his clothes so they did not require accessories to make them fashionable or complete, but Elsa Peretti's modern, abstract and organically shaped silver jewelry provided the perfect finishing touch to any Halston outfit. Halston encouraged and, some say, assisted and directed Peretti's designs. More than just complementary, his clothes and the softly curved, sensual lines of her jewelry were a marriage of spirit and mutually flattering minimalist looks.

"I am closer to Halston's clothes than any designer, perhaps because I know him better," said the model-turned-jewelry-designer, who was also one of his closest friends. "I feel very much myself in his clothes."

Their names and looks were so closely linked that when Halston added some jewelry pieces of his own design to his first Seventh Avenue collection, the press incorrectly jumped to the conclusion that the two had parted ways. "I simply needed more jewelry," explained Halston, who had also begun designing belts and handbags for his licensed lines.

"Jewelry," Halston believed, "should take the real approach—real silver, real gold, not only for aesthetic reasons, but because it is also a good investment."

Other than in Native American jewelry, silver was not considered serious jewelry when Peretti and Halston began showcasing her silver pieces in his collections. Her first piece, a silver teardrop pendant, had been created before she started modeling for the designer. That was followed up with silver bracelets striped with ivory, a series of organic shapes in silver, such as the bean and heart pendants and handbags, and a spectacular rattlesnake-shaped silver belt. Halston reportedly paid to have the first prototypes made for Peretti's horseshoe and elliptical belt buckles. Her diamonds by the yard, tiny diamonds spaced out on delicate gold chains, were worn either as chokers or in rope-length multiples.

"I saw him spend a full evening taking a pair of snub-nosed pliers and actually making that gold mesh that became a bra, and it became a very important product for her," says Mike Lichtenstein.

OPPOSITE:
Elsa Peretti's metal mesh bra from Fall 1975 collection.
BELOW:
Elsa Peretti's heart-shaped black lacquered evening bag, June 1976.
BOTTOM:
Two sizes of Elsa Peretti's silver flask-on-a-chain worn with angora/wool knit shirt from Fall 1972 collection.

No discussion of Halston's fashions would be complete without touching upon the costumes he designed for various theatrical productions. It may have started as a sideline to his larger and more commercial projects, but it was one he took seriously and found creatively challenging. A consummate showman himself, he fully understood the power and impact clothes could have on a theatrical presentation. When he stopped actively designing for Halston Enterprises, costume design became his fashion lifeline, the central focus of his creative efforts.

Most of the garments he made for films, TV, Broadway shows or live concerts were adapted from his custom and ready-to-wear collections. In 1973, when Lauren Bacall was in London appearing in *Applause*, the musical version of *All About Eve*, it was decided that a television version would be taped in London to be aired in the United States on March 15. Bacall, an old friend and devoted customer, asked Halston to design a wardrobe of twelve costume changes for the show.

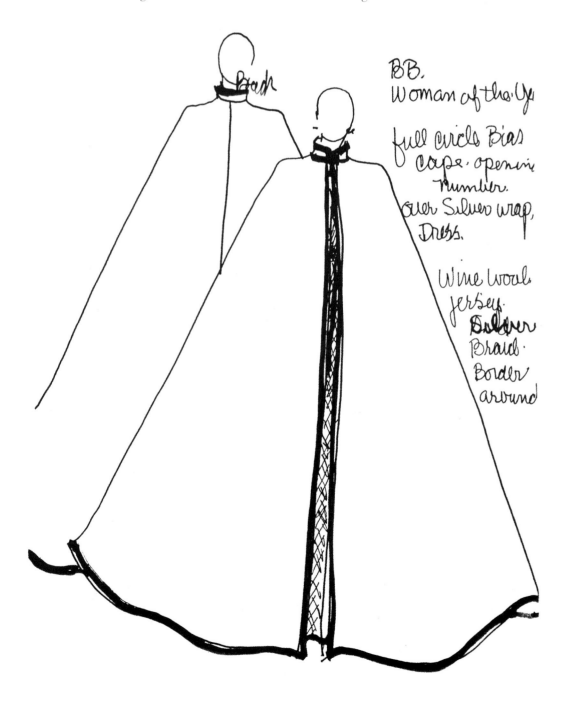

Working together via transatlantic telephone conferences, Halston designed clothes that "not only have to move well and take the beating they're subjected to in strenuous dance numbers, but they also must sustain the mood of the scenes. It's important for costumes in plays to reflect situations, not personal taste."

The color palette he used was unusual for him: "I used every bright color around to make each scene look different. There are colors I might not dream of using otherwise."

From the Summer 1973 collection, he made Bacall a narrow chiffon caftan for the finale, and a slinky, draped, pale blue silk jersey evening dress with a wrapped waist for the scene where her character, Margo Channing, receives the Tony Award. A brilliant red jersey jumpsuit and boa was prescribed for the dramatic scene where a drunk Margo asks everyone to leave her party. A halter-neck, bias-cut short dress and fringed jacket that was worn in a very active dance number was also in the wardrobes of Jackie Onassis and Pamela Harriman.

Other outfits for *Applause* included a beige cashmere coat with a big collar for the Connecticut scenes, a sunny yellow daytime shirtdress, a lavender nightgown and bed jacket, pink chiffon hostess pajamas and a bold blue sequined femme fatale evening gown. All was accessorized with Elsa Peretti's seashell shoulder bag, snake and wrap belts, and ivory, gold and silver bracelets and rings.

He later designed Bacall's costumes for the Broadway musical *Woman of the Year* and for the film *The Fan* costarring James Garner, but at his request, did not receive an on-screen credit.

OPPOSITE:
Halston's original sketch for a bias-cut wool jersey cape worn by Lauren Bacall in the musical Woman of the Year.
BOTTOM:
Lauren Bacall and the cast of Woman of the Year *during production of "I Love NY" ad.*

Halston was eminently qualified to dress Jacqueline Bisset in her role as the wife of *The Greek Tycoon*, loosely based on the life of Jacqueline Onassis. This being his first major film assignment, he was charged with designing the wardrobe but, according to Bill Dugan, also volunteered to instruct Bisset on what Jackie would or would not do. Set in the year it was filmed, Halston told *WWD*, "Ely Landau, the producer of the film, contacted me and I was thrilled. I only stated I couldn't have anything to do with nostalgia. This is all 1977. The clothes are of this period and an extension of my designs."

For four days, Halston and Bisset were locked away in his Sixty-eighth Street showroom discussing the thirty costumes needed for the film. "I will make a point to dress emotionally," she said at the time. "I think people make drastic mistakes in movies when they contradict the plot by wearing the wrong color."

"Everything for the film was made to order because nothing he had previously made worked," says Jacqueline Bisset. "He had to rethink his whole concept for me, which surprised him a lot." As for their personal chemistry, she says, "There was some give and take. He was very grand in some ways and very charming in others."

BELOW:
Halston and Jacqueline Bisset selecting fabrics for her costumes for the film The Greek Tycoon.
OPPOSITE:
Halston's original sketch for costume for The Greek Tycoon, *and Jacqueline Bisset (inset) wearing the same outfit.*

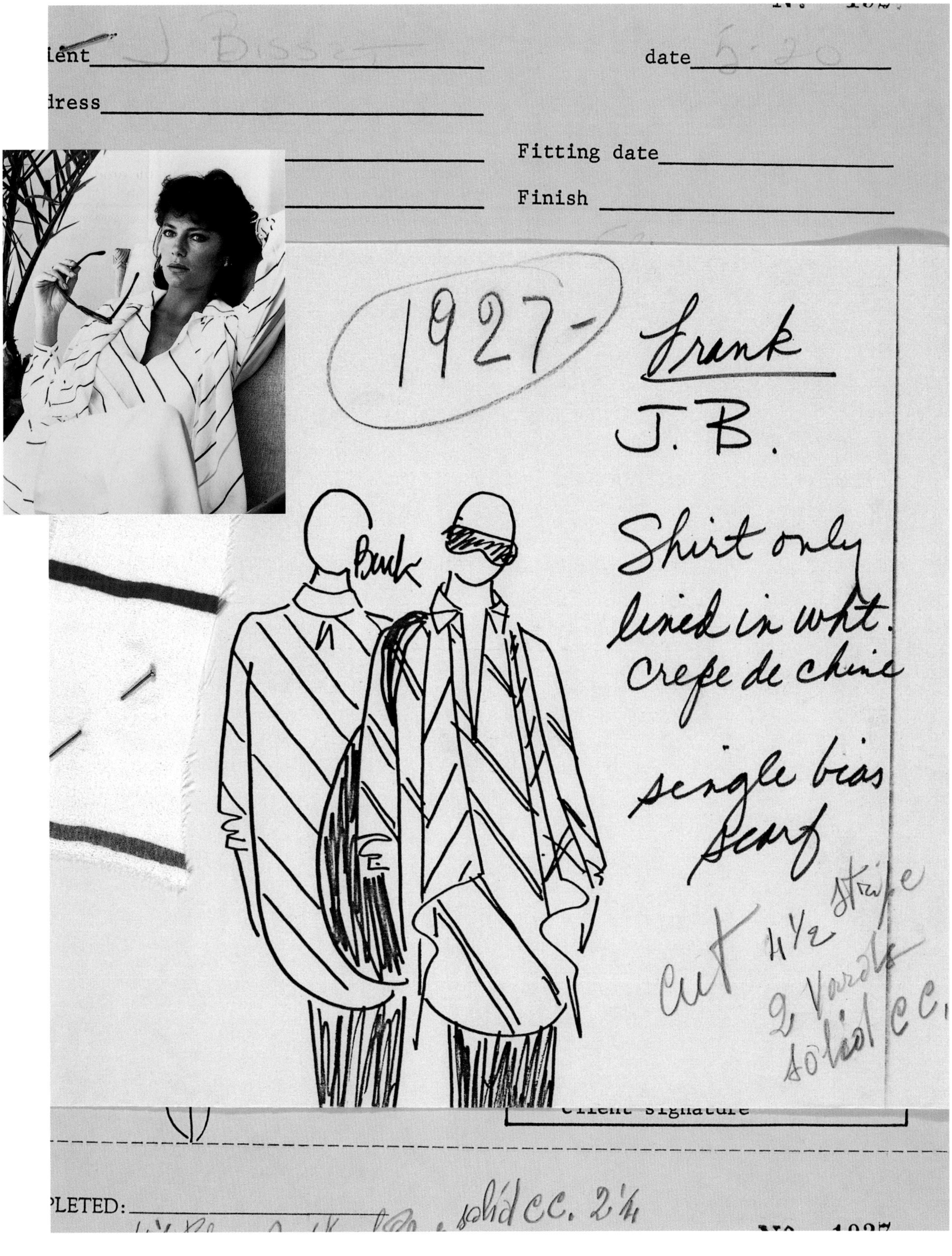

Client_____J. Bissett_____   date___5·20____

dress_____

Fitting date_____

Finish _____

(1927-)   Frank
         J. B.

Back

Shirt only
lined in wht.
crepe de chine

single bias
scarf

Cut 4½ stripe
2 yards
solid c.c.

client signature

PLETED:_____ solid c.c. 2¼

That same year, Halston replaced the costume designer that had been hired to design Liza Minnelli's wardrobe for the stage musical *The Act.* "That was Halston's first real, from start to finish, show," says Minnelli. "The producer had had problems with couture designers before, so they wouldn't listen to me when I asked them if we could use Halston. Luckily, I had five bags with me, a set of Vuitton luggage. I said to him, 'This is my entire wardrobe for my life. This is all I have. And it was all designed by Halston and it fits in five bags. Does that make a difference?'" She started pulling clothes out of her bags, "things that would completely take you through the day into night."

Halston quickly stepped in to help his friend. "We were doing a show about Las Vegas and there wasn't a light on the stage. The clothes were dull," Minnelli remembers. "Halston said, 'Well, then, the clothes just have to sparkle.' I am a performer; I

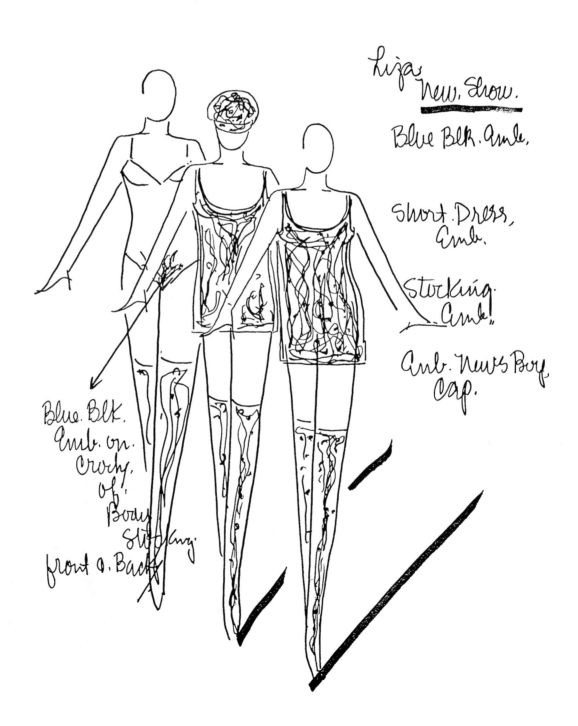

sweat when I perform, so Halston said. 'We're going to make the costumes look as wet as you get, kiddo.' That's how everything shined."

In addition to Liza's costumes, Halston made luxurious red bathrobes for the cast to wear backstage so "the whole theater was red."

Akira Maki was assigned to accompany Liza and her twenty costumes for the show during her national tour, which included stops in Chicago, San Francisco and Los Angeles, and then during the first two weeks after it opened in New York. He was working round-the-clock to fix things that did not please Liza or that required repair after a performance. While in California, Halston intercepted a call from a friend of Akira's asking if the assistant would be back in New York for his birthday, because his friends were planning a party. Halston paid for Akira's return to New York and waiting for him was champagne, chocolates and a dozen red roses from Halston and Liza.

"When Liza was going to perform, one month before, the entire staff worked just for her," says Yutaka Hasegawa. "Everything stopped for that project. Sometimes there were fifty people there."

Liza's costumes for *Cabaret* were completely remade using the highly skilled talents of Halston's Indian embroiderers. Bill Dugan recalls that for the "apple" jacket, the fruit was hand painted on chiffon and the beadwork sewn on top.

In addition to designing her entire street wardrobe and the costumes for all her subsequent musical concerts and performances, Halston also designed the costumes for her film appearances in *Arthur* and *New York, New York*.

"Everything was pull on, one piece," Minnelli describes. "A piece of Velcro here and in a second, it's on, and off you go."

One of the design projects Halston took on after he was no longer designing a collection was for Liza Minnelli's three-week engagement at New York's Carnegie Hall in May 1987. She opened the show wearing a short white slip dress and matching kimono jacket that were completely embroidered with beads, pearls and sequins. In the second act, Minnelli wore a long red velvet strapless concert dress with layers and layers of pink tulle. She had only twenty-seven seconds to change from that into a blue-black honeycomb-embroidered pullover that shimmered like stars under the strong stage lights. Halston chose the colors, keeping in mind the red and gold colors of the newly refurbished music hall.

BELOW:
Liza Minnelli wearing Halston-designed costume in film New York, New York, *in 1977.*
OPPOSITE:
Halston's original sketch for Liza Minnelli's concert costume, 1980.

Illustrations of Liza Minnelli's Halston wardrobe from the how-to notebook he created for her.

"Halston was one of my closest and dearest friends. At a time when I was at my lowest ebb, he stood by me. If it were not for his belief in me, and his support of my school and dance company, they would not exist today."

—MARTHA GRAHAM

OPPOSITE:
Martha Graham wearing Halston's teiki sequin caftan, with her dance company in 1984.
OVERLEAF:
Halston's costumes for the Martha Graham Dance Company ballet Frescoes. *Photograph Francesco Scavullo*

Halston's affiliation as costume designer for the Martha Graham Dance Company was truly a labor of love. There was a bond between the two artists that went well beyond their love of the arts, more along the lines of a mother-son relationship. They both shared an appetite and curiosity for life, and as a dancer, Graham revered the body and its coverings as much as Halston. Their fifteen-year collaboration began with costumes but concluded with Halston becoming the financial savior of the Graham dance troupe.

In her autobiography, *Blood Memory*, which Graham partly dedicated to Halston, she recounted how the two first met, when Graham was already a septuagenarian. They were introduced when she needed something to wear to present the Capezio Dance Award: "Halston suggested a wonderful earth-colored cashmere caftan and a darker natural poncho over it. I loved it. I felt as if I had always worn it. Halston understood the drape of fabric and the body's movement beneath it; he understood elegance."

Rather than return the dress to Halston, which was just a loan, she asked Halston if she could buy it, but pay it off monthly. Halston said, "Martha, if I cannot give you that dress, there is nothing in the world I can give you."

Their mutual love for fabrics helped continue their friendship. For most of her career, Graham had designed all the costumes her dancers wore. Now she was crippled with arthritis and could no longer shop the fabric stores the way she used to. Halston invited her to his workroom to look at fabrics, but because of the condition of her hands she always wore gloves and commented that she could not feel the fabrics, or use her hands. Halston replied, "Martha, let me be your hands."

From that point on, Halston made almost all of the costumes for her dance troupe, remaking and restyling the old ones, many of which were so threadbare and poorly made that dancers were going on stage with safety pins holding them together.

Halston and Graham would confer about the look she wanted. The dancers would run through their numbers for the designer in his showroom, stretching and bending in their larger-than-life movements, so he could see what the costumes needed to do in order to accommodate them. Then he or Joe Eula would sketch the ideas, or Halston might drape fabrics on the models themselves. All the garments were made in Halston's workrooms, completely free of charge. The first sample of each costume was usually draped by the designer himself.

"Martha Graham and Halston were alike, they were both perfectionists, both demanding, but they didn't just demand and not do it themselves. I saw him sew hats for her ballets until his hands were bleeding. That's how strongly he cared for her," says his personal secretary, Faye Robeson.

"When Martha was here, Halston was like a little child, asking millions of questions," remembers Akira Maki. "She talked so softly to him and he used to listen to every word."

Halston redesigned or reedited almost all of the costumes for the ballets Graham's troupe was performing, making them more stylish where before they served their purpose in a classic way. In Agnes de Mille's book *Martha: The Life and Work of Martha Graham*, she said Halston was the first of Graham's patrons to have "ever put their name on anything of hers, or interfered in any way. His thumb mark was on every ballet. He altered the entire pictorial aspect of her theater."

"The challenge of making 40 to 60 costumes was inspiring," said Halston after completing his first wardrobe for the ballet *Lucifer*, which starred Rudolf Nureyev and Margot Fonteyn. "Martha Graham is such a strong creative force. In serious business I don't often have the chance to do fantasy. Therefore, to design fantasy costumes was a whole new world for me. I loved it. I hope to continue in this new field."

Halston saw the difference between theater design and the kind of clothes he usually designed: "Many times a [theater] dress has to be mounted on an underpinning, a leotard, for instance, so it won't move around or bunch up. For Martha, I created some frontier dresses which suggest the period, but which are really contemporary dresses. They are complicated, unlike street dresses, because they are built on a leotard base. They move completely freely with the body—and yet they stay in place when the dancers perform in them. You can throw your arm upward and the line isn't spoiled. The dress isn't pulled out of shape. I had to make sure the dancers wouldn't be restricted in their movement. I think the dancing costume is the most complicated kind of costume there is in the theater."

For *Lucifer*, Halston hand painted some fabric to have a mottled look for Fonteyn's costume, which also included a snake headdress and body tights. Nureyev's costume "consisted of a gold, jewel-studded jockstrap and an Ace bandage wrapped around a foot which was injured. Lucifer's cape, designed by Halston, looked like a bedspread made for a king. The jockstrap . . . was the same sort of royal affair," said the review in the *New Yorker* magazine.

Later in 1975, Halston designed the costumes for a ballet based on *The Scarlet Letter*, which the *New York Daily News* said were some of the most elaborate that Graham has ever shown and in which "Hester's incriminating letter 'A' was inexplicably gold."

The dress Halston designed for Mary Queen of Scots in the ballet titled *Episodes* was huge but "so light that the dancer moves easily among the other dancers. It is also so cleverly constructed that when the choreography calls for the dancer to leave it, the costume stands uninhabited onstage, upright on its own," described Edith Loew Gross in *Vogue* magazine.

OPPOSITE:
Halston's original sketch for Martha Graham Dance Company costume for Clytemnestra.
BELOW:
Benefit fashion show at Bloomingdale's for Martha Graham Dance Company. Halston-designed costume for Episodes *ballet, October 1981.*

What Halston found fascinating about designing these period costumes and those for *Clytemnestra*, which takes place in ancient Greece, was "to get the essence of something that has perhaps been done before and do it in a contemporary new way. In other words, the dresses that we made for the theater, which is really sort of an exaggeration of life and things, all may stretch and you just put them on like a bathing suit, but then when you see them they're the most elaborate things you've ever seen."

For *Acts of Light* in 1981, Halston "dressed the performers in golden tissue which almost reduced the work to a cosmetic display," said Agnes de Mille. "The men throughout the program seemed more naked than they ever had been before."

"She could do it all," said Halston about Graham in 1980 when he designed all the costumes for her season at the Metropolitan Opera House. "She is a genius at dance, at theater, at costumes, at lighting. There is nothing she can't do."

And there was nothing he would not do for her. For *Frescoes*, Halston's team worked all night and day to change the costumes because, as he describes, "When we finally saw the costumes in action, well, they just didn't work. So in a day and a half, I had to redo all the designs myself. And the workroom stayed open till midnight. I worked till six in the morning. I came back at nine and we worked all day. The new costumes barely were finished by the time we had to go to the Met to dress everyone at seven P.M. I'm talking about sixty people!"

BELOW:
Halston receiving the third annual Martha Graham Award from First Lady Betty Ford who is wearing a Halston sequined dress, May 1979.
OPPOSITE:
Halston's original sketch for three-layer caftan made for Martha Graham to wear to the Metropolitan Museum of Art's Costume Institute gala.

"When one of my dancers goes onstage in a Halston costume, it is beautifully made, inside and out, and adds to the integrity of the movement. It must reveal the body, reveal the beautiful line of the waist, the hips, the shoulders, the turn of the head. The costume must speak to all of these things," said Graham in her autobiography.

Halston planned and footed the bill for many benefits for Graham, and he became her escort to art and government affairs. He traveled to Paris to see her awarded France's Chevalier of the Legion of Honor and to see the dance company perform three works—*Phaedra's Dream, Acts of Light* and *Seraphic Dialog*—at the Paris Opera, all featuring Halston's costumes. For his efforts for Graham, he was presented with the third annual Martha Graham Award by Mrs. Gerald Ford on May 21, 1979.

Graham recalled one incident that exemplified Halston's generosity: "We were rehearsing in a theater and we had to stop at a crucial time because of union rules. And he asked our company director, 'Why is she stopping?' and he said, 'She can't afford to pay the double time.' And Halston said, 'That's ridiculous. I'll pay it.' And he did . . ."

In talking about Halston in her autobiography, which was written after his death, Graham described him in such a way that you knew she completely understood the man and his art. She called him "a strange, gentle and fierce man. Fierce because he would only settle for the best. If you couldn't give your best, then too bad for you. He made it very clear in the beginning. Halston believed as did I that the only sin was mediocrity."

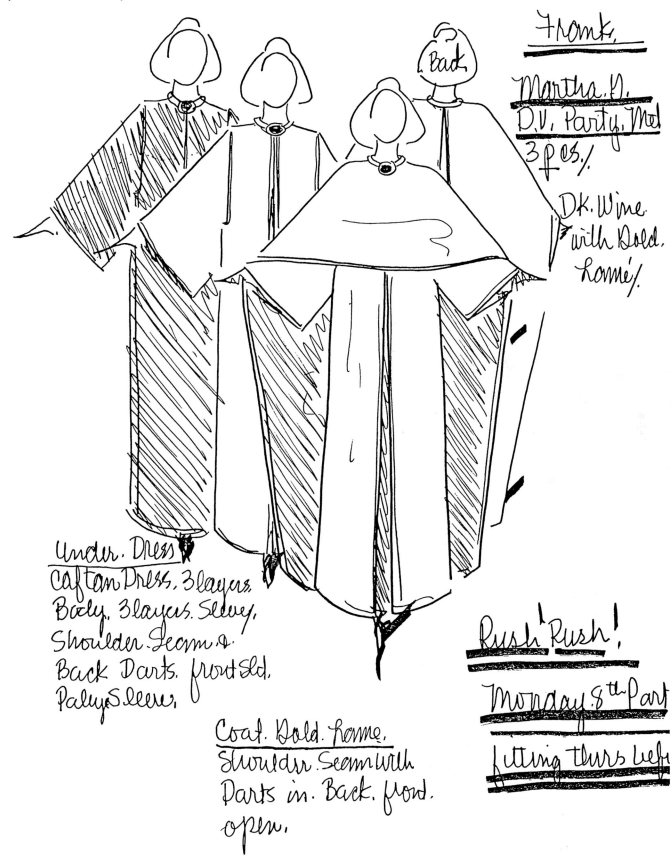

HALSTON REVISITED

It took a few years for the rest of the fashion world to catch up with Halston. The minimalism that Halston conceived and uniquely offered in the late 1960s and 1970s was applauded in the mid and late 1980s and 1990s as the very definition of modern fashion. Credit was given where credit was due.

HALSTON HAUNTS SEVENTH AVENUE, said the front page of *WWD* on April 21, 1989. "Halston may be out of the Seventh Avenue scene, but his spirit is everywhere." The photo spread showed pieces from Halston's collections from ten to fifteen years before. They were astoundingly similar to those from the recent collections of such design notables as Bill Blass, Oscar de la Renta, Donna Karan, Michael Kors, Louis dell'Olio for Anne Klein, Ralph Lauren, Carolyne Roehm, Marc Jacobs and Isaac Mizrahi.

IT'S STILL WORKING, declared the headline in *W* magazine in July 1996. "Halston's groundbreaking style of 20 years ago is as valid now as it was then."

Gucci's Tom Ford, one of the leaders of the Halston renaissance, looked back to the future of fashion, noting, "The way people dressed then was so modern—sensible, clean, simple, spare, practical, minimal, functional. But luxurious." A different era, but the message still rings true.

Within his own lifetime, Halston saw his own designs newly appreciated and revived. "I think it's great that people consider me interesting enough to copy. That mood still exists in fashion. If I were to do something now, I would continue my style," he said, while in the midst of legal struggles to recapture the company that bore his name.

A few years later, he acknowledged as a matter of fact that "the experiment was mine. It was revolutionary in its day. I made the change from very structured clothes to a more casual look and fashionable women picked up on it. I still think my look was the most attractive and sensible. Whether it was cashmeres, jersey, the strapless, chiffon, it was about a total look. Clothes should be practical, glamorous, functional and spare. . . . I'm proud. I'm happy," he said of those who copied his designs. "It proves it still works. I think it will work forever. Certain people have formed whole businesses on my look. They might have the effect, but not the cause. They haven't had to experiment."

OPPOSITE:
Halston, December 1978.
BELOW:
Front page of WWD, *April 21, 1989.*
OVERLEAF:
From Halston retrospective exhibit, "Absolute Modernism," held at the Museum at FIT, October 1991.

CHRONOLOGY

1932 Born Roy Halston Frowick on April 23 in Des Moines, Iowa.

1952 Moved to Chicago. Studied fashion illustration at night at Chicago Art Institute. Worked days as window dresser at Carson Pirie Scott department store. Made hats in spare time.

1953 André Basil provided him with a hat display in his Ambassador Hotel hair salon.

1957 February 18—Basil and Halston moved to a larger salon on the third floor of 900 Michigan Avenue, called the Boulevard Salon.

Received first national press coverage in *Women's Wear Daily.*

1958 Moved to New York to work for milliner Lilly Daché.

1959 Left Lilly Daché to work in Bergdorf Goodman's custom millinery salon.

1960 Received first cover of *Harper's Bazaar* magazine for his millinery.

Designed pillbox hat that Jackie Kennedy wore to John Kennedy's presidential inauguration.

1962 Won first Coty Fashion Critics Award for millinery.

1966 June 28—Fashion show of first clothing collection for Bergdorf Goodman.

Opened Halston boutique at Bergdorf Goodman.

1968 January 12—Last day worked for Bergdorf Goodman.

April 25—Incorporated own business, Halston Ltd., with temporary headquarters in his apartment.

September 26—Formed ready-to-wear and made-to-order company called Halston Ltd. with financial backing from Mrs. Estelle Marsh Watlington.

December 2—Opened showroom at 33 East Sixty-eighth Street designed by Angelo Donghia. Showed first solo apparel collection.

1969 March 6—Opened first boutique on third floor of Bloomingdale's department store.

October 13—Won second Coty Award, a special award for the total look of his first solo collection.

Sponsored Charles James retrospective benefit fashion show at Electric Circus in New York's East Village.

1970 Hired Charles James as "technical consultant."

1971 Won third Coty Award, a Winnie.

January—First appearance of Aquasuede fabric (later renamed Ultrasuede) in raincoat for Spring 1971 collection.

1972 February 7—Opened Halston boutique on corner of Sixty-eighth Street and Madison Avenue.

May—Formed partnership with Guido De Natale and Ben Shaw. Created ready-to-wear company called Halston Originals located at 550 Seventh Avenue.

May 22—Showed first Halston Originals collection for Fall 1972, including first Ultrasuede shirtdress style #704.

August 21—*Newsweek* cover photo and story: "Ease and Elegance Designed by Halston."

October—Received fourth Coty Award, a Return Award.

1973 November 5—Signed contract with Norton Simon Inc. (NSI) to purchase Halston Originals and Halston Ltd., his trademarks and exclusive design services, creating a new company called Halston Enterprises.

November 28—French-American fashion gala at the Palace of Versailles, France.

1974 First appearance of single-seam dress in Spring 1974 collection.

June—Received fifth Coty Award; inducted into the Hall of Fame.

November—The Skimp appears on cover of *Women's Wear Daily.*

1975 Launched Halston fragrance in Elsa Peretti–designed bottle through the Max Factor division of NSI.

1976 March—Opened first store outside of New York in Water Tower Place, N. Michigan Avenue, Chicago, with benefit fashion show at Art Institute.

March 22—Savage bathing suit photographed for cover of *Time* magazine with cover story "American Chic in Fashion."

June—Won Fragrance of the Year Award from the Fragrance Foundation.

Launched two men's fragrances called Z-12 and 1-12.

1977 April—Introduced bodystocking for Fall 1977.

Received Tony Award nomination for costume designs for Liza Minnelli in the Broadway musical *The Act.*

1978 January—Moved offices to twenty-first floor of Olympic Tower.

August—Opened first West Coast boutique in South Coast Plaza, Orange County, California.

1979 April—Showed first Halston Sportswear collection.

May—Received the third Annual Martha Graham Award at ceremony at Lincoln Center.

Given special citation by Coty American Fashion Critics Award nominating committee, for development of a total American look.

1980 September 4—Begins three-continent around-the-world tour. Halston is first American designer to visit and show American fashions in the People's Republic of China. In Tokyo, launched Japanese licensed line with Kosugi Sangyo Co. In Paris, introduced fragrance.

1981 January—Filmed episode of *Love Boat* television series featuring fashion designers.

1982 September—Signed multimillion-dollar licensing agreement to produce and sell women's, men's, children's and home furnishings products for exclusive distribution in JCPenney stores, called Halston III.

1983 June 7—Showed first Halston III women's sportswear and dress collection for JCPenney for Summer 1983 at the American Museum of Natural History.

July—Esmark, Inc. acquired Norton Simon, Inc. and its Halston Enterprises division.

1984 May—Beatrice Foods Cos. acquired Esmark, Inc., making Max Factor and its Halston and Orlane units a division of its International Playtex, Inc. division.

October 4—Halston signed letter of intent with Playtex to regain ownership of his made-to-order and ready-to-wear businesses.

1986 November—Revlon Group signed definitive agreement for purchase of Halston Enterprises and Halston Fragrances from BCI Holdings.

1988 November—Tested positive for AIDS.

1989 Moved to California.

December—Sold Manhattan town house.

1990 March 26—Died in sleep at age fifty-seven of complications from AIDS.

June—Memorial in Lincoln Center organized by Liza Minnelli.

August—Revlon, Inc., suspends women's apparel design operations of Halston Enterprises, Inc., and closes Olympic Tower offices.

1991 February—Special tribute to Halston at Council of Fashion Designer's of America's annual awards presentation.

October—Retrospective of Halston's work at Museum at Fashion Institute of Technology, titled "Halston: Absolute Modernism."

1992 Halston and Borghese brands anonymously purchased from Revlon for estimated $125 million, and formed into Halston Borghese Inc.

1993 Halston Borghese Inc. dedicated Halston Archives and Study Room at the Fashion Institute of Technology.

NOTES

75   *We have such rapport*—New York Times, 5/12/76

      I wanted to take all the fancy stuff off her—People, 6/20/77

78   *I'm giving women what they want*—New York Times Magazine, 2/11/73

MASTER MILLINER

81   *As if he were trying to figure out*—New York Times Magazine, 2/11/73

      We all wondered how and why he did it—Newsweek, 8/21/72

84   *Intricate manipulations with silks*—Women's Wear Daily, 2/19/57

      The first time I saw Halston he was a baby—Gaines, 1991, p 46.

85   *I was doing the John Mills wedding*—Women's Wear Daily, 1/9/68

      When I first came to America—Oscar de la Renta in the WWD obituary, 3/28/90

89   *I had the advantage of the terrific schooling*—Esquire, August 1975

      I learned about fashion at Bergdorf Goodman's—New York Times Magazine, 2/11/73

      They'd spend the afternoon at Bergdorf's trying on hats—New York Times Magazine, 2/11/73

      The only direction I gave Halston—Graham, 1997, p. 392

90   *We made about 120 hats for her*—Women's Wear Daily, 1/9/68

      She's the most interesting, good-looking public figure—Women's Wear Daily, 9/16/65

92   *A hat is a head covering*—New York Times, 7/6/65

94   *He was probably the greatest hatmaker in the world*—New York Times Magazine, 2/11/73

96   *High fashion is a losing proposition these days*—Newsweek, 2/11/63

FASHION'S FIRST MINIMALIST

101   *Revolution is out*—Women's Wear Daily, 9/16/64

103   *I really don't understand beads*—Women's Wear Daily, 12/3/68

      No one who ever worked in fashion at that time—Mirabella, July 1990

      All the parts that the stores and customers—Women's Wear Daily, 12/3/68

104   *I'm tired of flat, skin-tight clothes*—New York Post, 6/16/70

      He's an engineer of fashion—Women's Wear Daily, 6/16/70

109   *The American look in fashion is coming to the fore*—Women's Wear Daily, 5/3/76

      Halston is doing for fashion in the 1970s—New York Times, 9/13/72

      Halston could be called the American counterpart—New York Times Magazine, 1/6/80

      The shadow of—New York Times, 12/15/78

110   *Balenciaga was really the great one*—RAM Report, April 1978

      Balenciaga and Givenchy are the fathers—Women's Wear Daily, 1/9/68

      I'm not putting everyone on Seventh Avenue down—Women's Wear Daily, 12/7/71

      The way they arrange their flowers—New York Times, 12/8/76

      People have become more conservative—Women's Wear Daily, 1/3/77

111   *You may not find Halston inventing*—Newsweek, 8/21/72

112   *Fashion is dull*—Women's Wear Daily, 9/16/64

      About the only objections competitors are able to raise—New York Times, 2/9/73

      Many fashion authorities feel that Halston's impact—New York Times Magazine, 2/11/73

113   *I just think bias is more sexy*—RAM Report, April 1978

114   *For a long, sweeping gown*—Women's Wear Daily, 9/16/64

121   *It has everything*—Videofashion, June 1979

126   *I love the idea of a ruffle*—Women's Wear Daily, 6/12/80

133   *Halston has introduced a whole new generation*—New York Times, 9/29/76

141   *One thing that is always interesting to a designer like myself*—Videofashion, June 1979

144   *Today in designing there are many*—Women's Wear Daily, 12/7/77

147   *I have to be involved in every aspect*—Vogue, 1980

149   *Like pantyhose*—Women's Wear Daily, 12/14/70

      When you wore Halston's pajamas to a dinner party—Mirabella, 1995, p. 151

154   *To take a lady from the dentist*—Women's Wear Daily, 6/15/78

      His success could be judged—New York Times, 9/13/72

159   *If I wanted to be more dressed*—Mirabella, 1995, p. 151

160   *Halston brings back woolies*—New York Post, 4/29/77

      This is something I've been working on for years—Women's Wear Daily, 4/27/77

165   *I think the one-piece dress is the most useful*—Women's Wear Daily, 7/10/74

      Sexy sells—New York Times Magazine, 4/9/78

168   *Nearly everybody's wearing miniskirts these days*—New York Times, 6/7/69

      I tried all lengths, long and short—Women's Wear Daily, June 1969

      Everyone is testing my below-the-knee length—Women's Wear Daily, 7/14/69

169   *When a woman of a certain age*—RAM Report, April 1978

      Women talk with their legs—Videofashion, June 1979

      The coat should have a little bit of a fuller proportion—Women's Wear Daily, 7/10/74

      Without ever raising a skirt—Women's Wear Daily, 11/1/79

      The story goes—Newsweek, 11/18/74

      I haven't been able to get off the phone—Women's Wear Daily, 11/6/74

170   *Chiffon is the most beautiful feminine fabric*—Women's Wear Daily, 8/25/75

176   *I like all colors*—Videofashion, June 1979

178   *I always make a lot of red*—W, 8/5/77

      It was ivory and it was meant to be ivory—Women's Wear Daily, 8/9/82

A Halston follower doesn't really need a lot of clothes—New York Times, 3/27/79

179 *I think the secret is to limit the colors—Women's Wear Daily, 3/27/79*

A woman with a limited wardrobe—Women's Wear Daily, 5/8/76

Essential pieces included—New York Times, 4/20/80

Career dressing should be conservative—Women's Wear Daily, 3/27/79

Halston's travel essentials included—W, 3/30/79

Halston was an American designer—Karl Lagerfeld in the WWD obituary, 3/28/90

186 *So many people think I'm plain Jane—Women's Wear Daily, 5/3/76*

The light reflected around the face—New York Times Magazine, 9/23/79

198 *I think the dream is always mink—Women's Wear Daily, 3/27/79*

201 *I am closer to Halston's clothes than any designer—Women's Wear Daily, 12/29/71*

Jewelry should take the real approach—Women's Wear Daily, 12/29/71

203 *It's important for costumes in plays to reflect situations—Chicago Tribune, 3/11/73*

These are colors I might not dream of using otherwise—Washington Post, 3/13/79

210 *Halston was one of my closest and dearest friends—Martha Graham through Ron Protas, the Associate Artistic Director of her company, in the WWD obituary, 3/28/90*

215 *The challenge of making 40 to 60 costumes was inspiring—Women's Wear Daily, 6/26/75*

Many times a dress has to be mounted—Attitude, September 1986

Lucifer's cape, designed by Halston, looked like—The New Yorker, 7/7/75

The costume stands uninhabited onstage—Vogue, June 1980

216 *To get the essence of something that has perhaps been done before—Videofashion, June 1979*

She could do it all—Women's Wear Daily, 4/22/80

When we finally saw the costumes in action—Attitude, September 1986

We were rehearsing in a theater and we had to stop—Vogue, June 1980

HALSTON REVISITED

219 *I think it's great that people consider me—W, 11/29/85*

The experiment was mine—Women's Wear Daily, 4/21/89

222 *The thing about a designer's big breakthrough—New York Times, 6/2/9823*

225 *He was truly a modernist—Lynn Manulis in the WWD obituary, 3/28/90*

BIBLIOGRAPHY

BOOKS

Coleman, Elizabeth Ann. *The Genius of Charles James.* New York: Holt, Rinehart & Winston, 1982.

De Mille, Agnes. *Martha: The Life and Work of Martha Graham.* New York: Random House, 1956, 1991.

Francis, Mark, and Margery King. *The Warhol Look.* New York: Bullfinch Press, Little, Brown and Co. 1997.

Gaines, Steven. *Simply Halston.* New York: Putnam, 1991.

Graham, Katherine. *Personal History.* New York: Vintage, 1997.

Graham, Martha. *Blood Memory.* New York: Doubleday, 1991.

Hackett, Pat. *The Andy Warhol Diaries.* New York: Warner Books, 1989.

Haden-Guest, Anthony. *The Last Party.* New York: William Morrow, 1998.

Herald, Jacqueline. *Fashions of a Decade: The 1970s.* New York: Facts on File, 1990.

Herndon, Booton. *Bergdorf's on the Plaza.* New York: Knopf, 1956.

Heymann, C. David. *Liz: An Intimate Biography of Elizabeth Taylor.* New Jersey: Birch Lane Press, Carol Publishing Group, 1995.

Mair, George. *Under the Rainbow: The Real Liza Minnelli.* New Jersey: Birch Lane Press, Carol Publishing Group, 1996.

Martin, Richard. *The St. James Fashion Encyclopedia: A Survey of Style from 1945 to the Present.* Detroit: St. James Press, 1996.

McDowell, Colin. *Hats: Status, Style and Glamour.* New York: Rizzoli, 1992.

Milbank, Caroline Rennolds. *New York Fashion: The Evolution of American Style.* New York: Harry N. Abrams, 1989.

Mirabella, Grace. *In and Out of Vogue.* New York: Doubleday, 1995.

Walz, Barbara, and Bernadine Morris. *The Fashion Makers.* New York: Random House, 1978.

PERIODICALS

Chicago Tribune

Cosmopolitan

Daily News Record

Harper's Bazaar

Life

Los Angeles Times

Newsweek

New York Daily News

The New Yorker

New York Post

New York Times

RAM Report

San Francisco Chronicle

Signature

Time

Vogue

Women's Wear Daily

INDEX

CREDITS

iii: Photograph ©Horst; vi–vii: *Women's Wear Daily*/Fairchild Publications; x: ©Harry Benson; xii: © *The New Yorker* Collection, 1978. Dana Fradon from cartoonbank.com. All Rights Reserved; xiii: *Women's Wear Daily*/Fairchild Publications; xiv: Robin Platzer, Twin Images; xv: © Anton Perich; xvi: ©Neal Barr; 2: R. Prigent/Sygma; 6 top: Robin Platzer, Twin Images; 6 bottom: *Women's Wear Daily*/Fairchild Publications; 9: Donghia Furniture/Textiles Ltd.; 12: *Women's Wear Daily*/Fairchild Publications; 13: ©Newsweek, Inc. All Rights Reserved. Reprinted by permission. Photograph by Lawrence Fried/The Image Bank ©1972; 16: Dustin Pittman/*Women's Wear Daily*/Fairchild Publications; 17: ©Harry Benson; 18 top: Courtesy of Guido De Natale; 18 bottom left: Mark Ellidge/Sipa Press; 18 bottom right: *Women's Wear Daily*/Fairchild Publications; 19 left: Illustration ©Joe Eula. Courtesy of the Halston Archives, Museum at the Fashion Institute of Technology, New York; 19 right: Mark Ellidge/Sipa Press; 23 below: Courtesy of Pillowtex Corporation; 23 bottom: Courtesy of Hartmann Luggage; 24–25: *Women's Wear Daily*/Fairchild Publications; 26 right: ©1999 Andy Warhol Foundation for the Visual Arts/ARS, New York; 26 below: Art ©Larry Rivers/Licensed by VAGA, New York; 29: © Arnold Newman; 30: Darlene Rubin/*Women's Wear Daily*/Fairchild Publications; 32 below: Reprinted with permission from Montgomery Ward; 32 bottom: Courtesy of the Air Transportation Association; 33: Lynn Karlin/*Women's Wear Daily*/Fairchild Publications; 34: Courtesy of the Girl Scouts of the U.S.A.; 35: Courtesy of Avis Rent-A-Car; 36: Tony Palmieri/*Women's Wear Daily*/Fairchild Publications; 37 top: ©Jade Alpert; 37 bottom: Courtesy of Kosugi Sangyo Co. Ltd., Tokyo, Japan; 39: Stanley Papich; 40: *Women's Wear Daily*/Fairchild Publications; 41 left: AP/World Wide Photo; 41 below: Sal Traina/*Women's Wear Daily*/Fairchild Publications; 42: *W* magazine/Fairchild Publications; 46 below left: Ichiro Fujimara/*Women's Wear Daily*/Fairchild Publications; 46 below right: *Women's Wear Daily*/Fairchild Publications; 46 bottom left: R. Prigent/Sygma; 46 bottom right: R. Prigent/Sygma; 47: R. Prigent/Sygma; 48: *W* magazine/Fairchild Publications; 49 below: Kenneth Paul Block; 49 below left: ©Rico Puhlmann; 54: Courtesy of Kosugi Sangyo Co. Ltd., Tokyo, Japan; 55:

©1976 Time Inc.; 56: Courtesy of Kosugi Sangyo Co. Ltd., Tokyo, Japan; 57: ©1999 Andy Warhol Foundation for the Visual Arts/ARS, New York; 58: Courtesy of the Halston Archives, Museum at the Fashion Institute of Technology, New York; 59: *PEOPLE Weekly* is a registered trademark of Time Inc., used with permission; 60: CORBIS/Bettmann; 61: From the collection of Alan Purcell; 63: Tony Palmieri/*Women's Wear Daily*/Fairchild Publications; 65 top: *Women's Wear Daily*/Fairchild Publications; 65 bottom: Tony Palmieri/*Women's Wear Daily*/Fairchild Publications; 66: Robin Platzer, Twin Images; 67 left: ©Douglas Kirkland; 67 below: CORBIS/Bettmann; 69: Alan Berliner/*Women's Wear Daily*/Fairchild Publications; 70: CORBIS/Bettmann; 71: CORBIS/Bettmann; 72: *Women's Wear Daily*/Fairchild Publications; 73 left: Lawrence Fried/The Image Bank ©1972; 73 center top: Photograph Francesco Scavullo; 73 center bottom: Photograph Francesco Scavullo; 73 right: Lawrence Fried/The Image Bank ©1972; 74: CORBIS/Bettmann; 75: AP/World Wide Photo; 77: Photograph Francesco Scavullo; 78–79: *W* magazine/Fairchild Publications; 80: Cover photograph by Richard Avedon. Courtesy of *Harper's Bazaar*; 83: Courtesy of Peg Zwecker; 87: CORBIS/Bettmann; 88: CORBIS/Bettmann; 91: CORBIS/Bettmann; 92 below: Cover photograph by Richard Avedon. Courtesy of *Harper's Bazaar*; 92 bottom: ©1962 Condé Nast Publications Inc. Courtesy of *Vogue*. Photograph by Gene Laurent; 93: ©Neal Barr; 94: Cover photograph by Richard Avedon. Courtesy of *Harper's Bazaar*; 95: Condé Nast Publications Inc. Courtesy of *Vogue*. Photograph by Bert Stern; 96 top: Stanley Papich; 96 bottom: ©Gösta Peterson; 97: Condé Nast Publications Inc. Courtesy of *Vogue*. Photograph by Bert Stern; 99: Stanley Papich; 100: Photograph Francesco Scavullo; 102 both: Stanley Papich; 103: Stanley Papich; 104: Photograph by Irving Solero. Courtesy of the Museum at the Fashion Institute of Technology, New York; 105 left: Condé Nast Publications Inc. Courtesy of *Mademoiselle*. Photograph by André Carrera; 105 top right: The Fashion Group International Archives; 105 bottom right: Condé Nast Publications Inc. Courtesy of *Vogue*. Photograph by Penati; 106: Courtesy of the Halston Archives, Museum at the Fashion Institute of Technology, New York; 107: *Women's Wear Daily*/Fairchild Publications; 108: Kenneth Paul Block/*Women's*

Wear Daily/Fairchild Publications; 109: Illustration Joe Eula; 111: *W* magazine/Fairchild Publications; 115 below: Courtesy of the Halston Archives, Museum at the Fashion Institute of Technology, New York; 115 right: *Women's Wear Daily*/Fairchild Publications; 116 left: Tony Palmieri/*Women's Wear Daily*/Fairchild Publications; 116 right: Preliminary drawings by Deborah L. Hernandez, Amarante Consulting, using Karat CAD designer. Final drawings by Jason Snyder using Adobe Illustrator; 118 right: Stanley Papich; 118 from top: Preliminary drawings by Deborah L. Hernandez, Amarante Consulting, using Karat CAD designer. Final drawings by Jason Snyder using Adobe Illustrator; 119 right: *Women's Wear Daily*/Fairchild Publications; 119 from top: Preliminary drawings by Deborah L. Hernandez, Amarante Consulting, using Karat CAD designer. Final drawings by Jason Snyder using Adobe Illustrator; 120 right: The Fashion Group International Archives; 120 far right: Preliminary drawings by Deborah L. Hernandez, Amarante Consulting, using Karat CAD designer. Final drawings by Jason Snyder using Adobe Illustrator; 122–23: ©Harry Benson; 124 right: Stanley Papich; 124 above: Preliminary drawings by Deborah L. Hernandez, Amarante Consulting, using Karat CAD designer. Final drawings by Jason Snyder using Adobe Illustrator; 125 left: Stanley Papich; 125 above: Preliminary drawings by Deborah L. Hernandez, Amarante Consulting, using Karat CAD designer. Final drawings by Jason Snyder using Adobe Illustrator; 127: Illustration Kenneth Paul Block/*W* magazine/Fairchild Publications; 128 right: Preliminary drawings by Deborah L. Hernandez, Amarante Consulting, using Karat CAD designer. Final drawings by Jason Snyder using Adobe Illustrator; 128 below: *Women's Wear Daily*/Fairchild Publications; 129 both: Dustin Pittman/*Women's Wear Daily*/Fairchild Publications; 130–31: ©Rico Puhlmann; 132 left: Sal Traina/*Women's WearDaily*/Fairchild Publications; 132 center: Stanley Papich; 132 right: Pierre Schermann/*Women's Wear Daily*/Fairchild Publications; 133: Stanley Papich. Courtesy of the Halston Archives, Museum at the Fashion Institute of Technology, New York; 134 top: Dustin Pittman/*Women's Wear Daily*/Fairchild Publications; 134 top right: Preliminary drawings by Deborah L. Hernandez, Amarante Consulting, using Karat CAD designer. Final drawings by Jason Snyder using Adobe

Illustrator; 134 above: Photograph by Irving Solero. Courtesy of the Museum at the Fashion Institute of Technology, New York; 135: *W* magazine/Fairchild Publications; 136–37: ©1976 Condé Nast Publications Inc. Courtesy of *Vogue*. Photograph by Duane Michals; 138 left: *Women's Wear Daily*/Fairchild Publications; 138 right: Stanley Papich; 139: *Women's Wear Daily*/Fairchild Publications; 140: Stanley Papich; 141: *Women's Wear Daily*/Fairchild Publications; 142–43: *W* magazine/Fairchild Publications; 144: Kenneth Paul Block/*Women's Wear Daily*/Fairchild Publications; 146: Tony Palmieri/*Women's Wear Daily*/Fairchild Publications; 149: Stanley Papich. Courtesy of the Halston Archives, Museum at the Fashion Institute of Technology, New York; 150: Stanley Papich; 151 left: Condé Nast Publications Inc. Courtesy of *Vogue*; 151 right: Stanley Papich; 152 both: Stanley Papich; 153 both: Stanley Papich. Courtesy of the Halston Archives, Museum at the Fashion Institute of Technology, New York; 154 left: Sal Traina/*Women's Wear Daily*/Fairchild Publications; 154 center: Pierre Schermann/*Women's Wear Daily*/Fairchild Publications; 154 right: *Women's Wear Daily*/Fairchild Publications; 155: © Neal Barr; 156–57: ©Gösta Peterson; 158 left: Stanley Papich; 158 center: *Women's Wear Daily*/Fairchild Publications; 158 right: Pierre Schermann/*Women's Wear Daily*/Fairchild Publications; 159: Kenneth Paul Block/*W* magazine/Fairchild Publications; 160: Stanley Papich; 161: Sal Traina/*Women's Wear Daily*/Fairchild Publications; 162–63: ©Harry Benson; 164 both: Stanley Papich; 165: Stanley Papich; 166 both: Stanley Papich; 167: Kenneth Paul Block/*W* magazine/Fairchild Publications; 168 both: Stanley Papich; 171: Stanley Papich; 172 left: Lynn Karlin/*Women's Wear Daily*/Fairchild Publications; 172 center: Pierre Schermann/*Women's Wear Daily*/Fairchild Publications; 172 right: Pierre Schermann/*Women's Wear Daily*/Fairchild Publications; 173 left: Pierre Schermann/*Women's Wear Daily*/Fairchild Publications; 173 right: ©1972 Condé Nast Publications Inc. Courtesy of *Vogue*; 175: Stanley Papich; 176: ©1976 Condé Nast Publications Inc. Courtesy of *Vogue*. Photograph by Jacques Malignon; 177: Photo Patrick Demarchelier for *Harper's Bazaar*; 180 all: Stanley Papich; 181 both: Stanley Papich. Courtesy of the Halston Archives, Museum at the Fashion Institute of Technology, New York; 182 all: Stanley Papich; 183 both: Stanley Papich; 185: *Women's Wear Daily*/Fairchild Publications; 186 above: Peter Simmins/*Women's Wear Daily*/Fairchild Publications; 186 right: Photograph by Irving Solero. Courtesy of the Museum at the Fashion Institute of Technology, New York; 187 left: Stanley Papich; 187 right: Lynn Karlin/*Women's Wear Daily*/Fairchild Publications; 188 both: Stanley Papich; 189: Stanley Papich; 190: Stanley Papich. Courtesy of the Halston Archives, Museum at the Fashion Institute of Technology, New York; 191: Stanley Papich; 192–93: ©Rico Puhlmann; 194: ©Rico Puhlmann; 195 both: Stanley Papich. Courtesy of the Halston Archives, Museum at the Fashion Institute of Technology, New York; 196 left: Stanley Papich; 196 center: Stanley Papich; 196 right: Stanley Papich. Courtesy of the Halston Archives, Museum at the Fashion Institute of Technology, New York; 197 left: Stanley Papich. Courtesy of the Halston Archives, Museum at the Fashion Institute of Technology, New York; 197 right: The Fashion Group International Archives ; 198 below: ©Condé Nast Publications Inc. Courtesy of *Vogue*; 198 right: Stanley Papich; 199 below: Stanley Papich. Courtesy of the Halston Archives, Museum at the Fashion Institute of Technology, New York; 199 right: Photograph Francesco Scavullo; 200: Stanley Papich; 201 below: Pierre Schermann/*Women's Wear Daily*/Fairchild Publications; 201 bottom: ©1972 Condé Nast Publications Inc. Courtesy of *Vogue*. Photograph by David Bailey; 202: Courtesy of the Halston Archives, Museum at the Fashion Institute of Technology, New York; 203: AP/World Wide Photos; 204: ©Ken Regan/Camera 5; 205: Courtesy of the Halston Archives, Museum at the Fashion Institute of Technology, New York; 205 inset: Courtesy of the Everett Collection; 206: Courtesy of the Halston Archives, Museum at the Fashion Institute of Technology, New York; 207: Courtesy of the Everett Collection; 208–9: Illustrations by Michelle Dowgin. From the private collection of Liza Minnelli; 211: CORBIS/Bettmann; 212–13: Photograph Francesco Scavullo; 214: Courtesy of the Halston Archives, Museum at the Fashion Institute of Technology, New York; 215: *Women's Wear Daily*/Fairchild Publications; 216: CORBIS/Bettmann; 217: Courtesy of the Halston Archives, Museum at the Fashion Institute of Technology, New York; 218: Darlene Rubin/*W* magazine/Fairchild Publications; 219: *Women's Wear Daily*/Fairchild Publications; 220–21: Irving Solero. Courtesy of the Halston Archives, Museum at the Fashion Institute of Technology, New York; 223: ©Rico Puhlmann; 226–27: ©Duane Michals; 228: Illustration ©Joe Eula